THE TABERNACLE
THE TEMPLE
AND YOU

Second Edition

The Function of Man's
Body, Soul, and Spirit
As the Temple of God

RON HORDYK

Permissions

Scriptures taken from the Holy Bible, **King James Version.**
Public Domain. **(KJV)**

Scriptures taken from the Holy Bible, **English Standard Version**®.
Copyright © 2001 by Crossway, a publishing ministry of
Good News Publishers. Used by permission. **(ESV)**

Scriptures taken from the **New American Standard Bible**®.
Copyright © 1960,1962,1963,1968,1971,1972,1973,1975,1977,1995
by The Lockman Foundation. Used by permission. **(NASB)**

Scriptures taken from the Holy Bible, **New International Reader's Version**®.
NIrV Copyright © 1995,1996,1998, 2014 by Biblica Inc.™
Used by permission of Zondervan. All rights reserved worldwide. **(NIrV)**

Scriptures taken from the Holy Bible, **New International Version**®.
Copyright © 1973, 1978, 1984 International Bible Society.
Used by permission of Zondervan Bible Publishers. **(NIV)**

Scriptures taken from the **New King James Version**®.
Copyright © 1982 by Thomas Nelson, Inc.
Used by permission. All rights reserved. **(NKJV)**

Scripture taken from the **New Revised Standard Version Bible**®.
Copyright © 1989 National Council of the Churches of Christ
in the United States of America.
Used by permission. All rights reserved. **(NRSV)**

Scriptures taken from the Holy Bible, **New Living Translation**®.
Copyright © 1996, 2004, 2007 by Tyndale House Foundation.
Used by permission of Tyndale House Publishers Inc.
Carol Stream, Illinois, 60188. All rights reserved worldwide. **(NLT)**

Scriptures taken from the Holy Bible, **Today's New International Version**®.
TNIV Copyright © 2001, 2005 International Bible Society.
Used by permission of the International Bible Society.
All rights reserved worldwide. **(TNIV)**

The Tabernacle, the Temple, and You
Second Edition
Copyright ©2014, 2020 Ron Hordyk

ISBN 978-1506-909-83-7 PBK
ISBN 978-1506-909-84-4 EBK

LCCN 2014901955-02

December 2020

Published and Distributed by
First Edition Design Publishing, Inc.
P.O. Box 17646, Sarasota, FL 34276-3217
www.firsteditiondesignpublishing.com

ALL RIGHTS RESERVED. No part of this book publication may be reproduced, stored in a retrieval system, or transmitted in any form or by any means — electronic, mechanical, photo-copy, recording, or any other — except brief quotation in reviews, without the prior permission of the author or publisher.

To God,

Who—while I was a vile sinner—
saved me from sin, self, and Satan;
possessed me with the power of His presence;
elevated me to the position of a son;
and equipped me for the fulfilling of His purpose,
be the glory for ever and ever. Amen.

I give thanks for my family, friends,
and brothers and sisters in the Lord,
whom God used in my life
to shed the world while
being transformed into His image.

The Tabernacle
the Temple
and You

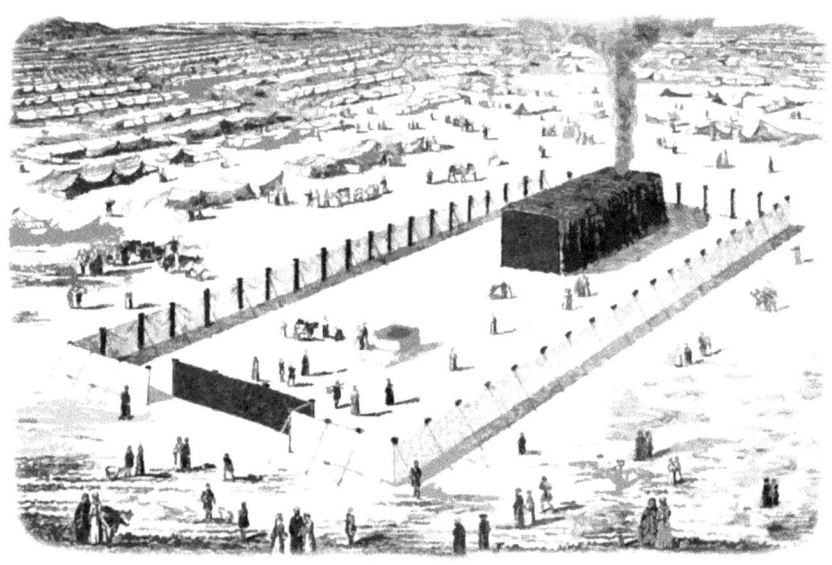

"A new day is coming," announces the Lord. "I will make a new covenant with the people of Israel. I will also make it with the people of Judah. It will not be like the covenant I made with their people long ago. That was when I took them by the hand. I led them out of Egypt. But they broke my covenant. They did it even though I was like a husband to them," announces the Lord. "This is the covenant I will make with Israel after that time," announces the Lord. "I will put my law in their minds. I will write it on their hearts. I will be their God. And they will be my people. A man will not need to teach his neighbor anymore. And he will not need to teach his friend anymore. He will not say, 'Know the Lord.' Everyone will know me. From the least important of them to the most important, all of them will know me," announces the Lord. "I will forgive their evil ways. I will not remember their sins anymore."

Jeremiah 31:31-34 NIrV

Contents

Preface		i
Lesson 1	God's Dwelling Place	1
Lesson 2	The Courtyard	21
Lesson 3	The Bronze Altar	41
Lesson 4	The Bronze Basin	61
Lesson 5	The Tabernacle	81
Lesson 6	The Holy Place	101
Lesson 7	The Gold Lampstand	121
Lesson 8	The Gold Altar of Incense	141
Lesson 9	The Gold Table of Showbread	261
Lesson 10	The Holy of Holies and the Ark	281
Lesson 11	Aaron's Staff That Budded	301
Lesson 12	The Two Stone Tablets	321
Lesson 13	The Gold Jar of Manna	341
Epilogue		369
Appendix		273

Preface

Over the years, many attempts have been made to draw lessons from the tabernacle concerning Christ, the Messiah. When reading about Jesus cleansing the temple in the Gospels, God directed me to consider that the tabernacle is about us, for we are the new temple of God:

> Do you not know **that you are the temple of God** and that the Spirit of God dwells in you? (1Co.3:16 NKJV)

Some narratives of Jesus' life are recorded only once, others twice or three times, but every Gospel records Jesus clearing the temple. Mark noted that the night before Jesus cleared the temple, He witnessed the venders in the courtyard closing up shop:

> So Jesus came to Jerusalem and **went into the Temple. After looking around carefully at everything**, he left because **it was late in the afternoon.** Then he returned to Bethany with the twelve disciples. (Mk.11:11 NLT)

I believe Jesus spoke with His Father in prayer about what He had seen, asking His Father how He should respond. This time of prayer would refute the claim that the temple episode was a spontaneous act. In John's account, Jesus took some cords to form a whip and cleared the temple:

> He found in the temple those who sold oxen and sheep and doves, and the moneychangers doing business. **When He had made a whip of cords, He drove them all out of the temple**, with the sheep and the oxen, and poured out the changers' money and overturned the tables. (Jn.2:14-15 NKJV)

Mark records that Jesus not only cleared the temple but also, after cleansing it, prevented anyone from re-entering with merchandise:

> On reaching Jerusalem, **Jesus entered the temple** area and began driving out those who were buying and selling there. He overturned the tables of the money-changers and the benches of those selling doves, **and would not allow anyone to carry merchandise through the temple courts**. (Mk.11:15-16 NIV)

Why did Jesus respond so severely on this occasion? First, **the common displaced the Holy:** the sacred temple became a common market with the bartering for better prices. Second, **the profane displaced the Holy:** from Jesus' perspective, the sacred temple became a place of robbery, for the prices of the sacrifices were greatly inflated. Finally, **the profane**

corrupted the Holy: the priests, who were to be holy, allowed the temple to be corrupted because they were silent concerning this wickedness. The chief priests and the teachers of the law were quick to accuse Jesus and His disciples of minor transgressions of the law but silent concerning the desecration of God's Temple. These guardians of the law probably allowed this blatant desecration of their most holy place because they received a percentage of that which was sold. Rather than applaud Jesus' actions, they were angered, taking it as a personal attack. When the Jews asked by what authority He had the right to cleanse the temple, Jesus replied, "Destroy this temple, and I will raise it up in three days" (Jn.2:19). John records:

> Then the Jews said, "It has taken forty-six years to build this temple, and will You raise it up in three days?" **But He was speaking of the temple of His body**. (Jn.2:20-21 NKJV)

Jesus' body was the temple of God; His body shared the same three elements as the temple: the courtyard, the Holy Place, and the Holy of Holies.

When the Holy Spirit descended in the form of a dove, Jesus' body became the temple of God. Jesus had a physical body:

> He went to Pilate and **asked for Jesus' body**. Then **he took the body down from the cross** and wrapped it in a long sheet of linen cloth and laid it in a new tomb that had been carved out of rock. (Lk.23:52-53 NLT)

Jesus' body contained His soul with the faculties of intellect, emotion, and will. His soul formed the Holy Place:

> "<u>My soul</u> is overwhelmed with sorrow to the point of death," he said to them. "Stay here and keep watch." Going a little farther, he fell to the ground and prayed that if possible the hour might pass from him. "Abba, Father," he said, "everything is possible for you. Take this cup from me. **Yet not what I will**, but what you will." (Mk.14:34-36 NIV)

Since Jesus was a spiritual man, His soul was fully submitted to His spirit. Jesus' spirit formed the Holy of Holies. When He died, we read:

> And when Jesus had cried out with a loud voice, He said, "**Father, 'into Your hands I commit <u>My spirit</u>.**'" Having said this, He breathed His last. (Lk.23:46 NKJV)

Even though Jesus was God, He became a man and had a body, a soul, and a spirit—in which the Holy Spirit dwelt. For, when Jesus was baptized, the Spirit descended upon Him and dwelt within Him:

> Now when all the people were baptized, **Jesus was also baptized**, and while He was praying, heaven was opened, and **the Holy Spirit descended <u>upon Him</u>** in bodily form like a dove, **and a voice came out of heaven, "You are My beloved Son**, in You I am well-pleased."
> (Lk.3:21-22 NASB)

This event is similar to when Moses set up the tabernacle and consecrated it. At that moment, the *skekinah* **glory of God**—the glory of the Presence of God—descended into the Holy of Holies:

> Then the cloud covered the tabernacle of meeting, and **the glory of the LORD filled the tabernacle.** (Ex.40:34 NKJV)

The *shekinah* glory of God accompanied His Presence and filled God's tabernacle. When Solomon finished building the temple and everything was consecrated to God, we read:

> When the priests withdrew from the Holy Place, **the cloud filled the temple** of the LORD. And the priests could not perform their service because **of the cloud, for the glory of the LORD filled his temple.**
> (1Ki.8:10-11 NIV)

The glory of the Presence of God moved from the tabernacle to the temple. When Jesus died, committing His Spirit to the Father, we read:

> And Jesus cried out again with a loud voice, and **yielded up His spirit.** And behold, **the veil of the temple was torn in two from top to bottom**; and the earth shook and the rocks were split. (Mt.27:50-51 NASB)

God tore the curtain in the temple that separated the Holy Place from the Holy of Holies. This tearing signified the passing of God's dwelling place from the temple in Jerusalem to its eventual location within His believers. The temple that Jesus initially raised up was His body; however, after His ascension, believers became the body of Christ, the temple of God:

> Do you not know **that you are God's temple** and that God's Spirit dwells in you? **If anyone destroys God's temple**, God will destroy that person. **For God's temple is holy, and you are that temple.** (1Co.3:16-17 NRSV)

We are the sacred temple of God! However, to understand the significance of the cleansing of the temple, we need to be reminded of a truth:

PREFACE

Jesus Christ is the same yesterday, and today, and for ever.
(He.13:8 KJV)

Jesus does not change; we know that what angered Him 2000 years ago will anger Him today. Since we are the temple of God, He will be angry when the common displaces the Holy. When the common things of life—food, clothing, work, or sports—displace our time with God, He will cleanse His temple. When the profane things—worldly movies, music, or books—displace our time to pray and read the Scripture, He will cleanse His temple. When the profane—pornography, drugs, gambling, or sexual immorality—corrupts the holy, He will cleanse His temple. Jesus cares as much for God's temple today as He did 2000 years ago. Just as Jesus cleansed the temple in Jerusalem from the corruption in His day, He will cleanse His temple today from evil:

> The reason the Son of God appeared was to destroy the devil's work. No-one who is born of God **will continue to sin**, because **God's seed remains in him**; he **cannot go on sinning, because he has been born of God**.
> (1Jn.3:8-9 NIV)

We cannot continue to sin because Christ, God's seed, lives in us. The Scriptures teach:

> **May God himself**, the God of peace, **sanctify you through and through.** May **your whole spirit, soul and body be kept blameless** at the coming of our Lord Jesus Christ. The one who calls you is faithful and *he will do it*.
> (1Th.5:23-24 NIV)

God promises to cleanse His temple. He also promises to keep it clean by preventing the common and the profane things from entering back into our lives:

> We know that **those who are born of God do not sin**, but **the one who was born of God protects them**, and the evil one does not touch them.
> (1Jn.5:18 NRSV)

If **we** are born of God (that is, we are His disciples), then Christ, the **one** born of God, protects us from Satan, who desires to regain control of our lives:

> No temptation has overtaken you but such as is common to man; and **God is faithful**, who **will not allow you to be tempted beyond what you are able**, but <u>with</u> the temptation **will provide the way of escape also, so that you will be able to endure it.** (1Co.10:13 NASB)

The previous Scriptures make promises on the foundation that God is faithful and will do everything that He has promised. However, God does not run a maid service and cleanse every person's life; He only cleanses His temple—the lives of His disciples. John, addressing the Laodicean church, wrote:

> Behold, **I stand at the door and knock**; if anyone hears My voice and **opens the door, I will come in to him** and will dine with him, and he with Me.
> (Re.3:20 NASB)

Christ told the Laodicean church that He did not live in them. Many Christians have neglected to release the control of their lives to Christ and become temples of God. If God's people are the temple of God, then parallels can be learned concerning the tabernacle, the temple, and His dwelling place, the lives of Christians. In AD 70, the temple in Jerusalem was destroyed by a Roman general named Titus. Why is it that in nearly 2000 years God has not rebuilt His temple—His dwelling place? There is no need to rebuild the physical temple since our hearts have become the temple of God in which His Spirit dwells. Notice the "I will" statements when Ezekiel wrote:

> For _I will_ take you out of the nations; _I will_ **gather you from all the countries and bring you back** into your own land. _I will_ **sprinkle clean water on you, and you will be clean**; _I will_ **cleanse you** from all your impurities and from all your idols. _I will_ **give you a new heart and put a new spirit in you**; _I will_ **remove** from you your heart of stone and give you a heart of flesh. And _I will_ **put my Spirit** in you **and move you to** follow my decrees and be careful to keep my laws.
> (Ez.36:24-27 TNIV)

God promised to give the Jews a new heart and to put His Spirit within them. Jesus said:

> You Samaritans worship what you do not know; we worship what we do know, **for salvation is from the Jews**. Yet a time is coming and has now come when the true worshippers **will worship the Father in spirit and truth**, for they are the kind of worshippers the Father seeks. **God is spirit, and his worshippers must worship in spirit and in truth**.
> (Jn.4:22-24 NIV)

Is our heart the new dwelling place of God in which He lives by His Spirit? Let us consider the similarities of His dwellings as we study *The Tabernacle, The Temple, and You.*

The Tabernacle

The Temple

And You

Second Edition

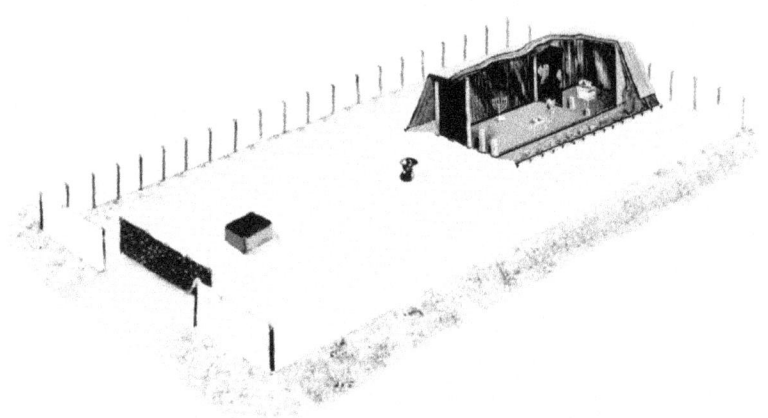

The Tabernacle

Moses set up the holy tent. He put the bases in place. He put the frames in them. He put in the crossbars. He set up the posts. He spread the holy tent over the frames. Then he put the coverings over the tent. Moses did it as the LORD had commanded him. He got the tablets of the covenant. He placed them in the ark. He put the poles through its rings. And he put the cover on it. The cover was the place where sin is paid for. Moses brought the ark into the holy tent. He hung the curtain to screen the ark where the tablets of the covenant are kept. Moses did it as the LORD had commanded him. He placed the table for the holy bread in the Tent of Meeting. It was on the north side of the holy tent outside the curtain. He arranged the loaves of bread on it in the sight of the Lord. Moses did it as the LORD had commanded him. He placed the lampstand in the Tent of Meeting. It stood across from the table on the south side of the holy tent. He set up the lamps in the sight of the Lord. Moses did it as the LORD had commanded him. He placed the gold altar for burning incense in the Tent of Meeting. He placed it in front of the curtain. He burned sweet-smelling incense on it. Moses did it as the LORD had commanded him. Then he put up the curtain at the entrance to the holy tent. He set the altar for burnt offerings near the entrance to the holy tent, the Tent of Meeting. He sacrificed burnt offerings and grain offerings on it. Moses did it as the LORD had commanded him. He placed the large bowl between the Tent of Meeting and the altar. He put water in the bowl for washing. Moses and Aaron and his sons used it to wash their hands and feet. They washed when they entered the Tent of Meeting or approached the altar. They did it as the LORD had commanded Moses. Then Moses set up the courtyard around the holy tent and altar. He put up the curtain at the entrance to the courtyard. And so Moses completed the work.   Exodus 40:18-33NIrV

Lesson 1

God's Dwelling Place

Man Is a Unique Creation

God created man as a unique creation. He created man in the image and likeness of Himself:

This is the written account of Adam's line. **When God created man, he made him in the likeness of God.** *He created them male and female and blessed them. And when they were created, he called them "man". When Adam had lived 130 years,* **he had a son in his own likeness, in his own image;** *and he named him Seth.* (Ge.5:1-3 NIV; Ge.1:26-27)

We can conclude that the design of man set him above the rest of creation. God made man with a process that was different from all other living beings. With all the other creatures, God spoke them into being; but with man:

The LORD God formed man **of the dust** *of the ground, and breathed into his nostrils* **the breath of life;** *and man* **became a living soul.**
(Ge.2:7 KJV)

Man was made with two elements: dust and breath/spirit of God. When combined, they created the third: a living soul. These three elements are known today as the three distinct parts of man: body, soul, and spirit:

May the God of peace himself sanctify you entirely; and **may your spirit and soul and body** *be kept sound and blameless at the coming of our Lord Jesus Christ. The one who calls you is faithful, and he will do this.*
(1Th.5:23-24 NRSV)

Body, soul, and spirit make us a trinity just like God; for God is a trinity of Father, Son, and Spirit. Animals do not have a spirit. When they die, they cease to exist:

The Egyptians are human, and not God; **their horses are flesh, and not spirit.** (Isa.31:3 NRSV)

The spirit of man separates mankind from the animals, for man has the ability to analyze, theorize, and synthesize. Animals adapt to their environment; however, mankind has the ability to alter their environment. The creative ability to process information in order to resolve situations is unique to man:

> **But it is a spirit in man**, And the breath of the Almighty **gives them understanding**. (Job 32:8 NASB)

The spiritual distinction between man and animals can be seen in the first task that God gave Adam. Animals could not create names:

> And out of the ground the LORD God formed every beast of the field and every bird of the sky, and **brought them to the man to see what he would call them; and whatever the man called a living creature, that was its name. And the man gave names** to all the cattle, and to the birds of the sky, and to every beast of the field... (Ge.2:19-20 NASB)

Man's spiritual ability to reason sets them apart from the animals:

> For what man knows the things of a man **except the spirit of the man which is in him**? Even so no one knows the things of God **except the Spirit of God**. (1Co.2:11 NKJV)

Man has the unique ability to reason the deeper questions of life.

The conception of human life is not just the uniting of an egg with a sperm, but also the creation of a spirit in the embryo. God claims responsibility for both processes in the conception of human life:

> Thus says the Lord, who stretches out the heavens, lays the foundation of the earth, **and forms the spirit of man within him**: (Zec.12:1 NKJV)

God has to create the spirit within a baby for human life to begin. A baby without a spirit is stillborn:

> **The spirit of God has made me**, and **the breath** of the Almighty gives me life. (Job 33:4 NRSV)

In this way, God created not only the first man and woman but also each person through the giving of a spirit in the womb. We do not die because our bodies cease to function; rather, we die because our spirit leaves our body:

> For **as the body without the spirit is dead**, so faith without works is dead also. (Ja.2:26 KJV)

God retains ultimate control of our spirit. When He gives the spirit, life is created; when He takes the human spirit away, death occurs. Both are the act of God:

> If it were his intention and he **withdrew his spirit and breath, all mankind would perish together** and man would return to the dust.
> (Job:34:14-15 NIV)

Since God controls life by the giving and taking of our spirit, God is the One Who retains ownership of our spirit:

> May the LORD, **the God of the spirits of all mankind**, appoint a man over this community. (Nu.27:16 NIV)

God's ownership of our spirit makes us accountable to Him. Once man's spirit is conceived, it is eternal and cannot be destroyed. Man's spirit makes them an eternal being. In death, the spirit returns to God—implying a tremendous responsibility for those who conceive:

> ... then the dust will return to the earth as it was, and **the spirit will return to God who gave it.** (Ec.12:7 NASB)

When Jesus raised Jairus' daughter from the dead, her spirit had already left and had to re-enter in order for her to return to life:

> But he took her by the hand and called out, "Child, get up!" **Her spirit returned,** and **she got up at once.** Then he directed them to give her something to eat. (Lk.8:54-55 NRSV)

Since our spirit is eternal, the question changes from, "Will we live eternally?" to, "Where will we spend eternity?" For, when we receive our new body and stand before God, we will be judged, and His judgment determines where we will spend eternity:

> And as it is appointed for men to die once, **but after this the judgment...**
> (He.9:27 NKJV)

Therefore, man was created in the likeness of God as a spiritual being and was designed to live with God forever.

THE PENALTY FOR EATING THE FORBIDDEN FRUIT

In the beginning, God would come from heaven and walk with Adam and Eve in His garden:

> **They heard the sound of the LORD God walking in the garden** at the time of the evening breeze, (Ge.3:8 NRSV)

They would walk with God just as one would walk with a close friend. When God placed Adam and Eve in His garden, He commanded them not to eat from the tree of the knowledge of good and evil:

> The LORD God commanded the man, "You may freely eat of every tree of the garden; but **of the tree of the knowledge of good and evil you shall not eat, for <u>in the day</u> that you eat of it <u>you shall die</u>**."
> (Ge.2:16-17 NRSV)

The tree of the knowledge of good and evil could be referred to as the tree of choice. As long as man did not know evil, he had no choice but to do good. Once man gained the knowledge of evil (choice), he would always be faced with the decision to obey or disobey God. One day, Satan possessed a snake and taught the woman the concept of evil—the possibility of disobedience to God. Satan asked whether there was any tree from which Adam and Eve were not allowed to eat, and Eve responded:

> "We may eat of the fruit of the trees in the garden; but God said, '**You shall not eat of the fruit** of the tree that is in the middle of the garden, **nor shall you touch it, <u>or you shall die</u>**.'" (Ge.3:2-3 NRSV)

Until this point in time, Eve never considered why she should eat of a fruit that would bring certain death. Eve knew the consequences for eating the fruit; however, once she learned the concept of evil, she could not resist the opportunity to become like God:

> "You will not surely die," the serpent said to the woman. "For God knows that when you eat of it your eyes will be opened, and **you will be like God, knowing good and evil**." (Ge.3:4-5 NIV)

The chance to become like God overpowered Eve's common sense. For, not only did she risk suicide by eating a fruit which she was convinced would kill her, but she also sought to commit murder by giving the fruit she considered deadly to her husband:

> When the woman saw that the fruit of the tree **was good** for food and **pleasing** to the eye, and also **desirable** for gaining wisdom, **she took some and ate it. She also gave some to her husband**, who was with her, and he ate it. **Then the eyes of both of them were opened, and they realized that they were naked**... (Ge.3:6-7 NIV)

Once mankind experienced choice—the ability to determine one's own destiny apart from God—Adam's and Eve's lives were altered by a new realm of possibilities. An example would be their reaction to nakedness.

The ability to choose between good and evil without the self-discipline of a holy nature enslaved man to sin. By eating the forbidden fruit, Adam and Eve became like God in only one way—knowing evil:

> Then the LORD God said, "**See, the man has become like one of us**, knowing good and evil"... (Ge.3:22 NRSV)

Knowing evil did not make man like God. God's nature is holy. God's holiness prevents Him from committing the evil He knows. The knowledge of evil apart from God's holy nature caused Eve's nature to be predisposed to sin—a sinful nature. The sinful nature was not a part of man at creation but came into being when they gained the knowledge of evil apart from a holy nature. Once they experienced evil, they were unable to regain the state of innocence they enjoyed in the beginning. In essence, God gave mankind the command in order to protect them from the power of sin. For without the nature of God, Eve's choice condemned her and her offspring to a life enslaved to sin:

> Therefore, **just as sin entered the world through one man**, and death through sin, and in this way **death came to all men, because all sinned**—for before the law was given, sin was in the world. But sin is not taken into account when there is no law. (Ro.5:12-13 NIV)

Sin as a power came into the world with man's new freedom to choose evil. Choice without a holy nature is not a freedom, but slavery:

> Jesus answered them, "Most assuredly, I say to you, **whoever commits sin is a slave of sin.** (Jn.8:34 NKJV)

Theologians speak of the ability to choose between good and evil as a great freedom, but, Biblically, it is taught as a powerful bondage:

> **They promise them freedom**, while they themselves **are slaves of depravity**—for **a man is a slave to whatever has mastered him.** (2Pe.2:19 NIV)

False teachers teach that the ability to choose between good and evil is the inherent right of all mankind, yet this lie is a denial of everything we experienced before we accepted Christ:

> **At one time we too** were foolish, disobedient, **deceived and enslaved** by all kinds of **passions and pleasures.** (Ti.3:3 NIV)

Many Christians forget their previous way of life. Before salvation, they were not only enslaved but also deceived. When Eve ate of the fruit, she became like God, knowing both good and evil and, at the same time, also died to the possibility of living a holy life. Through the ability to choose, we became consumed to exploit, to hate, to violate, to maim our fellow humans for our own self-gratification. Yet, many claim that without the ability to choose evil, we become a mere puppet. People do not realize that the inability to choose evil makes us like God:

> Therefore, hear me, you who have sense, **far be it from God that he should do wickedness**, and from **the Almighty that he should do wrong**. (Job 34:10 NRSV)

Many theologians teach that the ability to choose between good or evil is a superior trait over the ability to choose only good. If the ability to choose evil is superior, man would be superior to God; for God Himself would not, could not, and will not choose evil because evil is contrary to the holiness of His nature. The ability to choose between good and evil is not a superior trait, but an inferior one. Inability to choose sin is superior to choice, for God, Who is superior to mankind, cannot choose evil:

> For You are not a God **who takes pleasure in wickedness**; **No evil dwells with You.** The boastful shall not stand before Your eyes; **You hate all who do iniquity**. (Ps.5:4-5 NASB)

God's holy character finds evil repugnant and sin unacceptable, causing Him to be separated from those who do wrong:

> But **your iniquities have made a separation between you and your God**, And **your sins have hidden His face from you**, so that He does not hear. (Isa.59:2 NASB)

The reason why God no longer walked with man after He sent them out of His garden was because they had sinned. God is perfect, and sin is imperfection. Sin isolates us from our perfect God:

> Your eyes are too pure **to look on evil**; you **cannot tolerate wrong**. (Hab.1:13 NIV)

Man's sin prevented them from having a relationship with God. Moses was accredited with speaking to God face to face with only the curtain of the Holy of Holies separating them:

> So **the LORD spoke to Moses face to face**, as a man speaks to his friend. (Ex.33:11 NKJV)

Even though Moses would talk to God as a friend, when he asked to see the glorious God, he was denied that privilege. If Moses stood before the face of God, he would instantly be put to death, judged, and sent to hell. A sinful man, even Moses, could not stand before the face of our glorious God:

> But He said, "You cannot see My face, **for no man can see Me and live!"** (Ex 33:20 NASB)

Even though God did not allow Moses to see His face, He did allow Moses to look upon His back:

> But this is not true of my servant Moses; he is faithful in all my house. With him I speak face to face, clearly and not in riddles; **he sees the form of the LORD**. (Nu.12:7-8 TNIV)

Therefore, man's new ability to choose evil and God's inability to tolerate evil prevents mankind from experiencing the Presence of God:

> Make every effort to live in peace with all men and **to be holy; without holiness no one will see the Lord**. (He.12:14 NIV)

GOD RETURNS TO MAN

When God asked Moses to build the tabernacle, God was communicating that He was willing to have His Presence return to man. For the first 2500 years, man understood the concept of God but could not grasp that God was always with them. Around 1500 BC, God told Moses to make the tabernacle, a physical reminder that Israel was God's chosen people and that He chose to live among them. The meaning of the word *tabernacle* is "to dwell with God":

> And Jehovah appeareth unto him, and saith, "Go not down towards Egypt, **tabernacle in the land concerning which I speak unto thee**, sojourn in this land, and I am with thee, and bless thee, for to thee and to thy seed I give all these lands, and I have established the oath which I have sworn to Abraham thy father..." (Ge.26:2-3 Young's Literal Translation)

God uses the word *tabernacle* to mean "dwell." John uses the word *tabernacle* in his Gospel:

> And the Word became flesh, **and did tabernacle among us,** and we beheld his glory, glory as of an only begotten of a father, full of grace and truth. (Jn.1:14 Young's Literal Translation)

When God asked Moses to have the Israelites build a tabernacle for Him, God was attempting to dwell among His people while maintaining the minimum, but necessary, separation from them. When Moses was on Mount Sinai, God gave him the design for His tabernacle:

> This is why Moses was warned when he was about to build the tabernacle: **"See to it that you make everything according to the pattern shown you on the mountain."** (He.8:5 NIV)

The tabernacle was made while Israel camped at the base of Mount Sinai. When the tabernacle was set up for the first time, the *shekinah* glory of God descended upon it:

> He set up the court around the tabernacle and the altar, and put up the screen at the gate of the court. So Moses finished the work. Then **the cloud covered the tent of meeting**, and **the glory of the LORD** filled the **tabernacle**. Moses was not able to enter the tent of meeting because the cloud settled upon it, and **the glory of the LORD filled the tabernacle**.
> (Ex.40:33-35 NRSV)

God dwelt in the tabernacle until around 1000 BC. At that time, David desired to build a permanent temple for God but was denied the privilege because he had killed too many men in war. God commanded David's son Solomon to build the temple; however, it was not designed by Solomon:

> Then **David gave his son Solomon the plans** for the portico of the temple, its buildings, its storerooms, its upper parts, its inner rooms and the place of atonement. He **gave him the plans of all that the Spirit** had put in his **mind** for the courts of the temple of the LORD and all the surrounding rooms, for the treasuries of the temple of God and for the treasuries for the dedicated things.
> (1Ch.28:11-12 NIV)

God's Spirit gave David the plans for the temple. Once Solomon finished building the temple and had everything consecrated to God, the *shekinah* glory of God's Presence filled the temple:

> It happened that when the priests came from the holy place, the **cloud filled the house of the LORD**, so that the priests could not stand to minister because of the cloud, **for the glory of the LORD filled the house of the LORD**.
> (1Ki.8:10-11 NASB)

God descended into His temple and dwelt there until 585 BC, when God sent the Babylonians to punish the nation of Judah. When Judah refused to surrender to the Babylonians as the Lord had commanded, both Jerusalem and the temple were destroyed by the Babylonians. During the seventy years of Babylonian captivity, God gave Ezekiel, a priest of God, a vision of the specific measurements for the future temple in Jerusalem. When Ezra rebuilt the temple, it was based upon the design God gave to Ezekiel:

> The man said to me, "Son of man, **look carefully and listen closely and pay attention to everything I am going to show you**, for that is why you have been brought here. **Tell the house of Israel everything you see**."
> (Eze.40:4 TNIV)

When Ezra dedicated the temple around 500 BC, the *shekinah* glory of God never descended upon it. Haggai recorded that Ezra's temple never equaled the grandeur of Solomon's temple:

> **Who is left among you who saw this temple in its former glory? And how do you see it now? Does it not seem to you like nothing in comparison?**
> (Hag.2:3 NASB)

The Scriptures record that when the foundation of Ezra's temple was completed, the people who had seen Solomon's temple wept:

> **But many of the priests and Levites and heads of families, old people who had seen the first house on its foundations, wept with a loud voice when they saw this house**, though many shouted aloud for joy, so that the people could not distinguish the sound of the joyful shout from the sound of the people's weeping, for the people shouted so loudly that the sound was heard far away.
> (Ezra 3:12-13 NRSV)

In 19 BC, King Herod started to renovate the temple Ezra built, but it was not finished until AD 68. Herod was not a Jew but an Edomite. He rebuilt the temple to appease the Jews. Herod respected the sanctity of the temple by hiring over one thousand priests to complete all of the construction. As Haggai prophesied, this new temple's grandeur was even greater than the temple which Solomon had built. Jesus' disciples remarked on its grandeur:

> As he was leaving the temple, one of his disciples said to him, "**Look, Teacher! What massive stones! What magnificent buildings!**" "Do you see all these great buildings?" replied Jesus. "Not one stone here will be left on another; every one will be thrown down."
> (Mk.13:1-2 NIV)

God never descended with the *shekinah* glory to dwell in this temple either. Two years after the temple was completed (AD 70), a Roman general named Titus desired to stamp out rebellion in Jerusalem and, therefore, transformed the temple to a pile of rubble. For nearly 2000 years, there has not been any temple in Jerusalem. However, a future temple has been prophesied for Jerusalem:

> **Concerning the coming of our Lord Jesus Christ and our being gathered to him**, we ask you, brothers, not to become easily unsettled or alarmed by some prophecy, report or letter supposed to have come from us, saying that the day of the Lord has already come. Don't let anyone deceive you in any way, for that day will not come until the rebellion occurs and the man of lawlessness is revealed, the man doomed to destruction. He will oppose and will exalt himself over everything that is called God or is

worshipped, **so that he sets himself up in God's temple, proclaiming himself to be God.** (2Th.2:1-4 NIV; 2Ti.2:17-18)

Before the first resurrection and the rapture of God's people, the temple must be rebuilt, for the anti-Christ must reign from the temple and claim to be God. Prior to 1980, I heard that a new temple was being prepared. Everything is now ready to be erected on the temple mount—once the Dome of the Rock and the Muslim Mosque has been eradicated. However, this new temple will be the temple of the anti-Christ. Thus far, all God's dwelling places shared the same design, His heavenly design:

They offer worship in a sanctuary that is a sketch and shadow of the heavenly one; for Moses, when he was about to erect the tent, was warned, "See that you make everything according to the pattern that was shown you on the mountain." (He.8:5 NRSV)

God's temple on earth was a replica of His dwelling place in heaven. Therefore, God's design of an earthly dwelling place is very specific.

A COMMON DESIGN

God designed the temple with a purpose: that man could come to Him and not die. Since all of the dwelling places were designed by God, all of them had a common design of three distinct areas: the courtyard, the Holy Place, and the Holy of Holies. In fact, the tabernacle consisted of several series of three things, each having its function. In the courtyard was the first series of three: the bronze altar, the bronze basin, and the tabernacle itself. Within the courtyard, the altar was the farthest that a common man could go. Here, he would bring a sacrifice or offering which the priest would offer upon the altar, on the people's behalf:

If a member of the community sins unintentionally and does what is forbidden in any of the LORD's commands, he is guilty. When he is made aware of the sin he committed, he must bring as his offering for the sin he committed a female goat without defect. **He is to lay his hand on the head of the sin offering and slaughter it at the place of the burnt offering.** Then the priest is to take some of the blood with his finger and put it on the horns of the altar of burnt offering and pour out the rest of the blood at the base of the altar. He shall remove all the fat, just as the fat is removed from the fellowship offering, and the priest shall burn it on the altar as an aroma pleasing to the LORD. **In this way the priest will make atonement for him, and he will be forgiven.** (Le.4:27-31 NIV)

Only a priest could approach the bronze altar, the bronze laver, or the tabernacle. A priest was also commanded to enter the first room in the tabernacle (the Holy Place). In the Holy Place was the next series of three pieces of furniture: the gold lampstand, the gold altar of incense, and the gold table of showbread. Twice a day, a priest had to tend the lamps of the gold lampstand while burning incense on the gold altar:

> Aaron must **burn fragrant incense on the altar every morning when he tends the lamps**. He must burn incense again when he lights the lamps at twilight so incense will burn regularly before the LORD for the generations to come. (Ex 30:7-8 TNIV)

Once a week on the Sabbath, the priest had to change the twelve cakes of unleavened bread on the table of showbread:

> **This bread is to be set out before the LORD regularly, Sabbath after Sabbath,** on behalf of the Israelites, as a lasting covenant. (Le 24:8 TNIV)

The Holy Place would be visited by priests each day. However, the third room (the Holy of Holies) could only be entered by the High Priest once a year on the Day of Atonement (Yom Kippur). The Holy of Holies contained only one piece of furniture: the Ark of the Covenant. However, inside the ark were three articles: Aaron's staff that budded, the two stone tablets of the covenant, and a gold jar containing manna:

> Behind the second curtain was a tent called **the Holy of Holies**. In it stood **the golden altar of incense** and **the ark of the covenant** overlaid on all sides with gold, in which there were a golden urn holding the manna, and Aaron's rod that budded, and the tablets of the covenant; (He.9:3-4 NRSV)

Once a year, the High Priest would enter the Holy of Holies to sprinkle blood on the mercy seat, which was located between the two cherubim on the lid of the ark. The blood sprinkled on the mercy seat before the Presence of God brought forgiveness for the sins of the Jewish nation:

> Now when these things have been so prepared, the **priests are continually entering the outer** tabernacle performing the divine worship, but into the second, **only the high priest enters once a year**, not without taking blood, which he offers for himself and **for the sins of the people committed in ignorance**. (He.9:6-7 NASB)

According to the commands of God, without sprinkling the blood on the mercy seat, the atonement for the sins of Israel could not be made. God not only designed every one of His temples, but He also commanded a specific order for the worship in His temple. Any violation to this order would cause rejection by God and possible death to the priest who was officiating.

GOD LIVED AMONG HIS PEOPLE

God made the temple so that He could dwell amongst His people. If one would approach the nation of Israel in the desert, one would find the tabernacle in the very middle of the twelve tribes.

To the east we would find the tribe of Judah with the tribes of Zebulun and Issachar on either side.

To the south we would find the tribe of Reuben with the tribes of Simeon and Gad on either side.

To the west we would find the tribe of Ephraim with the tribes of Manasseh and Benjamin on either side.

To the north we would find the tribe of Dan with the tribes of Asher and Naphtali on either side.

The temple was for man's benefit to make them aware that God dwelt among them.

— God did not need a dwelling place. He is omnipresent and is not limited to one place at one time:

> *God, who made the world and everything in it, since He is Lord of heaven and earth, **does not dwell in temples made with hands.*** (Ac.17:24 NKJV)

The purpose of the courtyard was to keep a minimum amount of separation between God and man. Israel knew that God's Presence was near but not directly accessible. However, God did not live solely in the Holy of Holies; for when Solomon dedicated the temple, he concluded:

> *But will God really dwell on earth? **The heavens, even the highest heaven, cannot contain you.** How much less this temple I have built!*
> (1Ki.8:27 NKJV)

A temple could not contain God, for even King David said:

> *Where can I go from your spirit? Or where can I flee from your presence? If I ascend to heaven, **you are there**; if I make my bed in Sheol, **you are there**. If I take the wings of the morning and settle at the farthest limits of the sea, even there **your hand shall lead me, and your right hand shall hold me fast**.* (Ps.139:7-10 NRSV)

The courtyard provided a physical barrier that allowed God to dwell in the middle of His people without having to destroy them because of their sin. In this way, man was allowed to approach God in a limited way, which was better than living totally separated from Him:

> One thing I have asked from the LORD, that I shall seek: **That I may dwell in the house of the LORD all the days of my life,** To behold the beauty of the LORD, And **to meditate in His temple.** For in the day of trouble **He will conceal me in His tabernacle**; In the secret place **of His tent** He will hide me; He will lift me up on a rock. (Ps.27:4-5 NASB)

Therefore, the tabernacle was not built for God but for man. A limited access to God was provided to remove the risk of death because of sin.

GOD DEPARTED FROM HIS TEMPLE

God dwelt only in the Holy of Holies above the Ark of the Covenant, over the mercy seat. The Ark of the Covenant disappeared prior to the Babylonian desecration of the temple (600 BC) and has never again been seen on earth. Jeremiah prophesied concerning the disappearance of the ark:

> "In those days, when your numbers have increased greatly in the land," declares the LORD, **"people will no longer say, 'The ark of the covenant of the LORD.' It will never enter their minds or be remembered; it will not be missed,** nor will another one be made." (Jer.3:16 TNIV)

The loss of the ark presented Israel with a two-fold problem. First, without the Ark of the Covenant, the High Priest could not make atonement for the people's sins. Without the blood sprinkled on the mercy seat, the Jews could not secure the forgiveness of God for the sins of the nation of Judah. In fact, since the destruction of the temple, nearly two thousand years ago, no blood has been offered in the Holy of Holies for the sins of the people of Israel:

> **For the life of the flesh is in the blood**; and I have given it to you for making atonement for your lives on the altar; **for, as life, it is the blood that makes atonement.** (Le.17:11 NRSV)

According to the law of Moses, without the daily sacrifices and especially without the blood on the mercy seat, there was no forgiveness. Secondly, an even a greater issue was that without the ark, there was no place for God to dwell:

> Then put the atonement cover **on top of the Ark**. *I will meet with you there and **talk to you from <u>above</u> the atonement cover <u>between</u> the gold cherubim that hover over the Ark of the Covenant**. From there I will give you my commands for the people of Israel.* (Ex.25:21-23 NLT)

God's dwelling place on earth was in the Holy of Holies, between the cherubim and over the mercy seat. His Presence in the Holy of Holies was evident by the cloud which came upon the tabernacle. Once the cloud lifted, the Israelites knew that God wanted them to leave the area. God had to remove Himself from above the ark in order for the priests to disassemble the whole tabernacle complex:

> *Throughout all their journeys **whenever the cloud was taken up from over the tabernacle**, the sons of Israel would set out; but if the cloud was not taken up, then **they did not set out until the day when it was taken up**. For throughout all their journeys, the cloud of the LORD was on the tabernacle by day, and there was fire in it by night, in the sight of all the house of Israel.* (Ex.40:36-38 NASB)

The cloud was a visible reminder that God had residence in the tabernacle. The reason why the *shekinah* glory of God did not descend upon Ezra's temple was that without the ark and its mercy seat, God had no place to dwell. The Holy of Holies became an empty room without an appropriate place for God to dwell:

> *He and all his men set out from Baalah of Judah to bring up from there the ark of God, which is called by the Name, the name of the LORD Almighty, **who is enthroned between the cherubim that are on the ark**.* (2Sa.6:2 NIV; 1Sa.4:4; 1Ch 13:6; 2Ki 19:15; Ps 80:1; Isa.37:16)

Without the descending of the *shekinah* glory of God on Ezra's temple, God was declaring that He no longer dwelt in the temple. Therefore, God demonstrated His disapproval of Judah by withdrawing from the temple.

GOD'S FINAL TEMPLE

In the Old Testament, the people of Israel first worshiped in the tabernacle and later in the temple. However, they actually did not have access to God; only the priests were allowed at specific times to enter the Holy Place. The only other group of people who would experience the Presence of God was the prophets:

> *Surely **the Lord GOD does nothing unless <u>He reveals</u>** His secret counsel **to His servants the prophets**.* (Am.3:7 NASB)

God's Spirit would come upon the prophet and give a revelation, after which His Spirit would depart until the next revelation. God determined when the revelations would occur:

> Word came to Saul: "David is in Naioth at Ramah"; so **he sent men to capture him**. But when **they saw <u>a group of prophets prophesying</u>**, with Samuel standing there as their leader, **the Spirit of God came on Saul's men, and they also prophesied**. (1Sa.19:19 TNIV)

The priests had a regular but limited access to God, while the prophets had erratic but personal access to Him. The common people did not have any access to God. Through the prophets, God promised that one day all people would receive His Spirit:

> Afterwards, **I will pour out my Spirit on all people**. Your sons and daughters will prophesy, your old men will dream dreams, your young men will see visions. Even **on my servants, both men and women, I will pour out my Spirit in those days**. (Joel 2:28-29 NIV)

Many of the prophets spoke about God coming from behind the curtain and indwelling all His people:

> I will never again hide my face from them, when I **pour out my spirit upon the house of Israel**, says the Lord GOD. (Eze.39:29 NRSV)

God stated that He would no longer be hidden behind the curtain of the Holy of Holies but would give His Spirit to all who are the true Israel:

> **I will pour out My Spirit on your offspring** and My blessing on your descendants; (Isa.44:3 NASB)

The promise of God's Spirit dwelling in men is not just a limited imparting of His Spirit. The word "pour" was used to imply a generous over-flowing of His Spirit:

> **I will pour out on** the house of David and on the inhabitants of Jerusalem, **<u>the Spirit</u> of grace and of supplication**, so that they **will <u>look on Me</u>** whom **they have pierced**; and they will mourn for Him, as one mourns for an only son, (Zec.12:10 NASB)

These are great promises, but man has two problems. First, God is Holy, and man has a wicked heart:

> **<u>The heart is deceitful</u>** above all things, and **<u>desperately wicked</u>**; Who can know it? (Jer.17:9 NKJV)

If our holy God cannot dwell **among** people with a wicked heart, then He certainly cannot dwell **in** people with a wicked heart:

> The LORD saw **how great the wickedness of the human race** had become on the earth, and that **every inclination** of the thoughts **of the human heart** was **only** evil **all** the time. The LORD regretted that he had made human beings on the earth, and **his heart was deeply troubled.** (Ge.6:5-6 TNIV)

Second, man's spirit is dead and is no longer able to unite with God's Spirit. The penalty for eating the forbidden fruit was death on the day that they ate of it:

> You **must not eat from the tree** of the knowledge of good and evil, for **when you eat of it you will surely die**." (Ge.2:17 NIV)

In order for God to maintain His integrity, those who ate the forbidden fruit had to die that day. However, when Adam and Eve ate of that fruit, they were not totally annihilated. They did not die physically, for Adam continued to live until he was 930 years old. They did not die soulically; that is, they did not become brain dead, losing their intellect, emotion, and will. They continued to make choices. The day they ate the forbidden fruit, man died in their spirit. The body connects us to the physical world through our senses. Our soul is who we are with our personality and preferences shaped by our past experiences. But our spirit was meant to connect us with God. It died the day man ate the forbidden fruit. I must point out that man's spirit did not cease to exist, for if it were, we would have died physically as well:

> For just as **the body without the spirit is dead**... (Ja.2:26 NASB)

Man's spirit was deadened. For example, one day my son passed out at work. At the hospital, the doctors determined that his pancreas shut down and stopped producing insulin—Type A diabetes. The pancreas was still in his body; it just stopped working. He needed to use artificial insulin in order to live. Similarly, mankind died in their spirit's function and were unable to utilize all that God created their spirit to be. Since man's spirit was deadened, God promised a new covenant in the Old Testament:

> This **is the covenant** that I will make with the house of Israel after those days, says the LORD: I will **put My law in their minds**, and write it **on their hearts**; and I will be their God, and they shall be My people. No more shall every man teach his neighbor, and every man his brother, saying, 'Know the LORD,' for **they all shall know Me**, **from the least** of them **to the greatest of them**, says the LORD. (Jer.31:33-34 NKJV)

The new covenant guarantees that all His people will experience God's indwelling instead of just knowing about Him. In order for God to accomplish this phenomenal change, He needed to give man a new heart and a new spirit:

> I will give you **a new heart** and put **a new spirit** in you; I will remove from you your heart of stone and give you a heart of flesh. And **I will put my Spirit in you** and **move you** to follow my decrees and be careful to keep my laws.
> (Eze.36:26-27 TNIV)

God promised Israel a new heart, in order to create a place for Him to dwell, and a new spirit, so that man could have direct access to God. Because of His indwelling, God could empower people to live for Him. When Jesus dialogued with the Samaritan woman at the well, He promised that God would change the place of worship from the temple in Jerusalem to the personal level of worshiping through man's spirit:

> "**Our fathers worshiped on this mountain, but you Jews claim that the place where we must worship is in Jerusalem.**" Jesus declared, "Believe me, woman, a time is coming when you will worship the Father neither on this mountain nor in Jerusalem. You Samaritans worship what you do not know; we worship what we do know, for salvation is from the Jews. **Yet a time is coming and has now come** when the true worshipers **will worship the Father in spirit** and truth, for they are the kind of worshipers the Father seeks. God is spirit, and **his worshipers must worship in spirit** and in truth." (Jn.4:20-24 NIV)

Through the cleansing of man's heart and the rebirth of man's spirit, we have become the temple of God. When Jesus died, a significant event took place in the temple in Jerusalem:

> And Jesus cried out again with a loud voice, and **yielded up His spirit**. And behold, **the veil of the temple was torn in two from top to bottom**; and the earth shook and the rocks were split. (Mt.27:50-51 NASB)

God tore, from the top to the bottom, the curtain that separated the Holy Place from the Holy of Holies. Through this act, God was stating that He will no longer be separated from His people. This action had two effects: God came out to dwell within man, and man can have complete access to God. This tearing signified the passing of God's dwelling place from the temple in Jerusalem to its present location in the human heart:

> I pray that out of his glorious riches he may strengthen you with power through **his Spirit in your inner being**, so **that Christ may dwell in your hearts** through faith. (Eph.3:16-17 NIV)

With God's Spirit living in us, we have become the new temple of God:

> Don't you know that **you yourselves are God's temple and that God's Spirit lives in you?** If anyone destroys God's temple, God will destroy him; **for God's temple is sacred**, and you are that temple.
> (1Co.3:16-17 NIV; 2Co.6:16)

Christ's death cleansed our heart, and His resurrection enables our spirit to be born again:

> According to his great mercy, **he has caused us to be born again** to a living hope **through the resurrection** of Jesus Christ from the dead,
> (1Pe.1:3 ESV)

However, the Holy Spirit did not come until Jesus ascended into heaven:

> But this He spoke **concerning the Spirit**, whom those believing in Him would receive; **for the Holy Spirit was not yet** given, because **Jesus was not yet glorified**.
> (Jn.7:39 NKJV)

Ten days after Jesus ascended into heaven, on the day of Pentecost, the *skekinah* glory of God filled His present dwelling place—the hearts of His people:

> When the day of Pentecost came, they were all together in one place. **Suddenly a sound like the blowing of a violent wind came from heaven** and filled the whole house where they were sitting. They saw what seemed to be **tongues of fire that separated and came to rest on each of them. All of them were filled with the Holy Spirit...**
> (Ac.2:1-4 NIV)

The Spirit of God now lives in the heart of His people. If the Spirit of God lives in you, then you have become the temple of God with all the fullness of Him dwelling within you:

> For **in Christ all the fullness of the Deity lives** in bodily form, and **you have been given fullness in Christ**, who is the head over every power and authority.
> (Co.2:9-10 NIV)

Christianity was never meant to be a religion of rituals, rules, traditions, and theology; rather, it was meant to be God living in man as His new temple.

We are the new temple. The way to God is represented by the courtyard; our body is the tabernacle; our soul is the Holy Place; and our re-born spirit is the Holy of Holies. The next twelve lessons will help us comprehend the significance of becoming God's temple by His Spirit's indwelling.

Thinking It Through:

1. What is unique about the way God created man?

2. Since the forbidden fruit was not intrinsically evil, what caused the creation of the sinful nature?

3. What would be the psychological condition of a person who eats something that is known to bring certain death?

4. What caused the creation of the sinful nature in man? Why?

5. What is superior: free choice or the inability to choose sin?

6. Who designed the tabernacle? Why?

7. When did God depart from His temple in Jerusalem?

8. What confirms that we have become the temple of God?

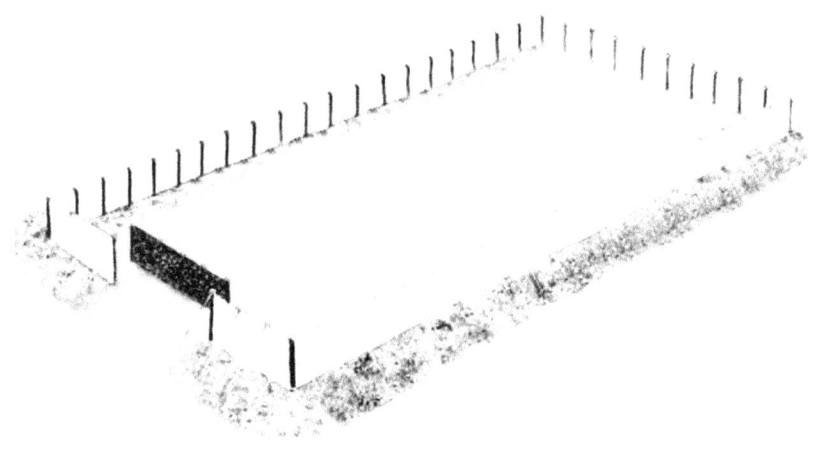

THE COURTYARD

Make a courtyard for the holy tent. The south side must be 150 feet long. It must have curtains that are made out of finely twisted linen. The curtains must be hung on 20 posts and 20 bronze bases. The posts must have silver hooks and bands on them. The north side must also be 150 feet long. It must have curtains with 20 posts and 20 bronze bases. The posts must have silver hooks and bands on them. The west end of the courtyard must be 75 feet wide. It must have curtains with ten posts and ten bases. The east end of the courtyard, toward the sunrise, must also be 75 feet wide. On one side of the entrance you must put curtains that are 22 feet six inches long. Hang them on three posts. Each post must have a base. On the other side you must also put curtains that are 22 feet six inches long. Hang them on three posts. Each post must have a base. For the entrance to the courtyard, provide a curtain that is 30 feet long. Make it out of blue, purple and bright red yarn and finely twisted linen. Have someone who sews skillfully make it. Hang it on four posts. Each post must have a base. All of the posts that are around the courtyard must have silver bands and hooks. They must also have bronze bases. The courtyard must be 150 feet long and 75 feet wide. It must have curtains that are made out of finely twisted linen. They must be seven feet six inches high. The posts must have bronze bases. Make all of the other articles used for any purpose in the holy tent out of bronze. That includes all of the tent stakes for the tent and the courtyard. Exodus.27:9-17 NIrV

Lesson 2

The Courtyard

Our Perspective

When Adam and Eve ate the forbidden fruit, they were sent out of God's garden and into Satan's kingdom, the world. For this reason, we will approach our study of the tabernacle from the perspective of man, who is on the outside in the Desert of Sin (Nu.33:11), and make our way to God. First, we must consider the courtyard. The courtyard implies an enclosed area. One might consider that the purpose of the courtyard wall was to keep the common people from approaching the tabernacle and from treating the holy complex as common through familiarity. If someone walked toward the tabernacle from the Desert of Sin to approach God, he would first have to walk through one of the twelve tribes of Israel. However, Israel did not contain twelve tribes but thirteen tribes. The thirteenth tribe was the tribe of Levi which acted as the buffer between the common people and God. Even though Jacob, whose name was changed to Israel, had only twelve sons, his son Joseph had a double blessing; for he did not receive one tribe as his representation but two. Joseph's two sons, Ephraim and Manasseh, became two separate tribes of Israel. The tribe of Levi was set apart from the other tribes when it rallied with Moses at the incident of the golden calf. When Moses came down from the mountain with the first two stone tablets of the law, he found the whole nation of Israel caught up in sin:

> *Moses turned and went down the mountain with the two tablets of the covenant law in his hands. They were inscribed on both sides, front and back. The tablets were the work of God; the writing was the writing of God, engraved on the tablets...* **When Moses approached the camp and saw the calf and the dancing, his anger burned and he threw the tablets out of his hands, breaking them to pieces at the foot of the mountain.**
> (Ex.32:15-16 NKJV)

When Moses had been up on the mountain for forty days, Israel had already rebelled against God by worshiping a golden idol in the form of a calf. Moses saw that the nation of Israel was out of control, and he knew that drastic measures were necessary to restore order:

> When Moses saw that the people were running wild (for Aaron had let them run wild, to the derision of their enemies), then Moses stood in the gate of the camp, and said, "**Who is on the Lord's side? Come to me!**" **And all the sons of Levi gathered around him.** He said to them, "Thus says the LORD, the God of Israel, 'Put your sword on your side, each of you! Go back and forth from gate to gate throughout the camp, and each of you kill your brother, your friend, and your neighbor.'" **The sons of Levi did as Moses commanded, and about three thousand of the people fell on that day.** Moses said, "**Today you have ordained yourselves for the service of the LORD,** each one at the cost of a son or a brother, and so have brought a blessing on yourselves this day." (Ex.32:25-28 NIV)

The day that the Levites rallied to Moses' call, they were set apart from the other tribes for God's special service in the tabernacle complex. The Levites were appointed to serve daily with the priests in the courtyard; both were constantly reminded by their work that their Holy God dwelt in the tabernacle. Their service made them the best choice to form a buffer that immediately surrounded the tabernacle on every side:

- **To the east** dwelt Moses, Aaron and the priests—who were the only ones who could enter the sanctuary.
- **To the south** dwelt the Kohathites—who were responsible for the furniture: the ark, the table, the lampstand, the altars, the articles used in the sanctuary, and the curtain for the Holy of Holies.
- **To the west** dwelt the Gershonites—who were responsible for the linens: the curtains and the tent with its coverings.
- **To the north** dwelt the Merarites—who were responsible for the hardware: the frames, crossbars, bases, posts, and pegs.

The buffer-zone created by the Levites was very significant because when Israel left Egypt, they already numbered 22,000 males, not including females:

> When Moses and Aaron counted the Levite clans at the LORD's command, the total number was 22,000 **males one month old or older**.
> (Nu.3:39 NLT)

Therefore, the Levites and the priests formed a barrier between the tabernacle and the people, preventing them from having casual access to it.

White Curtains

If someone approached the tabernacle from the north, west, or south, he would come to a wall consisting of a series of curtains made of finely-twisted white linen. White symbolizes purity, for in heaven, at the marriage supper of the Lamb, we also will be given pure, fine linen to wear:

> For the wedding of the Lamb has come, and his bride has made herself ready. **Fine linen, bright and clean, was given her to wear. (Fine linen stands for the righteous acts of the saints.)** (Re.19.7-8 NIV; Re.7:9)

When Christ arose from the dead, God sent an angel to roll back the stone in front of Jesus' tomb. Those who saw the angel recorded that he was wearing white:

> There was a great earthquake; **for an angel of the Lord, descending from heaven,** came and rolled back the stone and sat on it. His appearance was like lightning, and **his clothing white as snow.** (Mt.28:2-3; Ac.1:10 NRSV)

Most people have a favorite color that they like to wear. For God, His color of preference is white:

> As I watched, thrones were set in place, and an Ancient One took his throne, **his clothing was white as snow,** and the hair of his head like pure wool... (Da.7:9 NRSV)

God is holy—absolute, sinless perfection—and the color white represents His holiness. The Scriptures use the color white to signify sinless purity:

> Purify me with hyssop, and I shall be clean; Wash me, and **I shall be whiter than snow.** (Ps.51:7 NRSV; Re.20:11 Isa.1:18)

If someone approached the tabernacle complex, he would be confronted by a white-curtained wall—reminding him that God lived behind the curtain:

> He who is the blessed and only Sovereign, the King of kings and Lord of lords; who alone possesses immortality and **dwells in unapproachable light; whom no man has seen <u>or can see</u>.** (1Ti.6:15-16 NASB)

Therefore, the white linen curtain was to remind man that the almighty, holy God dwelt behind the curtain.

The Posts

The curtain was held up by posts of acacia wood with brass bases and silver hooks fastened to silver bands which went around the posts and held up the curtains:

The bases for the posts were bronze. The hooks and bands on the posts were silver, and their tops were overlaid with silver; so all the posts of the courtyard had silver bands. (Ex.27:17 TNIV)

The acacia wood of the posts that held up the curtain was not naturally found in the wilderness:

*I will plant trees in the barren desert—cedar, **acacia**, myrtle, olive, cypress, fir, and pine. I am doing this so **all who see this miracle** will understand what it means—that it is the LORD who has done this, the Holy One of Israel who created it.* (Isa.41:19 NLT)

The previous Scripture clearly states that the acacia tree, as well as the cedar, the myrtle, and the olive trees, were not found in the wilderness. The acacia wood was brought out of Egypt. When building the tabernacle, the people were not told to find acacia wood; rather, everyone who had acacia wood brought the wood from his personal effects:

*And **every man, who had in his possession** blue and purple and scarlet material and fine linen and goats' hair and rams' skins dyed red and porpoise skins, **brought them**. Everyone who could make a contribution of silver and bronze brought the LORD'S contribution; and **every man, who had <u>in his possession acacia wood</u>** for any work of the service, **brought it**.* (Ex.35:23-24 NASB)

The acacia wood used in the tabernacle symbolized mankind. Israel's exodus out of Egypt to the Promised Land symbolized mankind's exodus from Satan's realm to God's kingdom. In the same way that the nation of Israel was in slavery in Egypt for 400 years, mankind was enslaved to sin for 4,000 years, from the creation of the world until the death of Christ. The Scripture symbolically uses trees (wood) to denote a man's life:

*And he shall be **like a tree** planted by the rivers of water…* (Ps.1:3 KJV)

In the book of Daniel, God used a tree in a dream to represent Nebuchadnezzar's life. Daniel interpreted the dream:

Your Majesty, you are that tree! (Da.4:22 TNIV)

The posts were supported by bases made of bronze. The bronze speaks of man's sinful foundation—man is born with a sinful nature. The Bible tells us that once Adam and Eve gained the knowledge of evil, mankind was predisposed to sin. Man's sinful nature was the cause of the flood:

The LORD saw that the wickedness of humankind was great in the earth, and that <u>every</u> inclination of the thoughts of their hearts was <u>only</u> evil

continually*. And the LORD was sorry that he had made humankind on the earth, and **it grieved him to his heart***. (Ge.6:5-6 NRSV; Ro.5:12-13)

We are born sinful by nature. No one teaches children to do evil; evil is done naturally. However, in order to change a child's sinful practices, one has to teach and enforce positive behavior from birth while disciplining sin:

*Surely **I was sinful at birth, sinful from the time my mother conceived me**.* (Ps 51:5 NIV; Ge.8:21)

Man was under the control of sin from conception. They could not even stop doing the evil that they had come to hate:

*I know that **nothing good** lives in me, that is, in **my sinful nature**. For I have the desire to do what is good, but **I cannot carry it out**. For what I do is not the good I want to do; no, the evil I do not want to do—**this I keep on doing**. Now if **I do what I do not want to do**, it is no longer I who do it, but it is sin living in me that does it.* (Ro.7:18-20 NLT)

Before Paul received the Holy Spirit, he was controlled by his sinful nature: unable to do the good that he wanted to do and consistently compelled to do the evil he did not want to do. The sinful nature of man caused them to be disinterested in the things of God, leading them to rebel against Him:

*We have already charged that all, both Jews and Greeks, are under the **power** of sin, as it is written: "There is **no one** who is righteous, **not even one**; there is **no one** who has understanding, there is **no one who seeks God**. **All have turned aside**, together they have become worthless; there is **no one** who shows kindness, there is **not even one**."* (Ro.3:9-12 NRSV)

If a natural man would come to the curtain wall instead of the gate, his nature would draw him away, back into the Desert of Sin because man's sinful nature is inherently disinterested in the things of God:

*Their feet **run** to do evil, and they rush to commit murder. **They think only** about sinning. Misery and destruction always follow them. **They don't know** where to find peace or **what it means to be just and good**.* (Isa.59:7-8 NLT)

Mankind by nature is predisposed to do evil:

*All of us also **lived** among them **at one time**, gratifying **the cravings of our sinful nature and following its desires and thoughts**. Like the rest, we were by nature **objects of wrath**.* (Eph 2:3 NIV)

Every person born of Adam is controlled by the sinful nature. In the same way that the bronze bases held up the acacia posts, our sinful nature controlled mankind and predisposed them to sin:

*The mind of sinful man is death, **but the mind controlled by the Spirit** is life and peace; the sinful mind is hostile to God. It does not submit to God's law, nor can it do so. **Those controlled by the sinful nature** cannot please God.*
(Ro.8:6-8 NIV)

Since the sinful nature corrupts man's desires, the Bible uses bronze, an impure metal, to portray people who are corrupt:

*They are all hardened rebels, going about to slander. **They are bronze and iron; they all act corruptly**.* (Jer.6:28 NIV)

The metal of the bases was called "bronze," a combination of copper and tin. To God, both copper and tin which make the alloy bronze were considered dross, the worthless scum of metal:

*Son of man, the house of Israel has **become dross to me; all of them are the <u>copper, tin</u>**, iron and lead **left inside a furnace**. They are but the dross of silver.* (Eze.22:18 NIV)

When we were controlled by the sinful nature, we were corrupt and considered worthless dross by God. In fact, Ezekiel 16 uses the Hebrew word for *brass*, another alloy of copper, but modern English versions translate the word *brass* as "lewdness or lust":

*Thus says the Lord GOD, "Because **your '<u>brass</u>'** was poured out and your nakedness uncovered through your harlotries with your lovers and with all your detestable idols, and because of the blood of your sons which you gave to idols.* (Eze.16:36 Youngs Literal Translation)

The acacia wood supported by bronze bases represented man in his natural state, predisposed to sin. Therefore, the acacia wood supported by a bronze base represented man's life which was under the control of their sinful nature.

THE CURTAIN

The wall was made of a series of linen curtains and was not designed to physically keep people from the tabernacle, for a linen curtain could be easily cut with a sharp knife, just like a camping tent's wall, enabling an easy access to the tabernacle. However, God was not concerned with people breaching the curtain wall, for God warned the Israelites that those who would attempt to get near the tabernacle would die:

*From now on **the Israelites must not go near the tent of meeting**, or they will bear **the consequences of their sin and will die**.* (Nu.18:22 TNIV)

The almighty God would not allow anyone sinful to come near the tabernacle, for He is holy. God also commanded the punishment of death for a person who was caught trying to approach the tabernacle:

> So you shall appoint Aaron and his sons, and they shall attend to their priesthood; but **the outsider who comes near shall be put to death.**
> (Nu.3:10 NKJV)

Since the punishment for an unauthorized person approaching the tabernacle was death by God or by the priests and Levites, we must consider the purpose of the curtain wall. The wall was never to prevent the people from entering the courtyard but to guide man to enter by the gate. A person only needed to follow the wall until he came to the gate; he could then enter the courtyard without the fear of death. However, man's tendency has always been to move away from God, back to wandering in the Desert of Sin:

> All we like sheep <u>have gone astray</u>; We have turned, <u>every one, to his own way</u>; And the LORD has laid on Him the iniquity of us all. (Isa.53:6 NIV)

Israel, like the rest of mankind, was so apt to reject God and seek any other alternative that would justify their continuation in sin:

> There is a way which <u>seems right to a man</u>, but its end **is the way of death.** (Pr.14:12 NASB)

Many people choose their course in life not on the basis of truth but by their feelings—what resonates with their dreams and desires. The linen curtain symbolizes the spiritual blindness of man:

> But their <u>minds were made dull</u>, for to this day the <u>same veil</u> remains when the old covenant is read. It has not been removed, **because only in Christ is it taken away.** Even to this day when Moses is read, <u>a veil covers</u> their hearts. But whenever anyone turns to the Lord, <u>the veil is taken away.</u> (2Co.3:14-15 NIV)

Natural man could not understand the things of God because their hearts were rebellious against Him. We are unable to understand the ways of God when He reveals Himself to man. In other words, the activities within the courtyard only made sense from the perspective of the gate. The Spirit of God must convict us of sin and our need of a Savior before we will desire to come to Him and enter by the gate:

> People who aren't spiritual can't receive **these truths from God's Spirit.** It all sounds foolish to them and they can't understand it, **for only those who are spiritual can understand what the Spirit means.** (1Co.2:14 NLT)

God has to work within man in order for them to believe in Christ:

> *No one can come to Me <u>unless the Father who sent Me draws him</u>; and I will raise him up on the last day.* (Jn.6:44 NASB)

The reason why the linen curtain was 5 cubits (7.5 feet) high was to signify that the natural senses of the body—sight, hearing, taste, smell, and touch—will never be able to perceive the things of God:

> *These are the men who divide you, **who follow mere natural instincts and do not have the Spirit**.* (Jd.1:19 NIV)

A person does not turn to God because he intellectually considered all the facts; rather, God used our brokenness to cause us to reach out to Him. When we saw no other way to escape our empty way of life, we called out in desperation to a God we could not see. When we called out to God in our brokenness, God revealed His truth by His Spirit:

> *Now we have received, not the spirit of the world, but **the Spirit who is from God**, so **that we may know** the things freely given to us by God, which things we also speak, not in words **taught by human wisdom**, but in those **taught by the Spirit**, combining **spiritual thoughts with spiritual words**.* (1Co.2:12-13 NASB)

The understanding of Christianity is spiritually discerned and can only be gained by revelation through the Holy Spirit. Consider the disciples: even though Christ repeatedly spoke of His death and resurrection, they could not comprehend what He was saying. However, after His resurrection, Jesus enabled His disciples to understand:

> *Then he said to them, "These are my words that I spoke to you while I was still with you—that everything written about me in the law of Moses, the prophets, and the psalms must be fulfilled." **Then he opened their minds to understand the scripture**.* (Lk.24:44-45 NRSV)

John grants us insight into how Christ opened their minds:

> *So Jesus said to them again, "Peace to you! As the Father has sent Me, I also send you". And when He had said this, He breathed on them, and said to them, **"Receive the Holy Spirit."*** (Jn.20:21-22 NKJV)

Only after receiving the Holy Spirit did the disciples obtain the understanding of all that Christ had accomplished by His death and resurrection. Man's natural wisdom cannot comprehend the things of God:

> *No, we speak of God's secret wisdom, a wisdom that has been hidden and that God destined for our glory before time began. **None of the rulers of this age understood it, for if they had, they would not have crucified the Lord of glory**. However, as it is written: "**No eye has seen, no ear has heard, no mind has conceived what God has prepared for those who***

*love him"—but **God has revealed it to us by his Spirit.*** (1Co.2:7-10 NIV)

The body's senses only perceive that which surrounds it in the physical realm, and the mind interprets the information to form a logical conclusion. Natural man bases their conclusions on what they perceive and disregard the invisible—thereby, they disregard God:

> Now this I affirm and insist on in the Lord: you must **no longer live as the Gentiles live, in the futility of their minds**. They are **darkened in their understanding**, alienated from the life of God **because of their ignorance and hardness of heart.** (Eph.4:17-18 NRSV)

Today, if a non-believer would look upon the rituals of the tabernacle, he would be appalled at the senseless, sacrificial killing of many animals. He would focus on animals' rights and not on his need for a sacrifice to pay for his sins. Sacrifice is only understood within the context of sin—a violation of God's nature. To the atheist, since he does not believe that God exists, a sacrifice becomes a meaningless waste of life. The linen curtain represents man's inability to perceive the Gospel. Only those who realize their sin are willing to come to God in humility, and they will be granted the insight to understand Him. Jesus said:

> Anyone **who chooses to do the will of God** will find out **whether my teaching comes from God** or whether I speak on my own. (Jn.7:17 TNIV)

Obedience to God precedes the understanding of His purposes for the command. Christians gain understanding after doing the will of God, for God honors our obedience by granting understanding. However, those who need to understand before they submit to the Gospel will never understand, for understanding comes with the obedience to the Gospel:

> I pray that **you may be active in sharing your faith**, so **that you will have a full understanding of every good thing** we have in Christ. (Phm.1:6:NIV)

When we humble ourselves through obedience, God grants us understanding. Accordingly, only those who obeyed by entering the courtyard through the gate were able to see and understand God's truth. Hence, only the participants who brought sacrifices or offerings were able to observe and grasp the meaning of the ritual. Those spectators who refused to obey by entering the courtyard through the gate with a sacrifice would never understand. Therefore, the curtain was not to keep people out of the courtyard but was symbolic of man's inability to understand the things of God because they only perceived through their five senses.

Spiritual Blindness

The inability for mankind to perceive spiritual things is understandable because man does not have the aptitude to comprehend God. However, there are two dynamics to the curtain wall: man's natural ignorance of God which prevents man from coming to Him, and a spiritual deception by the "world forces of darkness" which diverts man's attention away from God. One is passive in that man simply cannot comprehend the things of God, but the other is active because man is being deceived. The world forces of darkness is a dynamic force which is actively working to prevent people from believing. These deceptive demons propagate lies to divert men from perceiving the truth:

> For our **struggle is not against flesh and blood**, but against the rulers, against the powers, **against the world forces of this darkness**, against the spiritual forces of wickedness in the heavenly places. (Eph.6:12 NASB)

The world forces of darkness promote an alternative to truth, such as evolution and atheism, to divert people away from the truth through false religions and philosophy. An example of this is found in psychology. Carl Jung, the father of analytical psychology, consulted spiritual guides (two of which were Philemon and Basilides) who revealed his methodology. These spiritual guides denied the affect of the spiritual realm on mankind, trying to solve man's problems by manipulating man's psyche or soul. The spiritual guides diverted man's focus away from the spiritual realm to the physical and soulical realms. Jung constantly met with spiritual entities, yet the people who follow his teachings deny the existence of the spiritual realm and its affect on mankind. Obviously, the spiritual realm propagates darkness:

> They are from the world; **therefore what they say is from the world, and the world listens to them**. We are from God. Whoever knows God listens to us, and whoever is not from God does not listen to us. From this we know the spirit of truth and **the spirit of error**. (1Jn.4:5-6 NRSV)

Secular people are mesmerized, influenced by the illusion that there is no God. This concept allows them to follow the passions and pleasures of their sinful nature:

> And you He made alive, who were dead in trespasses and sins, in which you once **walked according to <u>the course of this world</u>**, according to the prince

of the power of the air, **the spirit** who now works in the **sons of disobedience** (Eph.2:1-2 NKJV)

Satan works his deception in man through the world forces of darkness. This organized spiritual conspiracy attempts to divert as many people as possible from perceiving all that Christ has accomplished for them:

> And even if **our gospel <u>is veiled</u>, it <u>is veiled</u> to those who are perishing,** in whose case **<u>the god of this world</u> has blinded the minds of the unbelieving so that they might not see** the light of the gospel of the glory of Christ, who is the image of God. (2Co.4:4 NASB)

Satan, who is the god of this age, is accredited with blinding unbelievers' minds. Satan is responsible because his spiritual forces of wickedness act according to his mandate. A similar example would be the Muslims who accused George Bush of killing Iraqis, even though he never fired one shot. The commander-in-chief is responsible for his subordinates' actions just as Satan is responsible for his demons' actions, the actions that prevent people from comprehending the truth. This is clearly seen amongst the people in rescue missions who have heard the message of the Gospel many times but have never made Jesus the Lord of their lives. The Scripture attributes their lack of commitment to the activities of the devil:

> The seed is the word of God. The ones on the path are those **who have heard**; then **<u>the devil comes</u> and takes away the word from their hearts,** so that they may not believe and be saved. (Lk.8:11-12 NRSV)

Many people will deny that the world forces of darkness influenced them to reject the Gospel, for they claim that they themselves rejected the Gospel based on logic. However, the Scripture attributes this rejection of the Gospel to the working of a spiritual entity:

> And so **they could not believe**, because Isaiah also said, "<u>**He**</u> **has blinded their eyes and hardened their heart**, so that they might not look with their eyes, and understand with their heart and turn— and I would heal them." (Jn.12:39-40 NRSV)

A spiritual being blinds a person's mind and hardens his heart. Blindness prevents a person from perceiving and understanding, while hardening prevents him from accepting and acting on what he perceives. Rejecting salvation is more than an intellectual shortcoming; it is a result of a power of darkness:

> I am sending you to them **to open their eyes and turn them from darkness to light, and from the power of Satan** to God, so that they may receive

forgiveness of sins and a place among those who are sanctified by faith in me. (Ac.26:17-18 NIV)

The spiritual power of Satan causes a blindness which creates darkness, thus preventing people from understanding the importance of Christ. The world forces of darkness not only prevent people from accepting the truth but also divert people from the truth by presenting an alternative version of the facts. This in turn propagates false religions:

*And he laid hold of the dragon, the serpent of old, who is the devil and Satan, and bound him for a thousand years, and threw him into the abyss, and shut it and sealed it over him, so **that he should not deceive the nations any longer,** until the thousand years were completed; after these things he must be released for a short time.* (Re 20:2-3 NASB)

Deception is the act of misleading a person by causing him to believe something that is not true:

*So the great dragon was cast out, that serpent of old, called the Devil and **Satan, who deceives the whole world**; he was cast to the earth, and **his angels were cast out with him**.* (Re.12:9 NKJV)

Consider why the world accepts nearly every philosophy and religion except Christianity. When men use profanities, why do they usually only profane the name of Jesus Christ? Why do people not use the name of Ra, Zeus, Sakkra, Brahma, Allah, or some other false deity? This selective profanity is the evidence that there exists a spiritual conspiracy against the true God and His Son Jesus Christ:

*The Spirit clearly says that in later times **some will abandon the faith** and follow **deceiving spirits** and **things taught by demons**.* (1Ti.4:1 TNIV)

The world forces of darkness are masters of diversion, for they will promote any belief system other than the one true God. Many false religions promise an existence after death, but their methodologies to attain that existence or their descriptions greatly conflict with each other. The inconsistency of religions is clearly seen when Paul was confronted by the Athenian's attempt to find God:

*So Paul stood in the midst of the Areopagus and said, "Men of Athens, I **observe that you are very religious in all respects**. For while I was passing through and examining the objects of your worship, I also found an altar with this inscription, 'to an unknown God.'"* (Ac.17:22-23 NASB)

Religion is man's attempt to reach God by their own efforts. The world readily accepts as credible any religion other than Christianity, but that acceptance does not mean they are truth. Consider three people desiring to ride a bus to the next city. You may sincerely believe the bus will arrive at 1 PM, while I believe the bus will arrive at 2 PM. Yet, another person may believe that the bus will arrive at 3 PM. We all believe that the bus will take us to the next city, but we disagree on the particulars. While each of us is sincere in his belief, only one reality exists as to the time when the bus will actually arrive. Many religions promise an eternal existence. They cannot all be correct, for there is only one reality. Spiritual forces of darkness do not care what religion or philosophy you believe, as long as you do not believe in the only true God. The white curtain wall represented the spiritual agenda of Satan to keep people from finding the gate and believing the truth:

> *This wisdom is not that which comes down from above, but **is earthly, natural, demonic**.* (Ja.3:15 NASB)

Therefore, there is a natural inability in man to perceive God, but there are also the world forces of darkness who propagate other religions to prevent people from perceiving the true God.

THE GATE

Every morning the sun would rise in the east on the Israelites' camp. It would pierce the darkness, shine on the gate, illuminating the way to God:

> *For it is the God who commanded **light to shine out of darkness, who has shone in our hearts to** give **the light** of the knowledge of the glory of God in the face of Jesus Christ.* (2Co.4:6 NKJV)

God is light, and He is the One Who draws us to the gate:

> *He went on to say, "This is why I told you that **no one can come to me unless the Father has enabled them**."* (Jn.6:44 TNIV)

Before the light reached the gate, it shone on the tribe of Judah:

> *Now those who camp on **the east side toward the sunrise shall be of the standard of the camp of Judah**...* (Nu.2:3 NASB)

When Solomon continued to sin by worshiping other gods, the nation of Israel was divided into two nations: ten tribes which were known as the nation of Israel and two tribes, Judah and Benjamin, which became the nation of Judah. The ten tribes of Israel were scattered among the nations by the Assyrians—never to be a nation again. They were replaced by other people who were later called Samaritans. The capital city of the ten tribes was Samaria. The nation of Judah was sent into Babylon and exiled for 70 years because of their sin. Later the people of the nation of Judah returned to the land of Judah and were known as Jews:

> You worship what you do not know; we know what we worship, **for salvation is of the Jews**. (Jn.4:22 NKJV)

The dawn's first light fell on Judah and pointed to Jesus, Who was referred to as the King of the Jews because He was descended from David of the tribe of Judah.

The light shone past the tribe of Judah to the priests who actually ministered before God, for the priests' tents lay between the gate of the tabernacle and the tribe of Judah. The priests are symbolic of the sacrifices and, more importantly, the blood:

> Indeed, under the law almost everything is purified with blood, and **without the shedding of blood there is no forgiveness of sins.** (He.9:22 NIV)

Jesus came not only as a Jew, but He also came as the great and perfect high priest. He offered His own blood for our eternal redemption:

> **Christ came as high priest** of the good things that are already here, he went through the greater and more perfect tabernacle that is not man-made, that is to say, not a part of this creation. He did not enter by means of the blood of goats and calves; but **he entered the Most Holy Place once for all by his own blood, having obtained eternal redemption.** (He.9:11-12 NIV)

Today, the light reaches the gate. Jesus said:

> I am the gate. Whoever **enters by me will be saved.** (Jn.10:9 NRSV)

Jesus claimed to be the only way to God:

> Jesus said to him, "**I am the way,** the truth, and the life. **No one comes to the Father except through Me.**" (Jn.14:6 NKJV)

The gate is Christ, for He is the only way we can escape the Desert of Sin and come to God:

> **There is salvation in no one else;** for there is **no other name** under heaven that has been given among men **by which we must be saved.** (Ac.4:12 NASB)

Unlike the wall of the courtyard which was white, three colors were embroidered into the linen curtains of the gate:

> For the entrance to the courtyard, make a curtain that is 30 feet long. Make it from finely woven linen, and decorate it with beautiful embroidery **in blue, purple,** and **scarlet thread.** (Ex.27:16 NLT)

The colors of the embroidery in the gate were blue, purple, and scarlet, and they all pointed to Christ.

The first color blue spoke of heaven; Jesus came down from heaven:

> No one has ascended into heaven except **the one who descended from heaven, the Son of Man.** (Jn.3:13 NRSV)

The second color embroidered into the linen gate was purple, which spoke of Christ's royalty. Jesus was a descendant of David, the king of the Jews:

> Therefore Pilate said to Him, "So You are a king?" Jesus answered, **"You say correctly that I am a king.** For this **I have been born,** and **for this I have come into the world."** (Jn.18:37 NASB)

The third color embroidered into the linen gate was scarlet/red, which spoke of Christ's sacrifice. Jesus is not only the great high priest but also the Lamb of God Who took the sins of the world upon Himself:

> The next day he saw Jesus coming toward him and declared, **"Here is the Lamb of God who takes away the sin of the world!"** (Jn.1:29 NRSV)

Just as the gate was the only way for man to enter the tabernacle, Jesus is the only way to come to God.

To know the way to God is not sufficient; we must enter through the gate. The demons know the way to God, yet they persist in their rebellion:

> **You believe that God is one;** you do well. **Even the demons believe**—and **shudder.** (Ja.2:19 NASB)

A man could remain outside the tabernacle at the gate, but he would still be in the Desert of Sin and separate from God. Some people understand the Gospel but believe that the gravity of sin in their lives places them beyond the grace of God. In other words, even though they know the way to God, their sense of unworthiness prevents them from entering.

One day, Jesus was eating and drinking with people of questionable reputation:

> The Pharisees and their scribes began grumbling at His disciples, saying, **"Why do you eat and drink with the tax collectors and sinners?"** And Jesus answered and said to them, "It is not those who are well who need a physician, but those who are sick. **I have not come to call the righteous but sinners to repentance."** (Lk.5:30-32 NASB)

If you are convinced that you are a sinner, then Jesus is calling you to enter through Him, the gate. God does not want anyone to perish, for His desire for man to be reconciled with Him is the reason why Jesus came to the earth:

> For God so loved the world that he gave his only Son, **so that everyone** who believes in him may not perish but **may have eternal life.** (Jn.3:16 NRSV)

Some people believe that they need to change before they are worthy of Christ, but their logic is flawed. If you had done some horribly dirty work in your garden, would you wash in the sink before taking a bath in a clean tub? Of course you wouldn't! The bathtub exists to make you clean. In the same way, Christ came to save and cleanse sinners from their sin. No prewash is needed:

> But God proves his love for us in that **while we still were sinners Christ died for us.** (Ro.5:8 NRSV)

Jesus was once confronted with the fate of a prostitute whom the law commanded to be stoned. He told her accusers that the person who was without sin should throw the first stone. Her accusers left because they all had sinned:

> "Then neither do I condemn you," Jesus declared. "**Go now and leave your life of sin.**" (Jn.8:11 NIV)

When people accept Christ's death as payment for their sins, He begins to transform their attitudes, behaviors, and characters:

> You **used to live** in sin, just like the rest of the world, obeying the devil—the commander of the powers in the unseen world. He is the spirit at work in the hearts of those who refuse to obey God. **All of us used to live** that way, following the passionate desires and inclinations of our sinful nature. (Eph.2:3 NLT)

What prevents people from coming to God is an unwillingness to humble themselves, admit that they are sinners, and reach out to the Savior Who died for them. Whether a person commits one sin or a million sins, every sinner needs a Savior:

> For whoever keeps the whole law and yet stumbles at just one point **is guilty of breaking all of it.** (Ja.2:10 NIV)

The question is not what you have done or how many sins you have committed, but rather, what are you going to do about your sin?

> For there is no difference between Jew and Gentile--the same Lord is Lord of all and richly blesses all who call on him, for, "**Everyone who calls on the name of the Lord will be saved.**" (Ro.10:12-13 TNIV)

Even if you consider yourself the worst of sinners, Christ came into the world to be your Savior. No one is beyond the hope of what is offered on the other side of the gate:

> *For this is good and acceptable in the sight of God our Savior,* **who desires all men to be saved** *and to come to the knowledge of the truth. For there is one God and* **one Mediator between God and men, the Man Christ Jesus,*
> (1Ti.2:3-5 NKJV)

Therefore, regardless of the evil done in the past, it will never prevent anyone from entering the gate.

Repentance

The Israelites were in the Desert of Sin, which was symbolic of the power of sin that enslaved the whole of humanity:

> *Then they set out from Elim, and all the congregation of the sons of* **Israel came to** <u>the wilderness of Sin</u>, *which is between Elim and Sinai, on the fifteenth day of the second month after their departure from the land of Egypt.*
> (Ex.16:1 NASB)

Every man has a choice to either remain in the Desert of Sin or turn to God through Christ. The foundation of the Gospel is repentance, a turning away from a life of sin to a life in God, by believing in Christ:

> *Therefore, leaving the discussion of the elementary* principles *of Christ, let us go on to perfection,* **not laying again the foundation of repentance** *from dead works and of faith toward God...*
> (He.6:1 NKJV)

God does not want anyone to go to hell, but everyone must turn from his pursuit of sin to Christ:

> *The Lord is not slow in keeping his promise, as some understand slowness. He is patient with you,* **not wanting** <u>anyone</u> **to perish,** *but* **everyone to come to repentance.**
> (2Pe.3:9 NIV)

The Greek word for *repentance* means "a change of mind." If I went into a store to buy a shirt but changed my mind, did I leave the store with a shirt? No! Just as Israel had to change their mind and enter the gate of the tabernacle, we must change our minds and turn to God through Christ:

> *They tell* **how you turned to God** *from idols* **to serve the living and true God**,
> (1Th.1:9 TNIV)

The gate represented repentance, for there is no other way to come to God:

> I have declared to **both Jews and Greeks** that they must turn to God in **repentance** and have faith in our Lord Jesus. (Ac.20:21 NIV)

If you refuse to repent, you will die in your sin:

> I tell you, no; but **unless you repent you will all likewise perish**. (Lk.13:3 NKJV)

God, through the eternal Gospel, is calling all people to repent from their sin:

> While God has overlooked the times of human ignorance, **now he commands all people everywhere to repent**, (Ac.17:30 NRSV)

To pray a sinner's prayer and to acknowledge God will not bring us any closer to God. We must repent by turning to God, just as Israel was required to approach God by entering the gate:

> **Godly sorrow brings repentance that leads to salvation** and leaves no regret, but worldly sorrow brings death. (2Co.7:10 NKJV)

Many people are wearied of their life in sin. They know the truth about Christ, yet they refuse to turn to God. God is still calling:

> **Now repent of your sins and turn to God**, so that your sins may be wiped away.. (Ac.3:19-20 NLT)

Just as the sun drew man to the gate, God, Who changes our minds (repentance), draws us unto Himself:

> When they heard this, they had no further objections and praised God, saying, "So then, **God has granted** even the Gentiles **repentance unto life**." (Ac.11:18 NIV)

To stop at the gate and refuse to enter the courtyard left a person not only in the Desert of Sin but also void of the Presence of God:

> I preached that they should repent and turn to God and **prove their repentance by their deeds**. (Ac.26:20 NIV)

God promises that if we enter the gate (Jesus), we will not be disappointed:

> Peter said to them, "**Repent,** and be baptized every one of you in the name of Jesus Christ **so that your sins may be forgiven**; and **you will receive the gift of the Holy Spirit.**" (Ac.2:38 NRSV)

Therefore, let us repent of our wandering in the Desert of Sin, and let us enter the gate so that we may know and participate in the Presence of God.

Thinking It Through:

1. Where was the tabernacle situated in relationship to the camps of the tribes of Israel?

2. What does white linen represent?

3. What do the bronze bases of the posts represent?

4. What would happen if a man breached the white linen wall?

5. Since the curtain was made of linen, what was its purpose?

6. What two things prevent natural man from perceiving and knowing God?

7. What do the three colors found in the gate teach us?

8. What is the main lesson of the gate?

William Dickes 1816-1892

BRONZE ALTAR

Build an altar out of acacia wood. It must be four feet six inches high and seven feet six inches square. Make a horn stick out from each of its upper four corners. Cover the altar with bronze. Make all of its tools out of bronze. Make its pots to remove the ashes. Make its shovels, sprinkling bowls, meat forks, and pans for carrying ashes. Make a bronze grate for the altar. Make a bronze ring for each of the four corners of the grate. Put the grate halfway up the altar on the inside. Make poles out of acacia wood for the altar. Cover them with bronze. Put the poles through the rings. They will be on two sides of the altar for carrying it. Make the altar out of boards. Make it hollow. You must make it just as I showed you on the mountain.   Exodus 27:1-8 NIrV

Lesson 3

The Bronze Altar

Sacrifice

Once we enter through the gate, we find ourselves in the courtyard facing the bronze altar. This is the altar that was used for sacrifices and offerings:

> *Place the altar of burnt offering in front of the entrance to the tabernacle, the Tent of Meeting; place the basin between the Tent of Meeting and the altar and put water in it.* (Ex.40:6 NIV)

Since we cannot enter the tabernacle without approaching the altar, the altar is the first step in drawing near to God. After Adam and Eve sinned, they were banished from God's garden and sent into the world. The Scriptures teach that our sins separated us from God:

> *Your iniquities have separated you from your God; your sins have hidden his face from you, so that he will not hear.* (Isa.59:2 NIV)

God is holy and, therefore, cannot tolerate our sin in His presence:

> *For You are not a God who takes pleasure in wickedness;* **No evil dwells with You.** *The boastful shall not stand before Your eyes;* **You hate all who do iniquity.** (Ps.5:4-5 NASB)

Everyone descended from Adam has sinned:

> *Indeed, there is* **no one** *on earth who is righteous,* **no one** *who does what is right and never sins.* (Ec.7:20 TNIV)

To approach God without having dealt with our sin ensures that we will die:

> *For if you live according to the sinful nature,* **you will die;** (Ro.8:13-14 NIV)

God postponed the penalty of physical death for Adam and Eve's sin, but He killed animals to make a temporary covering for Adam and Eve:

> *The LORD God made garments of skin for Adam and his wife, and clothed them.* (Ge.3:21 NASB)

The first death experienced were the animals killed after Adam and Eve's sin. The first narrative after the fall of man is about sacrifice:

> When it was time for the harvest, Cain **presented <u>some</u> of his crops** as a gift to the LORD. Abel **also brought a gift—<u>the best</u> of the firstborn lambs from his flock**. The LORD accepted Abel and his gift, but he did not accept Cain and his gift. (Ge.4:3-5 NLT)

The Scriptures do not tell us why Cain and Abel offered sacrifices to God. Rather, the Scriptures teach us that the attitude of our heart is very important when making a sacrifice. After the world was destroyed by the flood, the first thing that Noah did after coming out of the ark was to offer a sacrifice:

> Then **Noah built an altar to the LORD**, and took of every clean animal and of every clean bird, **and offered burnt offerings on the altar.** (Ge.8:20 NKJV)

Noah offered a sacrifice for the sins of the former world. When Job thought his children might have sinned, he offered sacrifices for their sin:

> And when the feast days had run their course, Job would send and sanctify them, and **he would rise early in the morning and offer burnt offerings according to the number of them all**; for Job said, "It may be that my **children have sinned**, and cursed God in their hearts." (Job 1:5 NRSV)

Abram constantly sacrificed to God, for wherever he settled in the land of Canaan, he built an altar:

> The LORD appeared to Abram and said, "To your offspring I will give this land." **So he built an altar there to the LORD**, who had appeared to him. (Ge.12:7 NIV)

The Scriptures never record that God commanded these people to build an altar and offer sacrifices for their sin; the Scriptures only state that this was the people's practice. When God eventually gave Israel the law, He then gave specific instructions concerning the sacrifices of animals to atone for their sins:

> For **the life of a creature is in the blood**, and I have given it to you to make atonement for yourselves on the altar; **it is the blood that makes atonement for one's life**. (Le.17:11 TNIV)

Only the shedding of blood could atone for their sins, for only blood could bring the forgiveness of God:

> Indeed, under the law almost everything is purified with blood, and **without the shedding of blood <u>there is no forgiveness of sins</u>**. (He.9:22 NRSV)

Even though the kinds of sacrificial animals varied, the procedure remained the same:

> *If a member of the community sins unintentionally and does what is forbidden in any of the LORD's commands, he is guilty. When he is made aware of the sin he committed,* **he must bring as his offering for the sin he committed a female goat without defect. He is to lay his hand on the head of the sin offering and slaughter it at the place of the burnt offering.** *Then the priest is to* **take some of the blood with his finger and put it on the horns of the altar** *of burnt offering and pour out the rest of the blood at the base of the altar.* (Le.4:27-30 NIV)

An Israelite would place his hand on the head of the animal that was to be sacrificed. This action transferred his sins done in ignorance onto the animal, which would then die for the person's sin. Only physically-perfect animals could be used as a sacrifice for one's sins:

> **You shall not offer anything that has a blemish, for it will not be acceptable in your behalf.** *When anyone offers a sacrifice of well-being to the LORD, in fulfillment of a vow or as a freewill offering, from the herd or from the flock, to be acceptable* **it must be perfect; there shall be no blemish in it.** *Anything blind, or injured, or maimed, or having a discharge or an itch or scabs—* **these you shall not offer to the LORD or put any of them on the altar as offerings by fire to the LORD.** (Le.22:20-22 NRSV)

Therefore, animal sacrifice had been practiced since Adam and Eve's first sin, when God took the lives of animals and made a covering for them.

THE STRUCTURE

The bronze altar of sacrifice was made from acacia wood and overlaid with bronze. The acacia wood was brought out of Egypt and represented man. The Scriptures used this parallel:

> **Blessed is the man... He is like a tree** *planted by streams of water,* (Ps.1:1&3 NIV)

Bronze represented man's sinful nature which predisposed them to commit sin. The Scriptures used bronze to portray people who acted corruptly:

> *They are all hardened rebels, going about to slander.* **They are bronze and iron; they all act corruptly.** (Jer.6:28 NIV)

The Scriptures also teach that we are sinful from conception: even a fetus has a sinful nature:

> Surely I was sinful at birth, sinful from the time my mother conceived me. (Ps 51:5 NIV; Ge.8:21)

The acacia wood covered by bronze represented that man's life was predisposed to sin. In the Old Testament, animal sacrifices were required, but animal sacrifices could not pay for our sins and grant us forgiveness:

> For it is impossible for the blood of bulls and goats to take away sins. (He.10:4 NASB)

The death of an animal cannot cancel the sin of a man because the penalty for sin is death. An animal's death was only an interim substitute:

> Behold, all souls are Mine; the soul of the father as well as the soul of the son is Mine; The soul who sins shall die. (Eze.18:4 NKJV)

God would have preferred that Israel would not sin rather than sin and offer the appropriate sacrifice. The Scriptures state that God was never pleased with the animal sacrifices:

> Christ said, "You did not want animal sacrifices or sin offerings or burnt offerings or other offerings for sin, nor were you pleased with them" (though they are required by the law of Moses). Then he said, "Look, I have come to do your will." He cancels the first covenant in order to put the second into effect. For God's will was for us to be made holy by the sacrifice of the body of Jesus Christ, once for all time. (He.10:8-10 NLT)

Even though animal sacrifices were required by the law, God sought more than obedience as a response to sin; God wanted a change of heart:

> For you have no delight in sacrifice; if I were to give a burnt offering, you would not be pleased. The sacrifice acceptable to God is a broken spirit; a broken and contrite heart, O God, you will not despise. (Ps.51:16-17 NRSV)

The only acceptable sacrifice required was a change of heart and spirit; anything less was unacceptable to God. The sacrifices that Israel offered fell short of what God had desired but served as an interim substitute.

The dimensions of the altar pointed to what God ultimately desired to be placed on the altar:

> Therefore, I urge you, brothers and sisters, in view of God's mercy, to offer your bodies as a living sacrifice, holy and pleasing to God—this is true worship. (Ro.12:1 TNIV)

Our body contains our soul and spirit. God will only be pleased when we offer the whole of our being on the altar as living sacrifices. The height of the altar was **three** cubits, which represented the *tri*-unity of man:

> And the LORD God formed man of **the dust of the ground**, and breathed into his nostrils **the breath of life**; and **man became a living soul.**
> (Ge.2:7 KJV)

The dust formed the body, the breath formed the spirit, and man became a living soul. Hence, man is composed of a body, a soul, and a spirit:

> Now may the God of peace Himself sanctify you entirely; and **may your spirit** and **soul** and **body** be **preserved complete**, without blame at the coming of our Lord Jesus Christ. (1Th.5:23 NASB)

When Satan tempted Eve, he presented her with the opportunity to become like God:

> Then the serpent said to the woman, "You will not surely die. **For God knows** that in **the day you eat of it your eyes will be opened, and you will be like God**, knowing good and evil." (Ge.3:4-5 NKJV)

Eve ate of the fruit because she sought to become equal to God. However, her disobedience had a penalty:

> **You must not eat** from the tree of the knowledge of good and evil, **for when you eat of it you will certainly die.** (Ge.2:17 TNIV)

Man had to die the day they ate of the forbidden fruit. The moment she rebelled against God by reaching for the fruit, man's spirit died. Man's spirit was alive at creation, died in the fall, and now must be born again:

> Jesus replied, "I assure you, no one can enter the Kingdom of God **without being born** of water and **the Spirit**. Humans can reproduce only human life, but **the Holy Spirit gives birth to spiritual life**. So don't be surprised when I say, '**You must be born again.**'" (Jn.3:5-7 NLT)

When Adam sinned, his spirit died, and his deadened spirit was hereditarily passed on to his descendants. Every spirit of mankind is deadened at birth because of Adam's sin:

> For **the sin of this one man, Adam, brought death to many.** (Ro.5:15 NLT)

Mankind's spirit is dead, unable to have fellowship with God. Jesus referred to someone who did not follow Him as being dead:

> But Jesus said to him, "Follow Me, and **let the dead bury their own dead.**" (Mt.8:22 NKJV)

The Scriptures state that every person is born spiritually dead even though he is physically alive:

> **Once you were dead** because of your disobedience and your many sins. (Eph.2:1 NLT)

Our willful continuation in sin is the evidence that we are still spiritually dead:

> **When you were dead** in **your sins** and in the uncircumcision of **your sinful nature**, God made you alive with Christ. (Co.2:13 TNIV)

If we consistently continue to sin, the Scriptures declare that we are dead:

> Even though <u>we were dead</u> **because of our sins**, he gave us life when he raised Christ from the dead. (Eph.2:5 NLT)

Eve ate the forbidden fruit because she desired to become equal with God and to be enabled to do as she pleased. Living to do as we please is a sign of being spiritual dead:

> The widow **who lives for pleasure <u>is dead</u>** even <u>while she lives</u>. (1Ti.5:6 NRSV)

Therefore, the Scriptures teach that all mankind died in their spirit when Adam and Eve ate the forbidden fruit in the Garden of Eden.

RESTORING GOD BACK TO HIS RIGHTFUL PLACE

Man's spirit died the moment Eve sought to become equal with God. God is now calling all mankind to return back under His authority. He is calling us to stop living for ourselves and lay our body and soul on the altar, so that once again we can experience life in our spirit:

> For those **who want to save their life** will lose it, and **those who lose their life for my sake <u>will find it</u>**. For **what will it profit them if they gain the whole world** but forfeit their life? Or what will they give in return for their life? (Mt.16:25-26 NRSV)

When we lay our life on the altar, we restore God to His rightful place as Lord and allow Him to live in and control us. We cannot become a Christian without laying all that we are on the altar:

> <u>We know</u> that <u>our old self</u> was crucified with him so that <u>the body of sin</u> **might be destroyed**, and we might **no longer be enslaved to sin**. (Ro.6:6 NRSV)

Many Christians attend church but have never given Christ control of their life. They may refer to themselves as Christian, but what does Christ say about them? In Revelation, Jesus called the people who attended the church of Sardis dead:

> I know your deeds, that **you have a name that you are alive**, but **you <u>are dead</u>**. (Re.3:1 NASB)

To call yourself a Christian but continue to live for your own pleasure proves that you are not only dead but also deceived:

> For we also <u>once were</u> foolish ourselves, disobedient, **deceived, enslaved to <u>various lusts and pleasures</u>**, (Ti.3:3 NASB)

Christians **once were** enslaved to pleasure, but after placing their old life on the altar, they are now born again in the Spirit and clothed in the new self that lives to please God:

> You <u>were</u> taught to put away your <u>former</u> way of life, <u>your old self</u>, corrupt and **deluded by <u>its lusts</u>**, and **to be renewed <u>in the spirit</u>** of your minds, and **to clothe yourselves with <u>the new self</u>**, created according to the likeness of God **in true righteousness and holiness**. (Eph.4:22-24 NRSV)

We need to place the soul with its slavery to bodily pleasures on the altar, for the old must go before the new can come. Christians receive a new self:

> Do not lie to each other, <u>since</u> you <u>have</u> taken off your <u>old self</u> with its practices and <u>have</u> put on the <u>new self</u>, which is being renewed in knowledge in the image of its Creator. (Co.3:9-10 TNIV)

The moment we lay our lives on the altar, restoring God's control over our life, our spirit becomes alive and possesses eternal life:

> I tell you the truth, whoever hears my word and believes him who sent me **has eternal life** and will not be condemned; he has **crossed over <u>from death</u> to life**. (Jn.5:24 NIV)

We may think that we have lost our life by laying it on the altar; however, it is only after dying to self that can we truly live. The dilemma is that we do not know what we will gain until we have given up what we know:

> We know **that we have passed <u>from death</u> to life**, because we love each other. Anyone who does not love **remains in death**. (1Jn.3:14 TNIV)

Your spirit will not come alive as long as you retain control of your life. You must choose to deny yourself the right of self-rule, give your life to Christ, and follow His teachings:

> He called **the crowd** with **his disciples**, and said to them, "**If any want to become my followers, let them deny themselves** and take up their cross and follow me." (Mk.8:34 NRSV; Mt.16:24; Lk.9:23)

Christ demands that His disciples reinstate Him to His rightful place as Lord of their lives. His disciples must reject the self-rule that Adam and Eve sought when they ate the forbidden fruit.

One day, as the crowds were following Jesus, a man sought to become His disciple:

> As they were going along the road, someone said to him, "I will follow you wherever you go." And Jesus said to him, "**Foxes have holes, and birds of the air have nests; but the Son of Man has nowhere to lay his head.**"
> (Lk.9:57-58 NRSV)

To be a Christian, a person must be willing to deny himself the right to control his life and make Jesus Lord of his life:

> **I have been crucified with Christ and I no longer live**, but Christ lives in me. The life I live in the body, **I live by faith in the Son of God**, who loved me and gave himself for me. (Ga.2:20 NIV)

The first article that a person comes to in the courtyard is the bronze altar. You cannot come to God without placing yourselves on the altar:

> **If anyone comes to me** and does not hate father and mother, wife and children, brothers and sisters—**yes, even life itself--such a person cannot be my disciple**. (Lk.14:26 TNIV)

The Scripture teaches that until we lay our life on the altar, we will not be able to approach God.

THE DIMENSIONS: THE FRONT AND BACK

The Scriptural measurement for the length and width of the bronze altar was five cubits (8.5 feet). Each side personified our feet which have five toes. Our feet represent the path we have chosen for our life—our purpose for living and our dreams for the future. Our path was patterned after the world because we were controlled by sin, self, and Satan; but God promised that if we offer our body as a living sacrifice, He will transform us. A living sacrifice is a person who gives up his hopes and dreams, lays them on the altar, and lives God's plan for his life:

> "For I know the plans I have for you," declares the LORD, "**plans to prosper you** and not to harm you, **plans to give you hope and a future.**" (Jer.29:11 TNIV)

Our plans were self-centered; however, God now has a new plan for our life. First, we need to give up our own agendas:

> Then Jesus told his disciples, "**If any want to become my followers**, let them **deny themselves** and **take up their cross** and follow me. ...For what

> will it profit them if they gain the whole world but **forfeit their life** *(soul)*? Or what will they give in return for their life *(soul)*?" (Mt.16:24&26 NRSV)

Christ asks us not only to deny our self but also to take up our cross. Unless we take up our cross, we cannot be His disciple:

> And **whoever does not carry their cross** and follow me **cannot be my disciple.** (Lk.14:27 TNIV)

To understand what is meant by "their cross," we must grasp what the cross meant to the One Who said it. For Christ, the cross was His primary purpose for coming to earth:

> Now My soul has become troubled; and what shall I say, "Father, save Me from this hour"? **But for this purpose I came to this hour.** (Jn.12:27 NASB)

Christ was born to die on the cross for our sins. Christ knew the pain He was going to endure; and yet, the Bible tells us He was determined to go to Jerusalem:

> As the time approached for him to be taken up to heaven, **Jesus resolutely set** out for Jerusalem. (Lk.9:51 NIV)

Christ embraced the cross and ignored His personal cost. The cross was God's specific purpose for Christ's coming to the earth. Your cross is God's specific purpose for your life. Christ does not stop at asking for our soul/life to be sacrificed; He asks for all of our hopes and dreams to be placed on the altar as well.

A rich young man once came to Jesus and asked, "What must I do to inherit eternal life?" Jesus told him to keep the law, to which the man replied that he had kept it from his youth. We then read the following:

> Jesus, **looking at him, <u>loved</u>** him and said, "You lack one thing; go, sell what you own, and give the money to the poor, and you will have treasure in heaven; then come, follow me." When he heard this, he was shocked and **went away grieving, for he had many possessions**. (Mk.10:21-22 NRSV)

The young man was not willing to give up all that was important to him, and he started to walk away. Even though Jesus loved him, He did not go after the young man to offer a compromise but let him leave. The lesson to be learned is that we must place the plans we have for our lives on the altar, allow them to be consumed, and embrace God's purpose for our lives. God saved us for a new specific purpose:

> *God, who has saved us and called us to a holy life--not because of anything we have done but because **of his own purpose** and grace.*
> (2Ti.1:9 TNIV)

God's purpose for your life is different than His purpose for my life. I cannot fulfill God's purpose for your life, and you cannot fulfill His purpose for my life. Each person is saved for a specific purpose, and each purpose is equally important to Christ for the fulfillment of His overall plan:

> *We know that God causes all things to work together for good to those who love God, to **those who are called according to His purpose**. For those whom He foreknew, He also predestined to become conformed to the image of His Son,* (Ro.8:28-29 NASB)

The height of Christian arrogance is to think that Christ saved us so that we can enjoy life. The Scriptures state that He saved us in order that we would regain our former position of servants who live for their Master's will. Laying our life on the altar is not a theological exercise. Repentance is a one-time act of the transfer of control to God, and this control must be expressed in our daily walk:

> *Then he said to them all, "If any want to become my followers, let them deny themselves and **take up their cross daily** and follow me."* (Lk.9:23 NRSV)

We must embrace God's purpose for our life, for He has a plan for every day of our life:

> *For we are God's workmanship, created in Christ Jesus **to do good works, which God prepared in advance for us to do.*** (Eph.2:10 NIV)

Christ is asking us to make one decision that will affect every decision for the rest of our life. God has a purpose for every person who is His child, for we are called not just to live eternally with Him in heaven but also daily for Him on earth. The Scriptures explicitly state that God has a plan for every day of your life:

> *In him we were also chosen, **having been predestined according to the plan of him** who **works out everything in conformity with the purpose of his will**, in order that we, who were the first to put our hope in Christ, might be for the praise of his glory.* (Eph.1:11-12 TNIV)

Christ did not make a compromise for the rich young ruler, and He will not compromise for us either:

> *And He said to another, "Follow Me." But he said, "**Permit me first to go and bury my father.**" But He said to him, "Allow the dead to bury their own dead;*

but as for you, go and proclaim everywhere the kingdom of God."
(Lk.9:59-60 NASB)

Therefore, Christ gave up His glory in heaven to come to earth and endure the cross. He asks us to give up our dreams and sacrifice them on the altar. In doing so, God can fulfill His purpose for our life. We can walk to the bronze altar and lay our hopes and dreams upon it, or we can walk away from it like the rich young ruler. Jesus taught us:

Do not store up for yourselves treasures on earth, where moth and rust consume and where thieves break in and steal; but store up for yourselves treasures in heaven, where neither moth nor rust consumes and where thieves do not break in and steal. For where your treasure is, there your heart will be also... No one can serve two masters; for a slave will either hate the one and love the other, or be devoted to the one and despise the other. You cannot serve God and wealth. (Mt.7:19-21&24 NRSV)

We have a choice; however, our decision has eternal consequences. We cannot be His disciple without laying our dreams on the altar.

THE DIMENSIONS: THE LEFT AND RIGHT SIDES

The dimensions of both the east and west sides of the bronze altar were also 5 cubits (8.5 feet). Just as we have five toes on each foot, we also have five fingers on each hand, signifying the things we do:

*Pay them back what they deserve, O LORD, **for what their hands have done**.* (La.3:64 NIV)

All that we do is a reflection of who we are! In light of eternity, all that we have experienced or accomplished for Christ will be meaningless if we continue to live for self:

*Yet when I surveyed **all that my hands had done** and what I had toiled to achieve, **everything was meaningless**, a chasing after the wind; nothing was gained under the sun.* (Ec.2:11 NIV)

King Solomon lacked nothing and yet came to the conclusion that everything his hands had accomplished was meaningless. Today, many famous people who have no want come to the same conclusion. Their lives seemed meaningless, as is evident by their suicide in the height of their famed careers. Most people chase after "more"—more money, more women, more excitement—but when there is no "more" to pursue, they end their lives. They tried everything the world had to offer but came to the conclusion that their lives were empty and without meaning:

> For everything in the world--**the cravings** of sinful people, **the lust** of their eyes and **their boasting** about what they have and do--comes not from the Father but from the world.   (1Jn.2:16 TNIV)

Man will never find fulfillment in the things of this world. God is asking us to humble ourselves and return to the position of His servant, willing to live in obedience to His commands:

> Then he called the crowd to him along with his disciples and said: "**Whoever wants to be my disciple must deny themselves** and take up their cross and follow me."   (Mk.8:34 TNIV; Lk.9:23)

God is now asking us to die to the control by our soul and to return to man's rightful place of submission to Him. The call to follow Him is not something new; all of His disciples had to answer that call:

> As Jesus was walking beside the Sea of Galilee, he saw two brothers, Simon called Peter and his brother Andrew. They were casting a net into the lake, for they were fishermen. "**Come, follow me,**" Jesus said, "and I will make you fishers of men." **At once they left their nets and followed him**. Going on from there, he saw two other brothers, James son of Zebedee and his brother John. They were in a boat with their father Zebedee, preparing their nets. **Jesus called them, and <u>immediately</u> they left the boat and their father and followed him.**   (Mt.4:18-22 NIV)

The first disciples had to follow Jesus' command instantly. Jesus does not hold two standards, and His call is the same for us today. We must immediately follow Him:

> And **anyone who does not** carry his cross and **follow me <u>cannot be my disciple</u>**.   (Lk.14:27 NIV)

Following Jesus is different than taking up our cross. If we are not ready to follow Him, then we are not worthy of Him:

> "**And he who does not** take his cross and **follow after Me is not worthy of Me.**"   (Mt.10:38-39 NASB)

Our cross is God's specific will for each of us. However, Jesus' call to every Christian is to follow Him, which is His general will for the church. Do you remember when we used to play "Follow the Leader"? To know what it means to follow, we must look to our Leader:

> ...he comes so that the world may learn that **I love the Father and do exactly what my Father has commanded** me.   (Jn.14:31 TNIV; 15:10)

Christ, Who is equal to God, humbled Himself by becoming a man and obeyed His Father in everything, even to the point of death on a cross:

> *Your attitude should be the same as that of Christ Jesus:* **Who, being in very nature God, did not consider equality with God something to be grasped,** *but made himself nothing,* **taking the very nature of a servant,** *being made in human likeness. And being found in appearance as a man,* **he humbled himself and <u>became obedient to death</u>**—***even death on a cross****!*
> (Php.2:5-8 NIV)

Jesus' life could be summarized as a life of obedience to the Father. Christ gave up His place as Lord over all creation and lowered Himself from equality with God to become a man. Now Jesus is asking us to lower ourselves and return to the former position that man had at creation, a servant of God. There is no other choice. If you have not laid the control of your life on the altar with Christ as your Savior, then you will spend eternity in hell. Christ will not become your Savior without becoming your Lord. If He is not Lord of your life, He is not Savior either:

> *Although he was a son, he learned obedience from what he suffered and, once made perfect, he became* **the source of eternal salvation for all who obey him.** (He.5:9 NIV)

You cannot be saved unless you agree to submit to the Lordship of Jesus Christ, for a slave can only have one master. You must rid yourself of one master before another master can rule:

> *We are witnesses of these things, and so is* **the Holy Spirit, whom God has given to those who obey him.** (Ac.5:32 TNIV)

Christ explicitly stated that obedience is a condition to become His disciple:

> *"Therefore* **go and make disciples** *of all nations, baptizing them in the name of the Father and of the Son and of the Holy Spirit, and* **teaching them to <u>obey everything</u> I have commanded you."** (Mt.28:19-20 NIV)

What is excluded from everything? Nothing! We are called to obey without compromise everything that the Scriptures command in the New Testament. If you do not lay your "self" on the bronze altar and refuse to become his servant and obey Him, then you cannot be His disciple. True faith is always reflected in a reasonable response of obedience:

> *Through him and for his name's sake, we received grace and apostleship to call people from among all the Gentiles* **to the obedience that comes from faith.** (Ro.1:5 NIV)

FREE CHOICE

In many churches the concept of "free choice" is preached: "I don't have to do it if I don't want to," or "I have my right to choose." These people have not laid their lives on the altar. Jesus asked:

> *Why do you call Me, "Lord, Lord," and **do not do what I say**?*
> (Lk.6:46 NKJV)

You can believe in God and still be bound for hell:

> *You believe that God is one; you do well. **Even the demons believe—and shudder**.* (Ja.2:19 NRSV)

At one time the demons were in the Presence of God, yet they still continue in rebellion against Him. The Bible forms a direct relationship between true belief and obedience when it uses the Greek word *apeitheo*:

> apeitheo {ap-i-theh'-o} - KJV - believe not 8, disobedient 4, obey not 3, unbelieving 1; number of times used 16 (Online Bible Greek Lexicon)

This word means both "disbelief" and "disobedience." In 1 Peter 2, *apeitheo* is used twice in the same portion of Scripture:

> *To you then who believe, he is precious; but for **those who do not believe**, "The stone that the builders rejected has become the very head of the corner," and "A stone that makes them stumble, and a rock that makes them fall." They stumble because **they disobey the word**, as they were destined to do.* (1Pe.2:7-8 NRSV)

A "disobedient" Christian is an oxymoron. To claim to know God yet continue in disobedience is incongruent:

> *To the pure all things are pure, but to **those who are defiled and unbelieving** nothing is pure; but even their mind and conscience are defiled. **They profess to know God**, but in works **they deny Him**, being abominable, **disobedient**, and disqualified for every good work.*
> (Tit.1:15 NKJV)

We either deny our self, or we are denying Christ His Lordship.

Everyone starts life in disobedience to God. Note that the Scriptures use the past tense when describing our former life apart from Christ:

> *For we also **once were** foolish ourselves, **disobedient**, deceived, **enslaved to various lusts and pleasures**, spending our life in malice and envy, hateful, hating one another.* (Tit.3:3-4 NASB)

The Scriptures never teach that a Christian is free to disobey God. Instead, they teach that our disobedience brings the wrath of God upon us:

> You **were** dead in your transgressions and sins, **in which you used to** live when you followed the ways of this world and of the ruler of the kingdom of the air, the spirit **who is now** at work in those who **are disobedient**. All of us also lived among them at one time, gratifying the cravings of our sinful nature and following its desires and thoughts. Like the rest, **we were by nature objects of wrath**. (Eph.2:1-3 NIV)

You either deny yourself the right to choose, or you are denying Christ:

> For **of this you can be sure**: No immoral, impure or greedy person—such a person is an idolater—**has any inheritance in the kingdom of Christ and of God**. Let no one deceive you with empty words, for because of such things **God's wrath comes on those who are disobedient**. (Eph.5:5-6 TNIV)

To continue to disobey Christ is to deny Him Lordship and is proof that you are not a Christian. Consider the terms "us" and "those":

> For the time has come for judgment **to begin at the house of God**; and if it begins **with us** first, what will be the end of **those** who **do not obey** the **gospel of God**? (1Pe.4:17 NIV)

There are *those* who preach free choice. They do not realize that the Bible distinctly speaks of them as *those* who are denying Christ His Lordship:

> For certain individuals **whose condemnation was written about** long ago have secretly slipped in among you. They are ungodly people, who **pervert the grace of our God into a license for immorality** and **deny Jesus Christ our only Sovereign** and Lord. (Jd.1:4 TNIV)

In the southern states, there are churches who call themselves "Freewill Baptist Church." They claim Jesus as their Savior but refuse to be living sacrifices. They encourage rebellion to Jesus as Lord:

> There will also be false teachers among you, who will secretly introduce destructive heresies, **even denying the Master who bought them**, bringing swift destruction upon themselves. (2Pe.2:1 NASB)

God gave us a test to confirm if someone is a Christian:

> **Test yourselves to see if you are in the faith**; examine yourselves! Or do you not recognize this about yourselves, that Jesus Christ is in you— **unless indeed you fail the test**? But I trust that you will realize that **we ourselves do not fail the test**. (2Co.13:5-6 NASB)

This test is important to pass because failure means eternity in hell. Paul describes the test at the beginning of 2 Corinthians:

*Another reason I wrote you was to see if **you would stand the test** and **be obedient in everything**.* (2Co.2:9 TNIV)

The test of sincere Christianity is to be obedient in everything. If you refuse to deny yourself and lay your life on the altar with Jesus as your Lord, then, from the Scriptural definition, you are not a Christian:

*We know that **we have come to know him if we obey his commands**. The man who says, "I know him," **but does not do what he commands is a liar**, and the truth is not in him. But if anyone obeys his word, God's love is truly made complete in him. This is how **we know we are in him**: Whoever claims to live in him must walk as Jesus did.* (1Jn.2:3-6 NIV)

Eve pursued free choice when she ate the forbidden fruit. Are you going to follow her example? Or, are you going to come to God by way of the altar and become a living sacrifice, restoring Him as Lord of your life?

THE FOUR HORNS

The area of the bronze altar of sacrifice was accessible to the common man. The altar had four horns, one on each corner. The priest would sprinkle the blood of the sacrifice on the horns:

***The priest shall take some of the blood** of the sin offering with his finger and **put it on the horns of the altar of burnt offering**, and pour out the rest of its blood at the base of the altar of burnt offering.* (Le.4:25 NRSV)

The blood on the horns represented Christ, the Lamb of God whose blood allows us to approach the holy place:

*Therefore, brethren, since **we have confidence to enter the holy place by the blood of Jesus**.* (He.10:19 NASB)

The blood sprinkled on the horns offered mercy. These four horns represented the four Gospels. The Gospels clearly portray Christ crucified as the means by which we receive forgiveness. Jesus is the horn of our salvation:

*Blessed is the Lord God of Israel, for He has visited and redeemed His people, and has **raised up a horn of salvation** for us in the house of His servant David...* (Lk.1:68-69 NKJV; 2Sa.22:2-3)

The actual horns of the altar offered mercy. If someone accidentally killed a person, he could flee to the altar, hold on to the horns, and not be killed:

*But **Adonijah**, in fear of Solomon, went and **took hold of the horns of the altar**. Then Solomon was told, "Adonijah is afraid of King Solomon and is*

clinging to the horns of the altar. (1Ki.1:50-51 NIV)

The horns of the altar were intended to offer mercy to a person who killed someone, until the issue of guilt was determined:

> Anyone who strikes a man and kills him shall surely be put to death. However, if he does not do it intentionally, but God lets it happen, **he is to flee to a place I will designate**. But if a man schemes and kills another man deliberately, **take him away from my altar** and put him to death.
> (Ex.21:12-14 NIV)

Even though the horns prevented the death of an innocent person, they were never meant to protect the person who intentionally killed someone:

> Then news came to Joab, for Joab had defected to Adonijah, though he had not defected to Absalom. **So Joab fled to the tabernacle of the LORD, and took hold of the horns of the altar.** And King Solomon was told, "Joab has fled to the tabernacle of the LORD; there he is, by the altar." Then Solomon sent Benaiah the son of Jehoiada, saying, "Go, strike him down."
> (1Ki.2:28-29 NKJV)

Adonijah was offered mercy while he held the horns of the altar. However, Joab was killed holding those same horns. Just as the horns protected an innocent person from being killed, so the Gospel offers mercy and salvation to those who sincerely seek after God:

> For I am not ashamed of **the gospel**, for **it is the power of God for salvation to everyone who believes**, to the Jew first and also to the Greek.
> (Ro.1:16 NASB)

We are offered forgiveness for our sins if we respond to the death of Christ according to the Gospels; otherwise, our belief is in vain:

> By <u>**this gospel you are saved**</u>, **if you hold firmly to the word I preached to you. Otherwise, you have <u>believed in vain</u>**. (1Co.15:2 NIV)

The Gospel teaches that we must die to self in order to live, but if we believe in Jesus without denying ourselves, then we are disobedient to that which Jesus taught:

> This will happen when the Lord Jesus is revealed from heaven in blazing fire with his powerful angels. **He will punish those who** do not know God and **do not obey the gospel of our Lord Jesus.** (2Th.1:7-8 NIV)

The Gospel is that Jesus died on the cross to forgive us our sins and rose from the dead to live in us as Lord. To come to Jesus for forgiveness and to not lay our life on the altar is inadequate for salvation:

> For it is **time for judgment to begin with the household of God**; and if it begins with us first, what will be the outcome for <u>those who do not obey the gospel</u> of God? (1Pe.4:17 NASB)

The Gospel does speak of Jesus' death on the cross and the laying of everything we are and have on the altar:

> The kingdom of heaven **is like a treasure hidden** in the field, which a man found and hid again; and from joy over it he goes and **sells all that he has and buys that field**. (Mt.13:44 NASB)

The Scriptures speak of a sacrifice. If we are not willing to be a living sacrifice, then we really have not accepted the Gospel:

> Again, the kingdom of heaven is like a merchant **seeking beautiful pearls**, who, when he had found one pearl of great price, went and **sold all that he had and bought it**. (Mt.13:45-46 NKJV)

To make a half-hearted commitment to Christ is no commitment at all. To deny our self and follow Christ is taught throughout the New Testament:

> For Christ's love compels us, because we are convinced that one died for all, and therefore all died. And he died for all, **that those who live should <u>no longer live for themselves</u> but for him who died for them** and was raised again. (2Co.5:14-15 TNIV)

Many people believe in Jesus and desire heaven, but few are willing to lay their life on the altar:

> Another also said, "I will follow You, Lord; **but first permit me to say good-bye to those at home**." But Jesus said to him, "No one, after putting his hand to the plow and **looking back, is fit for the kingdom of God**." (Lk.9:61-62 NASB)

Jesus warns us:

> Enter through the narrow gate; for **the gate is wide and the road is easy that leads to destruction**, and there are **many who take it**. (Mt.7:13 NRSV)

The four horns on the altar represent the four Gospels, which all call us to die to self. Therefore, if you are not ready to meet the cost of the altar, then do not reach for the horns of the altar because they will not save you. Only after we have placed everything on the altar can we proceed to the bronze basin and approach God. Jesus said:

> In the same way, those of you who **do not give up everything you have cannot be my disciples**. (Lk.14:33 TNIV)

THINKING IT THROUGH:

1. What was the main purpose of the sacrifices in the Old Testament?

2. Why was God not pleased with animal sacrifices?

3. Why does the Scripture consider people dead while they are physically alive?

4. What does God want to be sacrificed?

5. What does it mean to deny yourself and pick up your cross?

6. Why is following Christ a prerequisite to being saved?

7. What does obedience have to do with Lordship?

8. What do we learn from the fact that the horns offered mercy to some but not to others?

Treasures of the Bible 1894

THE BRONZE BASIN

Make a large bronze bowl for washing. Make a bronze stand to put it on. Place the bowl between the Tent of Meeting and the altar. Put water in it. Aaron and his sons must wash their hands and feet with water from it. When they enter the Tent of Meeting, they must wash with water so that they will not die. They will come to the altar to serve me. They will bring an offering that is made to me with fire. When they do, they must wash their hands and feet so that they will not die. For all time to come, that will be a law for Aaron and the priests who are in his family line.   Exodus 30:18-21 NIrV

LESSON 4

THE BRONZE BASIN

THE WATER IN THE BASIN

A man would enter the gate of the tabernacle, into the courtyard, to bring a sacrifice to be offered on the altar. The altar was the closest that an ordinary Israelite could come to the tabernacle because only a priest could approach the bronze basin. The bronze basin was positioned between the bronze altar and the tabernacle:

> *You shall set the basin between **the tabernacle** of meeting and **the altar**, and **put water in it**.* (Ex.40:7 NKJV)

In the Old Testament, God commanded the shedding of blood for the forgiveness of sins. The bronze basin was filled with a specific kind of water for cleansing:

> *This is a requirement of the law that the LORD has commanded: Tell the Israelites **to bring you a red heifer without defect** or blemish and that has never been under a yoke. Give it to Eleazar the priest; it is to be taken **outside the camp** and **slaughtered** in his presence. Then Eleazar the priest is to take some of its blood on his finger and sprinkle it seven times towards the front of the Tent of Meeting. While he watches, **the heifer is to be burned**—its hide, flesh, blood and offal. The priest is to take some cedar wood, hyssop and scarlet wool and throw them onto the burning heifer... A man who is clean shall gather up the ashes of the heifer and put them in a ceremonially clean place outside the camp. They shall be kept by the Israelite community **for use in the water of cleansing; it is for purification from sin**.* (Nu.19:2-9 NKJV)

The ashes of the red heifer were mixed with water for the bronze basin. The red heifer was killed outside of the camp, which was symbolic of Christ Who died outside of the city:

> *So also **Jesus suffered and died outside the city gates** to make his people holy by means **of his own blood**.* (He.13:12 NLT)

The ashes of the red heifer used in the water for the bronze basin represented Christ, for only the blood of Christ can cleanse us from sin:

> But if we walk in the light as He is in the light, we have fellowship with one another, and **the blood of Jesus** Christ His Son **cleanses us from all sin**.
> (1Jn.1:7 NKJV)

Only water mixed with the ashes of the red heifer was approved by God to make the priests ceremonially clean:

> But **the man who is unclean and does not purify himself**, that person <u>shall be cut off</u> from among the assembly, because **he has defiled the sanctuary of the Lord**. The water of purification has not been sprinkled on him; **he is unclean**. (Nu.19:20 NASB)

According to the law, a refusal to be cleansed by water from the bronze basin meant that a person would be banished from the people of God.

SOLID BRONZE FROM MIRRORS

The basin was made from solid bronze and without any acacia wood. The Scriptures use bronze as an illustration of corruption:

> I have made you **a tester and a refiner among my people** so that you may know and test their ways. They are **all stubbornly rebellious**, going about with slanders; **they are bronze and iron, all of them act <u>corruptly</u>**.
> (Jer.6:27-28 NRSV)

Pure bronze represented sin in its purest form. Sin is a power, an entity unto itself; it influences all of man's actions:

> But **sin, <u>seizing</u> the opportunity** afforded by the commandment, **produced in me** every kind of coveting. For apart from the law, sin was dead. Once I was alive apart from the law; but when the commandment came, **sin <u>sprang to life</u> and I died**. (Ro.7:8-9 TNIV; Ro.5:12)

The lack of acacia wood in the bronze basin symbolized that sin as a power was not originally part of man at creation:

> Therefore, **just as sin came into the world** through one man, and death came through sin, and so death spread to all because all have sinned.
> (Ro.5:12 NRSV)

The pure bronze also signified that man was totally corrupted by sin:

> I know that **<u>nothing good lives in me</u>**, that is, **in my sinful nature**. I want to do what is right, **but I can't**. I want to do what is good, **but I don't**. I don't want to do what is wrong, **but I do it anyway**. But if I do what I don't want to

do, I am not really the one doing wrong; **it is <u>sin living in me</u> that does it.**
(Ro.7:18-80 NLT)

Sin as a power has enslaved every person descended from Adam:

> We have already charged that **all**, both Jews and Greeks, are **under <u>the power of sin</u>**, as it is written: "There is **no one** who is righteous, **not even one**; there is **no one** who has understanding, there is **no one** who seeks God. **All** have turned aside, together they have become worthless; there is **no one** who shows kindness, there is **not even one**." (Ro.3:9-12 TNIV)

God concluded that no person ever sought after Him, for all were under the power of sin. The basin was in the courtyard because sin's control was manifested through the body:

> We know that our old self was crucified with him **so that the <u>body of sin</u> might be destroyed**, and we might **no longer be <u>enslaved to sin</u>**. For whoever has died is freed from sin. (Ro.6:6 NRSV)

Sin's power and control over man's life must be washed away before we can approach God. The bronze used in the basin was of a specific quality, such as women used for mirrors:

> They **made the bronze basin** and its bronze stand **from the mirrors of the women** who served at the entrance to the tent of meeting. (Ex.38:8 TNIV)

A mirror is an object that allows us to see an accurate reflection of our self. The reflective nature of the bronze suggests that man must come to the realization of their sinfulness before they will be able to come to God. If we think that we are righteous and can approach God because of our own merit, we are deceived:

> **Every man's way is right <u>in his own eyes</u>, But the LORD weighs the hearts.** (Pr.21:2 NASB; Ga.6:3-4)

We do good things, but what are our motives behind our good deeds? God knows the thoughts of man and judges their intent:

> People **<u>may think</u> all their ways are pure, but motives are weighed by the LORD**. (Pr.16:2 TNIV)

A person does not go to hell for a lack of good deeds; he goes to hell for committing a sin. When we perceive our self from God's perspective, we will not only be humbled by our sinfulness, but also, out of humility, we will seek God's mercy. However, mankind is morally blind, thinking that they are good:

> *I have a message from God in my heart concerning the sinfulness of the wicked: There is no fear of God before their eyes. **In their own eyes they flatter themselves <u>too much to detect or hate their sin</u>.*** (Ps.36:1-2 TNIV)

If we are to approach God, we must have an understanding of what we are—wretched, blind, and poor. The church at Laodicea was blind by their assessment; they were self-deceived:

> *You say, "I am rich; I have acquired wealth and do not need a thing." **But you do not realize that you are wretched, pitiful, poor, blind and naked.** I counsel you to buy from me gold refined in the fire, so that you can become rich; and white clothes to wear, so that you can cover your shameful nakedness; and salve to put on your eyes, so that you can see.*
> (Re.3:17-18 NIV)

The Laodicean church thought that they were acceptable to God, yet God found them repulsive by their lack of holiness. If we are going to approach God, we need to begin to see ourselves from God's perspective:

> ***Blessed are the poor in spirit**: for theirs is the kingdom of heaven.*
> (Mt.5:3 KJV)

We must recognize how wicked we are in God's eyes before we will be willing to receive all that God offers:

> ***<u>If</u> my people** who are called by my name **humble themselves**, pray, seek my face, **<u>and</u> turn from their wicked ways**, **<u>then</u>** I will hear from heaven, and will forgive their sin and heal their land.* (2Ch.7:14 NRSV)

Only when we look into the mirror and see ourselves from God's perspective can we realize the need to receive what is offered at the basin. Therefore, we need to examine ourselves so that we can humbly come to the basin and receive purification from the sin in our life.

THE WASHING OF DEDICATION

After everything in the tabernacle was set up, the priests were ordained. If we desire to go beyond the altar to the tabernacle, we must become a priest. Only the priests can enter the Holy Place:

> *Then **you shall bring Aaron and his sons to the doorway of the tent of meeting and <u>wash them with water</u>**. You shall put the holy garments on Aaron and anoint him and consecrate him, that he may minister as a priest to Me. You shall bring his sons and put tunics on them; and you shall anoint them even as you have anointed their father, that they may minister as priests to Me; and **their anointing will qualify them for a perpetual priesthood** throughout their generations.* (Ex.40:12-15 NASB)

Aaron (the high priest) and his sons were required to wash with water in their ordination. When Jesus entered the world, He came not only as the perfect sacrifice but also as the great high priest:

> Therefore, since we have **a great high priest** who has passed through the heavens, **Jesus the Son of God**, let us hold fast our confession.
> (He.4:14 NASB)

Before Jesus could serve as a high priest, the law required that He be washed with water. Jesus came to John the Baptist to be baptized:

> Then Jesus came from Galilee to John at the Jordan, **to be baptized by him**. John would have prevented him, saying, "I need to be baptized by you, and do you come to me?" But Jesus answered him, **"Let it be so now; for it is proper for us in this way to fulfill all righteousness."** (Mt.3:13-15 NRSV)

Jesus, our high priest, was not baptized for the forgiveness of sins but to fulfill all righteousness. He came to be washed at the start of His ministry:

> This is the one I meant when I said, "A man who comes after me has surpassed me because he was before me." I myself did not know him, but **the reason I came baptizing with water was that he might be revealed to Israel.** (Jn.1:30-31 TNIV)

Not only is Jesus our great high priest, but when we become a Christian, we also become a priest:

> All glory to him who loves us and has freed us from our sins by shedding his blood for us. **He has made us a Kingdom of priests** for God his Father.
> (Re.1:5-6 NLT; Re.5:10)

Since all priests must be washed in their ordination, all Jesus' disciples had to be washed. Early in His ministry, while John the Baptist was still baptizing, Jesus withdrew with His disciples and baptized them:

> After this, **Jesus and his disciples** went out into the Judean countryside, where **he spent some time with them, and baptized**... (This was before John was put in prison.) (Jn.3:22-23 TNIV)

Prior to His death, Jesus baptized the twelve disciples, after which they started baptizing other followers who sought to become Jesus' disciples:

> The Pharisees heard that **Jesus was gaining and baptizing more disciples than John**, although **in fact it was not Jesus who baptized, but His disciples**. (Jn.4:1-2 NIV)

At the time of Jesus' ascension, the number of disciples reached 120 people:

> In those days Peter stood up among the believers (together the crowd **numbered about one hundred twenty persons**)... (Ac.1:15 NRSV)

All of the disciples were together during Pentecost when the promised Holy Spirit came upon them. After being filled with the Holy Spirit, Peter preached to a large crowd and concluded his sermon with the presentation of a new covenant:

> Peter said to them, "**Repent**, and **be baptized** every one of you in the name of Jesus Christ so **that your sins may be forgiven**; and **you will receive the gift of the Holy Spirit**. For **the promise is for** you, for your children, and for all who are far away, **everyone whom the Lord our God calls to him.**" (Ac.2:38-39 NRSV)

On the day of Peter's sermon, 3,000 people accepted Jesus' death as payment for their sin and were baptized. In the same way that the priests needed to be completely washed at the start of their ministry, believers need to be cleansed with water in baptism when they first believe:

> Then those **who gladly received his word were baptized**; and that day about **three thousand souls** were added to them. (Ac.2:41 NKJV)

If only the twelve apostles were able to baptize, each one would have had to baptize 250 people. However, since all believers are priests, each of the 120 disciples could have baptized 25 new converts on Pentecost. Jesus commanded His disciples how to make new disciples:

> Therefore, go and **make disciples** of all the nations, **baptizing them** in the name of the Father and the Son and the Holy Spirit. Teach these new disciples **to obey all the commands** I have given you. (Mt.28:19-20 NLT)

When a priest was first washed with water, he was ceremonially cleansed of all uncleanness. In the same way, when Paul accepted the Lord, he had to be washed in his baptism, washing away his sin:

> Now why do you delay? **Get up and be baptized, and <u>wash away your sins</u>**, calling on His name. (Ac.22:16 NASB)

If a priest was not washed in his ordination, he did not become a priest. The Scriptures teach that our obedience in water baptism is the proof of our belief. Baptism does not earn us salvation; rather, baptism is commanded by God in order to enter His covenant which saves us:

> God waited patiently in the days of Noah while the ark was being built. In it only a few people, eight in all, were saved through water, and this water symbolizes <u>**baptism that now saves you**</u> also— not the removal of dirt from the body but **the pledge** of a good conscience towards God. **It saves you by the resurrection of Jesus Christ**, (1Pe.3:20-21 NIV)

Baptism apart from the inner change does not save us because baptism is only the first step of obedience on our life-long journey as a Christian. Every journey begins with the first step, and without the first step, we have not started the Biblical journey of faith:

> He who **believes** and **is baptized will be saved**; but he who does not believe will be condemned. (Mk.16:16 NKJV)

Baptism without belief becomes nothing more than a bath of hollow ritual, but baptism done in response to faith brings salvation:

> But when the kindness and love of God our Savior appeared, he saved us, not because of righteous things we had done, but because of his mercy. **He saved us** through **the washing of rebirth** and renewal by the Holy Spirit, whom he poured out on us generously through Jesus Christ our Savior... (Ti.3:4-6 NIV)

In the model of the first church, baptism was administered the moment someone personally made the decision to follow Jesus:

> As they rode along, they came to some water, and the eunuch said, "Look! There's some water! **Why can't I be baptized**?" He ordered the carriage to stop, and **they went down into the water, and Philip baptized him**. (Ac.8:36&38 NLT)

The eunuch heard the Gospel and was baptized in the nearest water available. Baptism into the name of Jesus is always water baptism:

> When they arrived, they prayed for them that they might receive the Holy Spirit, because **the Holy Spirit had not yet come** upon any of them; **they had simply been baptized into the name of the Lord Jesus**. Then Peter and John placed their hands on them, and they received the Holy Spirit. (Ac.8:15-17 NIV)

Receiving the Holy Spirit does not negate the need for water baptism, for when the Gentiles received the Holy Spirit, Peter commanded that they be baptized:

> "Surely no one can stand in the way **of their being baptized with water**. They have received the Holy Spirit just as we have." **So he ordered that they be baptized in the name of Jesus Christ**. (Ac.10:47-48 TNIV)

The time of day, the people present, or the body of water in which you are immersed is of no consequence to your baptism:

> He took them the same hour of the night and washed their stripes. And **immediately he and all his family were baptized**. Now when he had brought them into his house, he set food before them; and he rejoiced, **having believed in God with all his household**. (Ac.16:33-34 NKJV)

No measurements or description for the bronze basin were given because any water will suffice. Cleansing with water was not optional for the priests of the Old Testament, and baptism is not optional for us if we want to be Jesus' disciples.

WE MUST GO TO THE BASIN

The Old Testament rituals could not cleanse the heart and conscience of man. However, the Old Testament regulations laid the foundation from which we can understand the New Testament realities:

> This is <u>an illustration for the present time</u>, indicating that the gifts and sacrifices being offered **were not <u>able to clear the conscience</u>** of the worshipper. They are only a matter of food and drink and **various ceremonial washings**—external regulations **applying until <u>the time of the new order</u>**. (He.9:9-10 TNIV)

The ceremonial laws could not cleanse Israel but were meant to teach the concepts of "clean" and "unclean" and God's method of cleansing. Christ was the ultimate sacrifice, and only He can cleanse our conscience:

> The blood of goats and bulls and the ashes of a heifer sprinkled on those who are ceremonially unclean sanctify them so that they are **outwardly clean**. How much more, then, will <u>**the blood of Christ**</u>, who through the eternal Spirit offered himself unblemished to God, <u>**cleanse our consciences**</u> from acts that lead to death, so that we may serve the living God! (He.9:13-14 TNIV)

The washing that we receive by our great High Priest Jesus cleanses our heart and evil conscience by the washing of our body with water in baptism:

> Since we have a great priest over the house of God, let us approach with **a true heart** in full assurance of faith, **with our hearts <u>sprinkled clean</u>** from an evil conscience and **our bodies <u>washed with pure water</u>**. (He.10:21-22 NRSV)

When we lay our life on the bronze altar, we offer ourselves to God, but God must do the cleansing of all that we were—removing of sin (bronze):

> Now **may the God** of peace **make you holy in every way**, and may your **whole spirit and soul and body** be kept blameless until our Lord Jesus Christ comes again. **<u>God will make this happen</u>**, for he who calls you is faithful. (1Th.5:23-24 NLT)

Jesus did not die to merely forgive us our sins; He died to purify us from all unrighteousness:

> **The grace of God** has appeared that offers salvation to all people. **It teaches us to say "No" to ungodliness and worldly passions, and to live self-controlled, upright and godly lives in this present age**, while we wait for the blessed hope—the appearing of the glory of our great God and Savior, Jesus Christ, who gave himself for us **to redeem us from all wickedness** and **to purify** for himself a people that are his very own, **eager to do what is good**. (Ti.2:11-14 TNIV)

We were wicked, but now we are purified by Christ of the "old":

> Therefore, if anyone is in Christ, he is a new creation; **the old has gone**, the new has come! (2Co.5:17 NKJV)

The Scriptures tell us that the old—the wicked bronze—has been washed away and that we have become a new creation.

The Scriptures clearly teach that the old must go before the new can come:

> No one puts **new wine into old wineskins**. For the old skins would burst from the pressure, spilling the wine and ruining the skins. **New wine is stored in new wineskins** so that both are preserved. (Mt.9:17 NLT)

The Holy Spirit cannot live in a sinful heart. Christians are new wine skins, and the Holy Spirit is the new wine. We need to know that the old is not simply gone but that the old has died, never to live again:

> Here is a trustworthy saying: **If we died with him, we will also live with him**; (2Ti.2:11 NLT)

The Scriptures use the words "if" and "died with Him" as a prerequisite to experiencing eternal life with Jesus. We find these terms used in Romans:

> Now **if we died with Christ**, we believe that **we shall also** live with Him, (Ro.6:8 NKJV)

If we died with Christ, only then can we have eternal life. The Scriptures state three times that our death with Christ must precede our life with Christ:

> **If** we have been **united with him like this** in **his death**, **we will certainly** also be united with him **in his resurrection**. (Ro.6:5 NIV)

The previous verse suggests how we died with Christ: "like this." To understand how we died with Christ, we need examine the context:

> Do you not know that **all of us who have been baptized into Christ** Jesus were **baptized into his death**? We were buried therefore with **him by baptism into death**, in order that, just as Christ was raised from the dead by the glory of the Father, **we too might walk in newness of life**. (Ro.6:3-4 ESV)

In our baptism, we died to the power of sin with all of its control over our life. The finality of the terms "buried with Him through/in baptism" is in the aorist tense, strengthening the permanency of dying to sin once for all time. Not only has the power of sin died with Christ in our baptism, but man's sinful nature also has been cut away:

> *In him* you were also circumcised, *in the **putting off of the sinful nature**, not with a circumcision done by the hands of men but **with the circumcision done by Christ, having been <u>buried with him in baptism</u>** and raised with him through your faith in the power of God,* (Co.2:11-12 NIV)

Baptism is our spiritual death certificate. The Scriptures state that we died with Christ and that the old is gone. The words "have been buried with him" is in the passive voice implying that God will do it. When we lay our life on the altar, we offer ourselves to God. In baptism, God puts the old to death.

The New Testament is not seen as a new law that we must keep by the determination of our will, but, rather, it is truth. The difference is that we do not legalistically follow the New Testament by dividing it into a specific number of "do's" and "do not's." The New Testament's only command is to love, and its truth teaches us how to love. Everything we do must be filtered by the Holy Spirit through the Scriptures to determine what we should "do." Since we now live by the Spirit, we have died to the law:

> *In the same way, my friends, **you <u>have died</u> to the law** through the body of Christ.* (Ro.7:4 NRSV; Ga.2:19)

The Ten Commandments were replaced by the Holy Spirit, Who personally convicts us of sin—both in what to "do" and what to "not do":

> *But now, **<u>by dying</u> to what once bound us, we have been released from the law** so that **<u>we serve</u> in <u>the new way of the Spirit</u>**, and not in the old way of the written code.* (Ro.7:6 TNIV)

Once we are baptized, we are now able to discern God's will through the Holy Spirit, which renders the law obsolete:

> *But if you are **led by the Spirit**, you are **not under** law.* (Ga.5:18 NKJV)

Not only did we die to the way that we determined what to do (law), but we also died to how we are to accomplish a life pleasing to God. The Jews kept the law by their own resolve—by their willpower to obey God's commands. The basic principles of this world assume that if a person is told to do something, he is expected to do it by himself. We must die to the basic principles of this world that suggest that we must stop sinning by our own effort:

> Since you <u>died</u> with Christ to <u>the basic principles of this world</u>, why, as though <u>you still</u> belonged to it, do you submit to its rules: "Do not handle! Do not taste! Do not touch!"? (Co.2:20-21 NIV)

A Christian has died to the basic principles of the world (self-righteousness) and now lives by relying on God to fulfill His promises:

> For <u>if you are trying</u> to make yourselves right with God by keeping the law, you **have been cut off from Christ**! You have **fallen away from God's grace**. But we who <u>live by the Spirit</u> eagerly <u>wait to receive</u> by faith the righteousness God has promised to us. (Ga.5:4-5 NLT)

Christians no longer try to overcome sin by their own effort, but they humbly confess their sin and ask God to transform their life. We rely on the Holy Spirit, Who lives in us and enables us to overcome our sin:

> For if you live according to the sinful nature, you will die; but if **by the Spirit you <u>put to death the misdeeds of the body</u>**, you will live, because **those who <u>are led</u> by the Spirit of God** are sons of God. (Ro.8:13-14 NIV)

Christians no longer live by the principles of the world that demand us to try harder; for we died, and the Holy Spirit lives in us. He cleanses us from our desire to sin.

There is a paradigm shift between the way the Jews lived and the way Christians live—the old self versus the new self. Our old self was always focused on "self"—"we" were the center of "our" universe: self-seeking, self-gratifying, self-governing, and even self-justifying. Christians died to the old self:

> We know that **our <u>old self</u> was crucified** with him so that the body of sin might be destroyed. (Ro.6:6 NRSV; Eph.4:22; Co.3:9)

Christians died to the self-centered life. When the Holy Spirit indwells us, our new self is a God-centered self—focused on living to please God:

> You **were taught** to put away **your former way** of life, your <u>old self</u>, corrupt and deluded by its lusts, and to **be** renewed in the spirit of your minds, and **to clothe yourselves with the new self**, created according **to the likeness of God in true righteousness and holiness**. (Eph.4:22-24 NRSV)

Christians are controlled by the Spirit and are predisposed to pleasing God.

The Jews, who saw God's laws as a series of choices, experienced sin as a power which enslaved them:

> For sin is the sting that results in death, and **the law gives sin its power**.
> (1Co.15:56 NLT)

The law presented God's will and forced man to make choices. Sin became a power in a person's life when he perceived that he had a choice between obedience and disobedience. Perceiving temptation as a choice empowers sin and enslaves mankind. Born-again Christians died to the power of sin; they no longer consider sin an option in their life:

> Shall we continue in sin... Certainly not! **How shall we who <u>died to sin</u> live any longer in it?** (Ro.6:2 NKJV)

Christians no longer see temptation as a choice:

> He Himself bore our sins in His body on the cross, **so that we might die to sin** and **live to righteousness**; for by His wounds you were healed.
> (1Pe.2:24 NASB)

By making Jesus Lord, offering our self on the altar, the power of sin has been overcome by the power of God's Presence within us:

> For **God is working in you**, giving you **the desire** and **the power to do what pleases him**. (Php.2:13 NLT)

Christ is the Lord of born-again Christians. They no longer perceive sin as a choice because God's power strengthens them to make the right choices:

> **His divine power** has given us **everything we need for a godly life**...
> (2Pe.1:3 TNIV)

With Christ as our Lord, we are obligated to obey Christ. We no longer consider temptations a choice.

Man is born with a sinful nature. The sinful nature came into being when man gained the knowledge of evil without possessing the holy nature of God. Man's sinful nature controlled them and predisposed them to sin. However, born-again Christians have crucified their sinful nature:

> Those **who belong to Christ** Jesus **have <u>crucified</u>** the sinful nature with its passions and desires. (Ga.5:24 NIV; Co.2:11)

When we are born again, we receive the Holy Spirit Who imparts the divine nature within us:

> He has given us great and precious promises. These are the promises that **enable you to share <u>his divine nature</u>** and escape the world's corruption caused by human desires. (2Pe.14 NLT)

A person can only have one nature. The Holy Spirit's divine nature displaces the sinful nature. Consequently, if the Holy Spirit lives in us, the sinful nature has been displaced and the Holy Spirit controls us:

> But you **are not controlled** by your sinful nature. You **are controlled** by the Spirit **if** you have the Spirit of God living in you. (And remember that those who do not have the Spirit of Christ living in them do not belong to him at all.) (Ro.8:9 NLT)

The sinful nature has been crucified, and we now live by the Holy Spirit:

> So I say, **walk by the Spirit**, and you **will not** gratify the desires of the sinful nature. (Ga.5:16 TNIV)

Now that our sinful nature has died, we no longer live by its desires. We now live in our new divine nature which desires to please God.

When Adam chose to follow Satan rather than God, he gave Satan the right to control him and all mankind. When God banished Adam from His garden, Adam was sent into the world—the kingdom of Satan:

> We know that we are from God, and **the whole world lies in the power of the evil one.** (1Jn.5:19 ESV)

The moment we make Christ our Lord, we are no longer citizens of Satan's kingdom and have become part of the Kingdom of God:

> For he has **rescued us from the kingdom of darkness** and transferred us into the **Kingdom of his dear Son.** (Co.1:13 NLT)

By changing our spiritual citizenship, Satan has lost his right to our life. The world—Satan's kingdom—has been crucified to all Christians:

> May I never boast of anything except the cross of our Lord Jesus Christ, **by which the world has been crucified** to me, and **I to the world**. (Ga.6:14 NRSV)

We are now part of the Kingdom of Heaven, and, as Christ's ambassadors, we have the authority to overcome Satan and his kingdom:

> I write to you, young men, because **you are strong**, and the word of God abides in you, and **you have overcome the evil one**. (1Jn.2:14 ESV)

While the bronze basin only ceremonially cleansed the priests, our Christian baptism cleanses all born-again believers from everything that caused us to sin. God used the words *died* and *crucified* in the previous verses in the aorist tense and twice in the perfect tense to signify that if we are born again, the act is done once and for all time. Therefore, the cleansing of a priest during ordination represented our baptism—an inner cleansing of the root causes of sin. This cleansing empowers us to live for God:

> **The old has passed away;** behold **the new has come.** (2Co.5:17 ESV)

A Constant Cleansing

The bronze basin was one of two articles in the tabernacle complex that was made of two parts:

> Make **a bronze basin**, with its **bronze stand**, for washing. Place it between the tent of meeting and the altar, and put water in it. (Ex.30:18 TNIV)

The one-time washing of a priest at their ordination was not enough. The bronze basin was placed between the bronze altar and the tabernacle to constantly remind the priests to wash their hands and feet with water before they approached either the bronze altar or the tabernacle:

> He set the basin between the tent of meeting and the altar, and put water in it for washing, with which Moses and Aaron and his sons **washed their hands and their feet.** When they went **into the tent of meeting**, and when they **approached the altar, they washed**; as the LORD had commanded Moses. (Ex.40:30-32 NRSV)

If they approached either the bronze altar or the tabernacle without washing from the basin, they would die:

> Make a bronze basin, with its bronze stand, for washing. Place it between the Tent of Meeting and the altar, and put water in it. **Aaron and his sons are to wash their hands and feet with water from it.** Whenever they **enter the Tent of Meeting,** they shall wash with water **so that they will not die.** Also, when they **approach the altar to minister by presenting an offering** made to the LORD by fire, they shall wash their hands and feet **so that they will not die.** (Ex.30:18-21 NIV)

Since God is holy, to approach Him in our uncleanness is to treat Him with contempt. God made provision for the priests' current uncleanness before approaching the bronze altar or the Holy Place:

> **Who may ascend** the hill of the LORD? **Who may stand in his holy place?** **He who has clean hands** and a pure heart, who does not lift up his soul to an idol or swear by what is false. (Ps.24:3-4 KNJV)

A priest could approach the tabernacle and enter the Holy Place because he was ceremonially clean. Having been baptized, Jesus clearly taught that the disciples were considered clean on the night He was betrayed:

> *You are already clean because **of the word** which I have spoken to you.*
> (Jn.15:3 NKJV)

Being baptized because of our obedience to the Word cleanses us:

> *Christ loved the church and gave himself up for her **to make her holy, cleansing her by the washing with water** through **the word**,*
> (Eph.5:25-26 TNIV)

However, there are two perspectives of cleansing, just as the basin consisted of two parts. One perspective of cleansing is a positional holiness—the way God views us. The other perspective of cleansing is a practical holiness—the way we live on earth:

> *For by one sacrifice **he has made perfect forever** those who are **being made holy**.* (He.10:14 TNIV)

Jesus is represented in the horns of the bronze altar because He has bought forgiveness for the sins we have committed. Jesus is also represented in the ashes of the red heifer in the waters of cleansing because He rose from the dead and has cleansed us of our desire to commit sin:

> *Both the one who **makes men holy** and those who **are made holy** are of the same family. So **Jesus** is not ashamed to call them brothers.*
> (He.2:11 NIV)

Christians are being made holy by Jesus. In our baptism, we die to the power of sin and our sinful nature so that sin no longer can reign in our heart. However, the remnants of sin, actions which we do out of habit from our past, must be dealt with:

> *My little children, I am writing these things to you **so that you may not sin**. But **if anyone does sin**, we have an advocate with the Father, Jesus Christ the righteous…* (1Jn.2:1 NRSV)

For Christians, sin is no longer probable because sin no longer **reigns** in our life, but acts of sin are possible to commit because **remnants** of our former life remain. The two perspectives can be seen in the following Scriptures:

> *For you **died**, and your life is hidden with Christ in God. When **Christ who is our life appears**, then you also will appear with Him in glory.*
> (Co.3:3-4 NKJV)

We died with Christ which is an accomplished fact. The pervious and following verses directly connect. The previous Scriptures state that "you died" to **reigning sin,** and the following Scripture is commanding us to "put to death our sinful actions"—**remnant sin:**

*Put to death, therefore, whatever belongs to your earthly nature: sexual immorality, impurity, lust, evil desires and greed, which is idolatry. Because of these, the wrath of God is coming. You **used to walk** in these ways, in the life **you once lived**. But **now** you must rid yourselves of all such things as these: anger, rage, malice, slander and filthy language from your lips. Do not lie to each other, since you **have taken off** your **old self with its practices** and **have put on** the new self, which is being renewed in knowledge in the image of its Creator.* (Co.3:5-10 NIV)

We have died to the power of sin (Ro.6:2-3) and have cut off our sinful nature (Co.2:11-12). Now we must put off the acts of sin—the remnant acts of our previous sinful life.

We have dealt with the reigning sin, but now we need to consider remnant sin. There are two attitudes in which people commit sin:

*If you see any brother or sister commit a sin that **does not lead to death**, you should pray and God will give them life. I refer to those whose sin **does not lead to death**. There is a sin **that leads to death**. I am not saying that you should pray about that. All wrongdoing is sin, and there **is sin that does not lead to death**.* (1Jn.5:16-17 TNIV)

The sin that leads to death leads to hell, and the other doesn't. John is not suggesting that one action is worse than another or that some sins are more acceptable than others. The difference between the sin that "does not lead to death" and the sin that "leads to death" is best understood in the terms *ignorance*, which says "I don't know," and *apathy*, which says "I don't care." The person who sins in ignorance **does not know** that he is sinning, but the person who sins with apathy **does not care** that he is sinning. These two attitudes toward sin were looked upon differently in the Old Testament, as well:

*Also **if one person sins unintentionally**, then he shall offer a one year old female goat for a sin offering. And the priest shall make atonement before the LORD **for the person who goes astray when he sins unintentionally**, making atonement for him that he may be forgiven.* (Nu.15:27-28 NASB)

Unintentional sin is forgiven, but intentional, continual sin is not forgiven. The Old Testament teaches about those who defiantly indulged in sin:

*But **anyone who sins defiantly**, whether native-born or foreigner, **blasphemes the LORD** and must be cut off from their people. Because **they have despised the LORD's word** and broken his commands, they must surely be cut off; **their guilt remains on them**.* (Nu.15:30-31 TNIV)

The sacrifice for unintentional sin brought forgiveness, but the person who defiantly sinned would not be forgiven—he had committed blasphemy against God. In the same light, if a Christian **defiantly or deliberately continues to sin**, his sins will not be forgiven:

> *If we deliberately keep on sinning* after we have received the knowledge of the truth, no **sacrifice for sins is left, but only a fearful expectation of judgment and of raging fire** that will consume the enemies of God.
> (He.10:26-27 NIV)

To deliberately continue to sin is the sin that leads to eternal death. In Christianity, the sins that do not lead to death are the sins committed unintentionally or in ignorance. When the Holy Spirit convicts us of the sin of ignorance, we need to respond in confession:

> *If we confess our sins, <u>he is faithful</u>* and just to **forgive us our sins**, and **to cleanse us from all unrighteousness**. (1Jn.1:9 KJV)

To confess is to agree with God that we have sinned. Through confession, we seek God's mercy and find forgiveness for our sins. Mercy is offered by the bronze altar of sacrifice, while grace is offered by the bronze basin. This grace cleanses us of the desire to continue in remnant sin:

> But if we walk in the light, as he is in the light, we have fellowship with one another, and **the blood of Jesus, <u>his Son, purifies us from all sin</u>**.
> (1Jn.1:7 TNIV)

Christ purifies His people, but in our confession, we must ask Him to complete His work of cleansing:

> **Let us draw near with confidence to the throne of grace**, so that we may receive mercy and **find grace to help in time of need**. (He.4:16 NASB)

We are not to respond to sin with an attempt to achieve holiness by our own effort. We are to respond to sin with an attitude of humility and ask for His grace to purify us of remnant sin. In a similar way to the priest washing his hands and feet before he went into the tabernacle, we need to wash our sins away. On the night that Jesus was betrayed, He washed the disciples' feet:

> Jesus replied, "**You don't realize now what I am doing. But later you will understand.**" "No," said Peter. "You will never wash my feet." Jesus answered, "**Unless I wash you, you <u>can't share life with me.</u>**"
> (Jn.13:6-8 TNIV)

Jesus said that if he did not wash the disciples' feet, they could have **no part of Him**. Neglecting this matter had eternal ramifications of being barred from eternal life with Christ. Jesus' words stressed the importance of what He was doing:

> Jesus answered, "A person who has had a bath needs only to wash his feet; his whole body is clean. And **you are clean**, though not every one of you." For <u>he knew who was going to betray him</u>, and that was why he said not every one was clean. (Jn.13:10-11 NIV)

All of the disciples were baptized by Jesus and, thereby, were considered clean. However, since their baptism, they had sinned. Hence, before His death and prior to the Lord's Supper, Jesus washed their feet to cleanse them from sin committed since their baptism. Jesus commands us to wash each others' feet, just as He washed the twelve disciples' feet:

> You call me Teacher and Lord—and you are right, for that is what I am. So if I, your Lord and Teacher, have washed your feet, **you also ought to wash one another's feet**. For I have set you an example, that you also should do as I have done to you. (Jn.13:13-15 NRSV)

Foot washing is similar to a priest washing his feet and hands before he approached the altar or the tabernacle. In the same way, we need to confess our sins the moment we are convicted; and prior to partaking of the Lord's Supper, we need to wash each others' feet (men washing men's feet/women washing women's feet). Foot washing cleanses people from their sins which were already confessed but committed since the previous foot washing. If we have something that is between us and another Christian, we must attempt to make things right before we partake. Therefore, the washing of the hands and feet of the priests before entering the Holy Place or approaching the altar was a foreshadowing of the foot washing which Jesus commanded to be done before the Lord's Supper.

Thinking It Through:

1. What made the water in the bronze basin special?

2. What does the basin which was made of pure bronze and without acacia wood represent?

3. From where did the bronze for the basin come, and what does the previous use of this bronze teach us?

4. What office does every Christian hold, and how does a person enter that office?

5. What is the difference between forgiveness and cleansing?

6. By dying with Christ, from what has a Christian been cleansed?

7. What is the difference between "reigning sin" and "remnant sin"?

8. What is the difference between the "sins that lead to death" and the "sins that do not lead to death"?

The Tabernacle

Make ten curtains out of finely twisted linen for the holy tent. Make them with blue, purple and bright red yarn. Have a skilled worker sew cherubim into the pattern... Make 50 gold hooks. Use them to join the curtains together so that the holy tent is all one piece. Make a total of 11 curtains out of goat hair to put over the holy tent... Make a covering for the tent. Make it out of ram skins that are dyed red. Put a covering of the hides of sea cows over that. Make frames out of acacia wood for the holy tent. Make each frame 15 feet long and two feet three inches wide... And make 40 silver bases to go under them. Make two bases for each frame... Also make crossbars out of acacia wood. Make five for the frames on one side of the holy tent. Make five for the frames on the other side. And make five for the frames on the west, at the far end of the holy tent. The center crossbar must reach from end to end at the middle of the frames. Cover the frames with gold. Make gold rings to hold the crossbars. Also cover the crossbars with gold. Set up the holy tent in keeping with the plan I showed you on the mountain. Make a curtain out of blue, purple and bright red yarn and finely twisted linen. Have a skilled worker sew cherubim into the pattern. Hang the curtain with gold hooks on four posts that are made out of acacia wood. Cover the posts with gold. Stand them on four silver bases. Hang the curtain from the hooks. "Place the ark of the covenant behind the curtain. The curtain will separate the Holy Room from the Most Holy Room... For the entrance to the tent make a curtain out of blue, purple and bright red yarn and finely twisted linen. Have a person who sews skilfully make it. Make gold hooks for the curtain. Make five posts out of acacia wood. Cover them with gold. And make five bronze bases for them.

Exodus 26:1-33NIrV

Lesson 5

The Tabernacle

Rights and Responsibility

The third item in the courtyard was the tabernacle itself. Once a person had left sin (the Desert of Sin), entered a covenant through Christ (the gate), made Christ Lord (laid his life on the altar), and been baptized (washed clean by the bronze basin), he became the temple of God (tabernacle):

> Do you not know that **you are a temple of God** and that **the Spirit of God dwells in you?** If any man destroys the temple of God, God will destroy him, for **the temple of God is holy**, and **that is what you are.** (1Co.3:16-17 NASB)

There is no other way to become the temple of God. Some trivialize the importance of coming to God in the manner that He has commanded. As we have seen in the previous chapters, if a priest came to the tabernacle in any way other than through the water of the basin, he would die:

> Make a **bronze washbasin** with a bronze stand. **Place it between the Tabernacle and the altar**, and fill it with water. Aaron and his sons will wash their hands and feet there. **They must wash with water whenever they go into the Tabernacle** to appear before the LORD and **when they approach the altar** to burn up their special gifts to the LORD—**or they will die**!
> (Ex.30:18-20 NLT)

Once a priest entered the tabernacle, there was little margin for error:

> The priests are to perform my service in such a way that they do not **become guilty and die** for treating it with contempt. I am the LORD, who makes them holy. (Le.22:9 TNIV)

A priest could die for several reasons. Consider a minor infraction:

> You shall **make for them linen undergarments** to cover their naked flesh; they shall reach from the hips to the thighs; Aaron and his sons shall wear them **when they go into the tent of meeting**, or when they come near the altar to minister in the holy place; or **they will bring guilt on themselves and die**. (Ex.28:42-43 NRSV)

The priests had to wear a specific type of undergarment; otherwise, they would die. To approach God was a great honor, which carried both great responsibilities and grave consequences. The church in the Western world has a very relaxed concept of God, almost to the point that they seem to think that God does not care about obedience. Think again! When Aaron and his sons first started to minister, two of Aaron's sons offered incense to God in a manner that was not according to His command:

> Now Aaron's sons, Nadab and Abihu, each took his censer, put fire in it, and laid incense on it; and **they offered unholy fire before the LORD, such as he had not commanded them**. And **fire came out from the presence of the LORD and consumed them, and they died** before the LORD. Then Moses said to Aaron, "This is what the LORD meant when he said, 'Through those who are near me I will show myself holy, and before all the people I will be glorified.'" (Le.10:1-3 NRSV)

Aaron had only four sons who could serve as priests; yet, without warning or hesitation, God took the lives of two of them. Aaron's sons were new to the position; yet, their error proved fatal:

> The names of the sons of Aaron were Nadab the firstborn and Abihu, Eleazar and Ithamar. Those were the names of Aaron's sons, **the anointed priests, who were ordained to serve as priests**. Nadab and Abihu, however, **fell dead before the LORD when they made an offering with unauthorised fire** before him in the Desert of Sinai. **They had no sons**; so only Eleazar and Ithamar served as priests during the lifetime of their father Aaron.
> (Nu.3:2-4 NIV)

A priest served in the tabernacle in reverent fear before the Presence of God. He knew that an error would cost him his life. The gravest mistake a person can make is to not take seriously what God said. God did not give us the Scriptures without forethought and purpose. When He dictated something by His Spirit to His prophets and apostles, He considered it important for us to know, which we must seriously consider.

THE DOOR

The tabernacle had two rooms: the Holy Place and the Holy of Holies. Our body is the temple of God with our soul being the Holy Place and our spirit becoming the Holy of Holies. Jesus said:

> I am the **way**, and the **truth**, and the **life**. No one comes to the Father **except through me**. (Jn.14:6 ESV)

The courtyard taught us the **way** to God; the Holy Place will teach us the **truth** about man's soul; and the Holy of Holies will teach us about **life** in our spirit. To come to God, we need to enter by the door of the tabernacle:

> For the entrance to the tent make a curtain of **blue, purple and scarlet** yarn and finely twisted linen—the work of an embroiderer. Make **gold hooks** for this curtain and **five posts of acacia wood overlaid with gold**. And cast **five bronze bases** for them. (Ex.26:36-37 NIV)

As with the gate of the courtyard, we find the curtains containing the colors blue, purple, and scarlet. The first color blue represented heaven: Jesus is God, Who came down from heaven. The second color purple spoke of Christ's royalty: Jesus was a king in the line of David. The third color scarlet/red spoke of His sacrifice: Jesus is the great High Priest and the Lamb of God. These three colors represented the work that Christ did to end the separation between God and man:

> For **Christ died for sins once for all**, the righteous for the unrighteous, **to bring you to God**. (1Pe.3:18 NIV)

We have already considered the colors in the gate of the courtyard. However, once through the door of the tabernacle, there is a change in the materials from outside of the tabernacle to the inside of the tabernacle. The bases of the columns of the curtained door were of the same metal as the bases of the posts that held up the curtained courtyard wall. The bases were made of solid bronze. Even though Christ changes us on the inside, we continue to live in a world of sin and will have to continue to overcome remnant sin—the habits formed by our sinful past:

> If we claim to be without sin, <u>we deceive ourselves</u> and the truth is not in us. (1Jn.1:8 ESV)

The Scripture never claimed that man would become perfect:

> My dear children, I write this to you **so that you <u>will not</u> sin**. But <u>if</u> **anybody <u>does</u> sin**, we have an advocate with the Father—Jesus Christ, the Righteous One. (1Jn.2:1 TNIV)

Since sin no longer **reigns** in our body, our natural tendency is to not sin; however, there will be actions that are **remnant** of our former life of which need to be convicted, confessed, and cleansed:

> For by one sacrifice **he has made perfect forever** those who **are being made holy**. (He.10:14 TNIV)

Hence, the five bronze bases are symbolic of the remnant sins which we will overcome with time through the power of the Presence of the Spirit.

Once we come to God through the entrance to the tabernacle, we begin to live for righteousness:

> He Himself bore our sins in His body on the cross, so that we **might die to sin** and **live to righteousness**; for by His wounds **you were healed**.
> (1Pe.2:24 NASB)

Everyone is born a sinner, with sin reigning in his life; however, the moment we become Christians, sin no longer reigns, and we are no longer viewed as sinners but as saints:

> God proves his love for us in that **while we still were sinners Christ died for us**. Much more surely then, now that **we have been justified** by his blood, will we be saved through him from the wrath of God. (Ro.5:8-9 NRSV)

We were sinners by the one act of Adam, but now we are made righteous by the one act of Jesus' death:

> For as **by one man's disobedience** many **were made sinners**, so also by **one Man's obedience** many **will be made righteous**. (Ro.5:19 NKJV)

The previous Scripture does not say that "the many will be viewed as righteous" but rather, "the many will be made righteous." Righteousness is not a position; it is a moral quality of life:

> Little children, let no one deceive you. Everyone **who does what is right** is righteous, just as he is righteous. (1Jn.3:7 NRSV)

Once we receive Christ into our life, our life is no longer characterized by sin—the bronze. A sinner is not saved but can be saved:

> You can be sure that **whoever brings the sinner** back **will save** that **person from death** and bring about the forgiveness of many sins.
> (Ja.5:20 NLT)

We are either a saint and righteous, or we are a sinner—but never both:

> If it is **hard for the righteous** to be saved, what will become of the **ungodly** and **the sinners**? (1Pe.4:18 NRSV)

Righteousness reigns in our lives because we are a new creation and have a new name:

> For God is not the author of confusion but of peace, **as in all the churches of the saints**. (1Co.14:33 NKJV)

The New Testament constantly refers to Christians as "saints" or "holy ones." Even at the end of time, Christians' lives are not characterized by disobedience but by obedience—holiness:

> This calls for patient endurance on **the part of the saints** who **obey** God's commandments and **remain faithful** to Jesus. (Re.14:12 NIV)

Once we have accepted Christ, a change takes place within our soul. This change is reflected in the way we live:

> We know that **anyone born of God does not continue** to sin; the One who was born of God **keeps them safe**, and the evil one cannot harm them.
> (1Jn.5:18 TNIV)

The change from a sinner to a saint is illustrated by the columns holding up the curtain at the entrance to the tabernacle. They were acacia wood overlaid in gold. In the courtyard the acacia wood was overlaid with bronze which represented a person without Christ under the control of the sinful nature:

> For **when we were controlled** by the sinful nature, the sinful passions aroused by the law were at work in our bodies, **so that we bore fruit for death**. (Ro.7:5 NIV)

Everyone is born with a sinful nature, but once we come to Christ, the sinful nature dies:

> Those who belong to Christ Jesus **have crucified the sinful nature** with its passions and desires. (Ga.5:24 TNIV)

Our sinful nature was cut away, no longer influencing our life:

> **When you came to Christ**, you were "circumcised," but not by a physical procedure. **Christ performed a spiritual circumcision—the cutting away of your sinful nature**. (Co.2:11 NLT)

To become the temple of God, we need to receive the divine nature which displaces our sinful nature:

> He has given us great and precious promises. These are the promises **that enable you to share his divine nature** and escape the world's corruption caused by human desires. (2Pe.1:4 NLT)

The wood was the same throughout the tabernacle complex, for it represented man. The difference was in the overlay: bronze represented our sinful nature while gold represented our new divine nature:

> *Those who are born of God **will not continue to sin**, because **God's seed** remains in them; **they cannot go on sinning**, because they have been born of God.* (1Jn.3:9 TNIV)

The gold overlaying the acacia wood signified a change in nature, and that change was the cause of a transformation in our attitude, behavior, and character. This change can be observed in Paul's missionary team:

> *You are witnesses, and so is God, of how **holy, righteous** and blameless **we were among you** who believed.* (1Th.2:10 NIV)

THE STRUCTURE: OUR FOUNDATION

The tabernacle was ten cubits high, thirty cubits long, and ten cubits wide. Silver bases formed the foundation of the tabernacle walls and had two sockets into which the tenons of the gold-covered boards of the wall fit. Consequently, the boards did not contact the dirt, but the silver bases supported the boards in their vertical position. All of the silver used in the tabernacle was gathered from a census taken at Mount Sinai:

> ***The silver obtained from those of the community who were counted in the census** was 100 talents and 1,775 shekels, according to the sanctuary shekel— one beka per person, that is, half a shekel, according to the sanctuary shekel, from everyone who had crossed over to those counted, twenty years old or more, a total of 603,550 men. **The 100 talents of <u>silver</u> were used to cast the bases for the sanctuary and for the curtain— 100 bases from the 100 talents, one talent for each base.*** (Ex.38:25-27 TNIV)

Whenever a census of the men was taken, each man had to redeem his life by paying half of a silver shekel:

> *When you take a census of the sons of Israel to number them, then **each one of them shall give <u>a ransom</u> for himself to the LORD**, when you number them, so that there will be no plague among them when you number them. …The rich shall not pay more and the poor shall not pay less than **the half shekel**, when you give the contribution to the LORD to <u>make atonement</u> for yourselves.* (Ex.30:12&15 NASB)

The silver bases formed the foundation of the tabernacle and symbolized the foundation of the Gospel, the redemptive work of Christ:

> *For <u>no other foundation</u> can anyone lay than that which is laid, which is **Jesus Christ**.* (1Co.3:11 NKJV)

Christ came to redeem us from our former way of life—belonging to the world. In the Old Testament, silver was the normal tender to redeem the life of every firstborn male:

> The first offspring of every womb, both man and animal, that is offered to the LORD is yours. But **you must redeem every firstborn son and every firstborn male of unclean animals**. When they are a month old, **you must redeem them at the redemption price set at five shekels of silver**, according to the sanctuary shekel, which weighs twenty gerahs.
> (Nu.18:15-16 NIV)

If someone's bull gored another person's slave, the compensation was paid in silver:

> If the ox gores a male or female servant, **he shall give to their master thirty shekels of silver,** and the ox shall be stoned. (Ex.21:32 NKJV)

Thirty pieces of silver was the redemption price of a slave. Zechariah prophesied the same amount, thirty pieces of silver, as the price that the Messiah's betrayer would receive:

> Then the LORD said to me, "Throw it to the potter, that magnificent price at which I was valued by them." **So I took the thirty shekels of silver and threw them to the potter in the house of the LORD.** (Zec.11:13 NRSV)

Zechariah's prophesy was fulfilled when Judas was promised thirty pieces of silver to betray Christ to the chief priests:

> Then one of the twelve, named Judas Iscariot, went to the chief priests and said, "What are you willing to give me to betray Him to you?" **And they weighed out thirty pieces of silver to him.** From then on he began looking for a good opportunity to betray Jesus. (Mt.26:14-16 NASB)

We have been redeemed by Jesus at the price of thirty pieces of silver.

To understand why Jesus was betrayed for thirty pieces of silver, we must consider that when Adam and Eve disobeyed God, God banished them from the garden into the world—Satan's kingdom:

> And he led Him up and showed Him **all the kingdoms of the world** in a moment of time. And the devil said to Him, "I will give You all this domain and its glory; for it **has been handed over to me, and I give it to whomever I wish."** (Lk.4:6 NASB)

Adam and Eve, by their own choice, sold themselves and all of their descendants into slavery to Satan:

> *Formerly, when you did not know God, **you were enslaved** to beings that by nature are not gods.* (Ga.4:8 NRSV)

When the Scriptures stated that we were enslaved to Satan, they meant that he had control over the whole of humanity:

> *We know that we are children of God, and that **the whole world is under the control of the evil one**.* (1Jn.5:19 NIV)

When the time came for Jesus to die, the priests offered to pay Judas the thirty pieces of silver to betray Jesus:

> *Jesus answered, "It is the one to whom I give this piece of bread when I have dipped it in the dish." So when he had dipped the piece of bread, he gave it to Judas son of Simon Iscariot. **After he received the piece of bread, Satan entered into him**. Jesus said to him, "Do quickly what you are going to do."* (Jn.13:26-27 NRSV)

Since Satan possessed Judas, Satan actually received the thirty pieces of silver through Judas. Satan's acceptance of the silver for Jesus' death was the redemption price to release all Christians from their slavery:

> *For **he has rescued us from the dominion of darkness** and brought us into the kingdom of the Son he loves, in whom **we have redemption**, the forgiveness of sins.* (Co.1:13-14 NIV)

Jesus redeemed and rescued us from Satan's authority. Even though Satan was paid in silver, which was the method of payment to redeem a slave on earth, it was Christ's death for which Satan received the payment that redeemed man. Hence, it was Christ's blood that ultimately redeemed us:

> *For you know that it was not with perishable things such as **silver or gold** that **you were redeemed** from the empty way of life handed down to you from your ancestors, but with the precious blood of Christ, a lamb without blemish or defect.* (1Pe.1:18-19 TNIV)

Christ personally redeemed us with His blood, granting us forgiveness of our sins:

> *In him **we have redemption** through his blood, **the forgiveness of sins**.* (Eph.1:7 TNIV)

The bases for the tabernacle walls were pure silver with no acacia wood. This implies that our redemption is purely a work of God:

> *No human being might boast in the presence of God. **He is the source** of your life in Christ Jesus, whom God made our wisdom and **our righteousness and sanctification and redemption**. Therefore, as it is written, "Let the one who boasts, boast in the Lord.* (1Co.1:29-31 ESV)

The pure silver represented God's work of redemption in the lives of mankind.

ACACIA WOOD COVERED WITH GOLD

The silver in the bases represented Christ's redemptive work; however, the gold that covered the boards of the walls represented Christ's sanctifying work:

> Our great God and Savior Jesus Christ, **who gave himself for us to redeem us** from all lawlessness and **to purify for himself a people** for his own possession who are zealous for good works. (Ti.2:13-14 ESV)

In the courtyard, the altar of sacrifice was acacia wood covered with bronze; but, in the tabernacle, all of the wood from Egypt was covered with gold. Pure gold is God's preferred building material:

> And the building of the wall of it was of jasper: and **the city was pure gold, like unto clear glass... and the street of the city was pure gold, as it were transparent glass.** (Re.21:18, 21 KJV)

Pure gold speaks of purity or divine holiness. Hence, in the tabernacle, the acacia wood from Egypt covered by gold symbolized natural man's attitudes, behavior, and character that is refined by God:

> **He will sit like a refiner of silver,** burning away the dross. **He will purify** the Levites, **refining them like gold and silver,** so that they may once again offer acceptable sacrifices to the LORD. (Mal.3:3 NLT)

Christians need to be purified from the remnants of sin in their life:

> In a large house there are articles **not only of gold and silver, but also of wood and clay;** some are for noble purposes and **some for disposal of refuse. Those who cleanse themselves** from the latter will be instruments for noble purposes, **made holy,** useful to the Master and prepared to do any good work. (2Ti.2:20-21 TNIV)

God must purify us before we can serve Him:

> The **refining pot is for silver** and the **furnace for gold,** but **the LORD tests the hearts.** (Pr.17:3 NKJV; Pr.27:21)

The previous verse gives us an indication of what the gold-overlaid boards represented—a pure heart. David wrote concerning the tabernacle:

> Who may ascend into the hill of the LORD? **Or who may stand in His holy place? He who has clean hands and a pure heart,** Who has not lifted up his soul to an idol, nor sworn deceitfully. (Ps.24:3-4 NKJV)

Only someone with a pure heart can stand in the Presence of God. The reason why a priest had to wash before entering the tabernacle was to ceremonially cleanse himself before coming to the Lord. David knew that he needed more than a ceremonially-clean heart:

> *Create in me a clean heart, O God*; *and renew a right spirit within me.*
> (Ps.51:10 KJV)

David, who had a heart that sought after God, asked for a pure heart. The Old Testament ceremonial washings were not able to cleanse the hearts of the Israelites because their hearts were bent on doing evil. Jesus taught that what went into one's stomach never made a man unclean, but what came out of his heart made him unclean:

> *Don't you see that whatever enters the mouth goes into the stomach and then out of the body?* **But the things that come out of the mouth come from the heart, and these make a man "unclean."** *For* <u>*out of the heart*</u> *come evil thoughts, murder, adultery, sexual immorality, theft, false testimony, slander.* **These are what** <u>**make a man "unclean"**</u>; *but eating with unwashed hands does not make him "unclean."* (Mt.15:17-20 NIV)

Israel benefited little when they went to the bronze basin for cleansing. Because this action could not cleanse their hearts, they continued to do evil. Their evil hearts caused them to repeat their sins; hence, the basin was only a place of ceremonial cleansing so that the priest could serve God.

God's evaluation of the condition of man's heart before the flood was that their heart was consistently evil:

> *The LORD saw how great man's wickedness on the earth had become, and that* <u>*every*</u> *inclination of the thoughts* <u>*of his heart*</u> *was* <u>*only*</u> *evil* <u>*all*</u> *the time.*
> (Ge.6:5 NIV)

In the Old Testament, every inclination of man's heart was only evil all the time. God identified the condition of man's heart in the book of Jeremiah:

> *The heart is deceitful above all things and* <u>*beyond cure*</u>. *Who can understand it?* (Jer.17:9-10 TNIV)

The heart of man was deceitful and without cure in the Old Testament. God called out to the Jews to change their heart:

> *Rid yourselves of all the offenses you have committed, and* <u>**get a new heart**</u> *and* **a new spirit. Why will you die, house of Israel?** *For I take no pleasure in the death of anyone, declares the Sovereign* LORD. **Repent and live!**
> (Eze.18:31-32 TNIV)

The Jew's problem was that they could not change their wicked hearts. However, God promised that one day He would give man a new heart that would enable them to naturally follow His commands:

> *I will sprinkle <u>clean water</u> on you, and <u>you will be clean</u>; I will cleanse you from all your impurities and from all your idols. I will give you <u>a new heart</u> and put a new spirit in you; I will remove from you your heart of stone and give you a heart of flesh. And I will <u>put my Spirit in you</u> and move you to follow my decrees and be careful to keep my laws.* (Eze.36:25-27 NIV; 11:19)

God promised that the Jews will be cleansed by water, through which they will receive a new heart. The Jews practiced circumcision of the flesh, while what they really needed was to be circumcised in their heart—a cutting away of all that was sinful:

> *But a Jew is one inwardly, and circumcision is a matter of the heart, <u>by the Spirit</u>, not by the letter.* (Ro.2:29 ESV)

In the New Testament, Christians are circumcised in their heart because the sinful nature is cut away:

> *In him you were also circumcised, in the putting off of the sinful nature, not with a circumcision done by the hands of men but with the circumcision done by Christ, <u>having been</u> buried with him in baptism.* (Co.2:11 NIV)

When Christians are baptized, they experience a spiritual circumcision of the heart—the cutting away of the sinful nature from the heart:

> *Since we have a great priest over the house of God, let us draw near with a sincere heart in full assurance of faith, having <u>our hearts sprinkled clean</u> from an evil conscience and our bodies <u>washed with pure water</u>.* (He.10:21-22 NASB)

For the first time since the fall of man, our heart is washed clean, which permits us to enter the Presence of God and live:

> *Blessed are the pure in heart, for they will see God.* (Mt.5:8 KJV)

Our heart must be cleansed if the Holy Spirit is going to dwell within us. Placing the Holy Spirit into a wicked heart would be similar to pouring new wine into old, leaky wineskins:

> *Nor do they put new wine into old wineskins, or else the wineskins break, the wine is spilled, and the wineskins are ruined. But they put new wine into new wineskins, and both are preserved.* (Mt.9:17 NKJV)

Purifying our heart does not save us; it only prepares a place for the Holy Spirit to dwell. The Holy Spirit's indwelling saves us. To purify our heart without the indwelling of the Spirit is a meaningless ritual:

> **When an evil spirit comes out of a man**, it goes through arid places seeking rest and does not find it. Then it says, "I will return to the house I left." When it arrives, it finds the house **unoccupied, swept clean and put in order**. Then it goes and takes with it seven other spirits more wicked than itself, and **they go in and live there**. And the final condition of that man is worse than the first. (Mt.12:43-45 NIV)

Our actions can only be altered by Christ, Who cleanses our heart. God could have chosen any method for cleansing, but He chose baptism, making baptism the only acceptable method of cleansing. The water does not cleanse; our faith in God's promise to cleanse us through baptism is what actually makes us clean:

> So God, who knows **the heart**, acknowledged them **by giving them the Holy Spirit,** just as He did to us, and made no distinction between us and them, **purifying their hearts by faith**. (Ac.15:8-9 NKJV)

We receive a pure heart by our faith in God's promise that baptism grants us a clean heart. The Scriptures teach that Christians pray to God from a pure heart:

> Flee from youthful lusts and pursue righteousness, faith, love and peace, with those who call on the Lord from **a pure heart**. (2Ti.2:22 NASB)

One of the differences between the old covenant and the new covenant is that the Jews had a wicked heart and Christians have a pure heart:

> But the goal of our instruction is love from **a pure heart** and **a good conscience** and a sincere faith. (1Ti.1:5 NASB)

The cleansing of our heart is not the end but the beginning: the necessary preparation for the indwelling by the Holy Spirit which affects change:

> But you **are not controlled** by your sinful nature. You **are controlled** by **the Spirit** if you have the Spirit of God living in you. (Ro.8:8-9 NLT)

The acacia wood covered in gold symbolized the change in the nature of the heart of man through Christ. Christians have a new divine nature.

THE COVERINGS

Four layers of coverings formed the roof of the tabernacle. The inner covering that formed the ceiling, could only be seen from the inside by the priests. It was made of finely twisted linen of blue, purple, and scarlet which symbolized the work that Christ completes within us. Even though the gate, the tabernacle's door, and the ceiling of the tabernacle were made with the same colors, the ceiling was different because cherubim were woven into its fabric. The Scriptures teach that in heaven God the Father is surrounded by the cherubim:

> Also before the throne there was what looked like a sea of glass, clear as crystal. In the centre, around the throne, **were four living creatures, and they were covered with eyes, in front and behind.** The first living creature was like a lion, the second was like an ox, the third had a face like a man, the fourth was like a flying eagle. **Each of the four living creatures had six wings and was covered with eyes all around,** even under his wings. Day and night they never stop saying: "Holy, holy, holy is the Lord God Almighty, who was, and is, and is to come." (Re.4:6-8 NIV)

Ezekiel saw these creatures in his vision, which he identified as cherubim:

> This is the living creature that I saw under the God of Israel by the river of Chebar; and **I knew that they were the cherubim.** (Eze.10:20 KJV)

The tabernacle was God's dwelling place; therefore, it was only natural that cherubim were incorporated into the fabric of the inner covering/ceiling. The cherubim reminded the priests that they had entered God's dwelling place on earth.

The second covering was made of goats' hair. Goats are independent, rebellious animals. The goats' hair represented the work of Christ in atonement for rebellious man. On the Day of Atonement, two goats were chosen to eradicate Israel's sin:

> He shall take the two goats and present them before the LORD at the doorway of the tent of meeting. **Aaron shall cast lots for the two goats,** one lot for the LORD and the other lot for the scapegoat. Then Aaron shall offer the goat **on which the lot for the LORD fell, and make it a sin offering.** (Le.16:7-9 NASB)

> When Aaron has finished making atonement for the Most Holy Place, the Tent of Meeting and the altar, he shall bring forward the live goat. **He is to lay both hands on the head of the live goat and confess over it all the wickedness and rebellion of the Israelites—all their sins—and put them on the goat's head. He shall send the goat away into the desert** in the care of a man appointed for the task. **The goat will carry on itself all their sins to a solitary place**; and the man shall release it in the desert. (Le.16:20-22 NIV)

One of the goats was sacrificed as a sin offering; the other goat was set free into the desert—taking the sins of the people with it. The book of Hebrews speaks about Christ as a high priest:

> For this reason **he had to be made like his brothers and sisters in every way**, in order that he might become a merciful and faithful high priest in service to God, and that **he might make atonement** for the **sins** of the people. (He.2:17 TNIV)

Only on the Day of Atonement was the high priest allowed to enter the Most Holy Place and place blood on the mercy seat. The blood was a sacrifice for the sins that Israel had committed the previous year. The blood was the foreshadowing of Christ's sacrifice:

> In this is love, not that we loved God but that he loved us and **sent his Son to be the atoning sacrifice** for our sins. (1Jn.4:10 NRSV)

The second goat was released into the desert and took with it the sins of the people. In a similar way, Jesus came to take away our sin:

> Everyone who practices sin also practices lawlessness; and sin is lawlessness. **You know that He appeared in order to take away sins**; and in Him there is no sin. (1Jn.3:4-5 NRSV; He.9:28)

Not only was Jesus the sacrifice for our sin, but He also took our sins away so that they can never be held against us again:

> **As far as the east is from the west**, So far has He removed our transgressions from us. (Ps.103:12 NASB)

Therefore, the covering of goats' hair symbolized Christ's work of atonement, which not only forgives man for their sin but also removes sin from man.

The third covering of rams' skin dyed red was placed on the covering of goats' hair. The rams' skin was symbolic of the male lamb which was killed at the Passover, whose blood was placed on the doorframe to have the angel of death pass over the house:

> Then Moses summoned all the elders of Israel and said to them, "Go at once and select the animals for your families and **slaughter the Passover lamb**. Take a bunch of hyssop, dip it into the blood in the basin and **put some of the blood on the top and on both sides of the door-frame.** Not one of you shall go out of the door of his house until morning. When the LORD goes through the land to strike down the Egyptians, **he will see the blood on the top and sides of the door-frame and will pass over that doorway,** and he will not permit the destroyer to enter your houses and strike you down. Obey

these instructions as a lasting ordinance for you and your descendants."
(Ex.12:21-24 NIV)

Egypt is symbolic of the kingdom of Satan. When the Passover lamb was killed, the blood was put on the doorframes of the Israelites' homes. The angel of death would pass over their homes when he saw the blood. If the doorframe were not covered in blood, then the firstborn in the house would die. The death of the Egyptians' firstborn sons enabled Israel to leave their bondage in Egypt. In the same way, Christ, Who is God's firstborn, was killed; and His blood freed us from both sin and Satan. Christ is our Passover lamb:

Your boasting is not good. Don't you know that a little yeast works through the whole batch of dough? Get rid of the old yeast that you may be a new batch without yeast— as you really are. **For Christ, our Passover lamb, has been sacrificed.** *Therefore let us keep the Festival, not with the old yeast, the yeast of malice and wickedness, but* **with bread without yeast, the bread of sincerity and truth.** (1Co.5:6-8 NIV)

The covering of rams' skins dyed red was symbolic of Christ's work of redemption which frees man from the world, the kingdom of Satan:

May I never boast except **in the cross of our Lord Jesus** *Christ, through which* **the world has been crucified to me,** *and* **I to the world.** *Neither circumcision nor uncircumcision means anything;* **what counts is the new creation** (Ga.6:14-15 TNIV)

Once we become a Christian, we are no longer of the world:

I have given them your word, and the world has hated them **because they are not of the world,** *just as I am not of the world.* (Jn.17:14 ESV)

Therefore, the red rams' skins symbolized Christ as the Passover lamb, Who died to redeem man from Satan's kingdom.

The final covering placed on the tabernacle was of an undefined animal. Not knowing the type of animal is significant. Some scholars speculate that the covering was of sea cows, porpoises, badgers, or another kind of animal. All we know is that the Hebrew word used for this type of skin had the attribute of being durable, for even sandals were made from it:

I clothed thee also with broidered work, and **shod thee** *with badgers' skin, and I girded thee about with fine linen, and I covered thee with silk.*
(Eze.16:10 KJV)

The nondescript skins remind us of the time when Adam and Eve first sinned, and God killed some unnamed animals to cover their nakedness:

> **The LORD God made garments of skin** for Adam and his wife, **and clothed them.** (Ge.3:21 NASB)

Some nondescript animals died in man's place to cover man's original sin. The lack of description prevents us from placing a greater importance on one animal above another. When the Israelites looked upon the tabernacle, they saw only this nondescript outer covering. Since the tabernacle symbolizes our body, when people look at Christians, what do they see? People see that Christians are from every nation and description:

> For God so loved the world that he gave his one and only Son, that **whoever believes in him** shall not perish but have eternal life. (Jn.3:16 TNIV)

The "whoever" in the previous verse means that any person can become a Christian. In God's covenant to Abraham, He made two promises:

> The LORD had said to Abram, "Go from your country, your people and your father's household to the land I will show you. I will make you into **a great nation**... and **all peoples on earth** will be blessed through you." (Ge.12:1-3 TNIV)

All the people in the world can be blessed if they believe on Christ. In heaven, people from every ethnic group will be represented:

> After this I looked, and there was a great multitude that no one could count, **from every nation, from all tribes and peoples and languages,** standing before the throne and before the Lamb, (Re.7:9 NRSV)

If we could look at the tabernacle structure, how would we describe it? If we looked at the Christians in heaven and tried to describe them, how would we describe them? The diversity in the appearance of Christians is limitless, for we come from every nation. Therefore, the top covering of the tabernacle was made of an unspecified animal and symbolized the diversity of Christians who form the church.

Our Body, God's Tabernacle

The tabernacle was built in approximately 1450 BC and was in use until approximately 950 BC when Solomon dedicated the temple. The tabernacle was not meant to be a permanent dwelling place for God, just as our bodies were not meant for eternity. A Christian's body is God's dwelling place:

> Or do you not know that <u>your body is a temple</u> of the Holy Spirit within you, whom you have from God? **You are not your own, for you were bought with a price.** So glorify God in your body. (1Co.6:19-20 ESV)

Jesus also spoke of His body as God's temple:

> Jesus answered them, "**Destroy this temple,** and I will raise it again in three days." They replied, "It has taken forty-six years to build this temple, and you are going to raise it in three days?" But <u>the temple he had spoken of was his body</u>. (Jn.2:19-21 TNIV)

When Jesus was born of Mary, He took on human likeness, having a body, a soul, and a spirit:

> Who, being **in very nature God**, did not consider **equality with God** something to be used to his own advantage; rather, he made himself nothing by taking the very nature of a servant, being <u>made in human likeness</u>. And being found **in appearance as <u>a human being</u>**, he humbled himself by becoming obedient to death—even death on a cross! (Php.2:6-8 TNIV)

Jesus' body died on the cross. Our physical body was not designed to enter heaven but to connect us to the present world, just as the tabernacle was God's temporary dwelling place on earth to connect with the Israelites:

> I think it is right to refresh your memory as long **as I live in the tent of this body**, because I know that **I will soon put it aside**, as our Lord Jesus Christ has made clear to me. (2Pe.1:13-15 TNIV)

Both our body and the tabernacle were created to be on earth for a short period of time:

> So we fix our eyes not on what is seen, but on what is unseen, since **what is seen <u>is temporary</u>**, but what is unseen is eternal. For we know that if **the <u>earthly tent we live in is destroyed</u>**, we have a building from God, an eternal house in heaven, not built by human hands... For while **we are in this tent**, we groan and are burdened, because we do not wish to be unclothed but to be clothed with our heavenly dwelling, **so that what is mortal may be swallowed up by life**. (2Co.4:18-5:4 TNIV)

Our physical body is the temporary tabernacle of God on the earth:

> What I am saying, brothers and sisters, is this: flesh and blood <u>cannot inherit the kingdom of God</u>, nor does **the perishable** inherit the imperishable. (1Co.15:50 NRSV)

The body will die, but man's soul and spirit will live forever. The tabernacle structure contained two rooms: the Holy Place and the Holy of

Holies. Man's body contains the soul and the spirit. Man's soul lives forever, for John saw the souls of Christians in heaven:

> When the Lamb broke the fifth seal, **I saw** underneath the altar **the souls of those who had been slain** because of the word of God, and because of the testimony which they had maintained; (Re.6:9 NASB)

Not only will our soul go to heaven but our spirit will return to God as well:

> Then **the dust will return to the earth** as it was, and **the spirit will return to God** who gave it. (Ec.12:7 NKJV)

At our death, the body is separated from our soul and spirit. However, our physical body is only made for life on this earth. When we are resurrected from the dead, we will receive a new body—a spiritual body:

> It is the same way **with the resurrection of the dead**. Our earthly bodies are planted in the ground when we die, but they will be raised to live forever... They are **buried as natural human bodies**, but they will be **raised as spiritual bodies**. (1Co.15:42-44 NLT)

When we die, our body is buried in the ground but is not changed until we receive a spiritual body in our resurrection—when Jesus returns on the clouds. Even though there is no physical change in our body when we become a Christian, our body has become the temple of God on earth:

> Do you not know **that your bodies are temples of the Holy Spirit**, who is in you, whom you have received from God? (1Co.6:19 TNIV)

Our body remains the same, but there is a dynamic change that takes place within man. Our soul becomes the new Holy Place. As we study the Holy Place in the tabernacle in the next four lessons, we will begin to understand how Christ changed our soul in its function, which also affects our body's actions.

Thinking It Through:

1. The priests who served in the Tabernacle had responsibilities and grave consequences. What do these teach us?

2. What does the bronze bases of the curtain door represent?

3. What did the acacis wood covered in gold represent?

4. What does the silver bases of the tabernacle represent?

5. What was the significance of using pure gold in the tabernacle?

6. Why were cherubim woven into the linen covering for the tabernacle?

7. Why did God leave the fourth outer layer of the tabernacle ambiguous/nondescript?

8. The tabernacle was a temporary dwelling place. What does this teach us about man?

The Bible and Its Story 1908

THE HOLY PLACE

The people of Israel did everything just as the LORD had commanded Moses. Then they brought the holy tent to Moses along with everything that belonged to it. Here are the things they brought. Hooks, frames, crossbars, posts bases, the covering of ram skins that were dyed red, the covering of the hides of sea cows, the curtain that screens the ark, the ark where the tablets of the covenant are kept, the poles and cover for the ark, the table for the holy bread with all of its articles, the holy bread, the pure gold lampstand with its row of lamps and everything that is used with it, the olive oil that gives light, the gold altar for burning incense, the anointing oil, the sweet-smelling incense, the curtain for the entrance to the tent, the bronze altar for burnt offerings with its bronze grate, its poles and all of its tools, the large bowl with its stand, the curtains of the courtyard with their posts and bases, the curtain for the entrance to the courtyard, the ropes and tent stakes for the courtyard, the sacred clothes for the priest Aaron the clothes for his sons when they serve as priests. The people of Israel had done all of the work just as the LORD had commanded Moses. Moses looked over the work carefully. He saw that the workers had done it just as the LORD had commanded. So Moses gave them his blessing. Exodus 39:32-43NIrV

Lesson 6

The Holy Place

A Model of Man

Since the tabernacle structure is our body, the Holy Place is our soul. The Holy Place had three articles: the gold lamp stand, the gold altar of incense, and the gold table of showbread. Our soul has three functions: our intellect (which gathers and processes information), our emotion/desires (which determine what we feel like doing), and our will (which completes the action through our body). Jesus said:

> You must **love the LORD** your God with all **your heart**, all **your soul**, and all **your mind**. This is the first and greatest commandment. (Mt.22:37-38 NLT)

Jesus commanded that we love God with our entire mind (intellect), our heart (emotion/desires), and our soul (will). All three functions of our soul must be placed on the altar. However, the Biblical model is only one model of how man processes information. For example, psychologists do not recognize man's spirit. Consequently, psychologists try to change the unacceptable behavior of men by focusing on the symptoms of man's psyche—soul. However, the soul is not the cause of our behavior; the soul's choices are only a symptom of a greater problem. When a medical doctor observes the symptoms in a person's body, he must discover the cause of the symptoms. One common error is to treat the symptoms but not cure the cause. For instance, a person who is suffering from extreme pain in the abdomen can be treated for the symptom by prescribing a strong pain killer. The symptom will go away. However, is the man really cured? No, he could die from appendicitis in a few days! The pain is real, but the pain is not the cause but a symptom of an illness. We can treat the pain quickly without curing the cause which will recur, or we can cure the cause. Both psychologists and Christians are concerned about the symptoms of man; however, psychologists focus on the symptoms, but Christians focus on the cause:

> See to it that no one takes you captive through **hollow and deceptive philosophy**, which depends on **human tradition and the basic principles of this world** rather than on Christ. For in Christ all the fullness of the Deity lives in bodily form, and **you have been given fullness in Christ,** who is the head over every power and authority. (Co.2:8-10 NIV)

I find it interesting that two groups of people with differing worldviews can look at the same data and reach totally conflicting conclusions. Once people deny the concept of God and His spiritual realm, their worldview will perceive everything from a physical origin. These people refer to the soul as the "psyche." They perceive all of man's problems as originating from the psyche and approach these problems through psychology on a soulical level. They only recognize a person's intellect, emotion, and will as they delve into a person's preferences, personality, and past. However, the idea of the soul is part of a Biblical model. The Bible teaches that man is predisposed to evil and that the cause of the evil in man needs to be addressed. The psychological model considers all mankind morally neutral and treats abnormal behavior primarily through psychotherapy or drugs, which suppress a person's psychological anomalies. Carl Jung, the founding father of analytic psychology, consulted spiritual guides (two of which were Philemon and Basilides) who formulated his theories. These spiritual guides denied the existence of the spiritual realm, proposing to solve man's problems by manipulating the psyche. Jung constantly met with spiritual entities, yet the spiritual guides diverted his focus from the spiritual realm to the physical and soulical realms. People who follow Jung's methods still deny the existence of the spiritual realm and its affect on mankind. The world is treating the symptoms—the anomalies of the psyche—and not the cause:

> Dear friends, I urge you, as foreigners and exiles, **to abstain from sinful desires, which war against your soul.** (1Pe.2:11 TNIV)

A spiritual battle is waged for every human soul, for Satan seeks to destroy and kill those who are made in God's image. We can try to overcome the symptoms of the sinful nature through some method of psychology, but the Scriptures teach that man without Christ will remain controlled by the sinful nature. This nature can only be put to death through Christ:

> Those who belong to Christ Jesus **have crucified the sinful nature with its passions and desires.** (Ga.5:24 NIV)

Psychologists concluded that Jeffrey Dahmer was a hopeless psychopath; but from a Biblical worldview, he was controlled by at least one demon. Jeffrey Dahmer was restored to wholeness through the acceptance of Christ before he was killed by his fellow inmates. One day Jesus also confronted a psychopath:

> And when He had come out of the boat, immediately **a man from the tombs with an unclean spirit met Him,** and he had his dwelling among the tombs. And no one was able to bind him anymore, even with a chain; because he had often been bound with shackles and chains, and **the chains had been torn apart by him, and the shackles broken in pieces, and no one was strong enough to subdue him.** And constantly night and day, among the tombs and in the mountains, **he was crying out and gashing himself with stones.** (Mk. 5:2-5 NASB)

The disciples did not subdue the man from the tombs and then send him for psychotherapy. Jesus, being God, used a Biblical model. He fully knew the spiritual realm and commanded the demons who controlled the man to depart from him, affecting an immediate change in behavior:

> For Jesus had said to him, **"Come out of this man, you evil spirit!"** Then Jesus asked him, "What is your name?" "My name is Legion," he replied, "for we are many." And he begged Jesus again and again not to send them out of the area. A large herd of pigs was feeding on the nearby hillside. The demons begged Jesus, "Send us among the pigs; allow us to go into them." **He gave them permission, and the evil spirits came out and went into the pigs.** (Mk.5:8-13 NIV)

You cannot counsel a demon. Psychologists continue to bully the soul through mind-altering drugs to suppress the demonic behavior. If man tries to deal with the symptoms of the soul, constant counseling or medication will be needed, for their effects are temporary. On the other hand, if we deal with the spiritual cause, the results can be permanent freedom:

> Then they came to Jesus, and **saw the one** who had been **demon-possessed** and had the legion, sitting and clothed and **in his right mind.** And they were afraid. (Mk.5:15 NKJV)

Our worldview and our model of a man formulate our approach to treating man's disorders. Through the Biblical approach, a person need not suffer recurring symptoms of his fallen condition but, rather, experience a permanent transformation through Christ living in him.

THE BODY, SOUL, AND SPIRIT

The body is composed of five senses: hearing, sight, smell, taste, and touch. Through these senses, we perceive the world around us, but the perceived information is processed by the soul. The **intellect** gathers the information from the five senses and processes it; the **emotion/desires** decide what one feels like doing; and the **will** dictates to the body how to respond with respect to the intellect and emotion. Adam's and Eve's spirits were alive in the Garden of Eden and had the capability to live in constant fellowship with God. Before Eve was tempted, her soul functioned as God intended:

> The woman said to the serpent, "From the fruit of the trees of the garden we may eat; but from **the fruit of the tree which is in the middle** of the garden, **God has said,** 'You shall not eat from it **or touch it, or you will die.**'"
>
> (Ge.3:2&3 NASB)

Eve was living by her spiritual faculties. Her spiritual intuition knew what God had said: that the fruit would kill her. Eve's spiritual conscience discerned the will of God: not to touch the fruit. Her spiritual communion caused her to disregard the fruit: it was just some tree in the middle of the garden. When Satan taught Eve the concept of evil, the sinful nature became alive. Eve rejected her spiritual faculties, for she coveted equality with God. Once Satan taught her the concept of evil, her soul changed from a spiritual dynamic to a soulical existence:

> When the woman saw **that the fruit of the tree <u>was good</u> for food and <u>pleasing</u> to the eye, and <u>also desirable</u> for gaining wisdom**, she took some and ate it. She also gave some to her husband, who was with her, and he ate it.
>
> (Ge.3:6 NIV)

With her spirit deadened, Eve used her soulical faculty of intellect to assume that the fruit of the forbidden tree was good for food and was the means for gaining wisdom. Through her soul's faculty of emotion, the fruit became pleasing to the eye, for she coveted to be like God. Finally, her soul's faculty of will, under the influence of her soul's intellect and emotion, picked the forbidden fruit, ate it, and gave some to her husband. Both Adam and Eve died spiritually that day:

> "...**the day you eat of it you will surely die.**" (Ge.2:17 NIV)

Once Eve's spirit died, she needed a new source of direction for her life/soul. Before being tempted, her spirit dictated the direction of her soul, which compelled her body to remain obedient to God. God intended man's soul to serve man's spirit. However, once mankind's spirit was deadened, they by default were controlled by their soul. After the fall, man's spirit died, and the soul needed a new purpose for life. Once mankind lost their spirit's faculties which focused on pleasing God, the soul found new purpose in the earthly realm by pleasing the body through sensuality. Man's soul took control of their body; however, the body's sensuality actually controlled the soul. The soul became a pawn of the body's senses. In some Biblical translations, to live for the pleasing of the body's senses is referred to as "walking in the flesh." The Gentiles lived for sensuality:

> So I tell you this, and insist on it in the Lord, that you must no longer live as the Gentiles do, **in the futility of their thinking.** ...Having **lost all sensitivity**, they have given themselves **over to sensuality** so as to **indulge in every kind of impurity**, with a **continual lust for more.** (Eph.4:19 NIV)

The Gentiles, who were ignorant of God, were consumed by sensuality, the pleasing of their bodily senses. Satan takes these normal pleasures and warps them to a destructive extreme, which produces an antisocial behavior. The world delves into the anomalies of the soul not recognizing the true cause: their deadened spirit. The Scriptures teach that man's spirit died, and refers to man as dead:

> As for you, you <u>were dead</u> in your transgressions and sins, in which you used to live when you followed the ways of this world and of **the ruler of the kingdom of the air, the spirit** who is now at work in those who are disobedient. **All of us also** lived among them at one time, **gratifying the cravings of our sinful nature** and following its desires and thoughts... **God, who is rich in mercy, made us alive with Christ** even when we <u>were dead</u> in transgressions. (Eph.2:1-5 NIV)

Mankind's spirit died when Adam and Eve fell into sin:

> For **as in Adam all die**, so also in Christ shall all be made alive.
> (1Co.15:22 ESV)

Adam could not pass on what he did not possess; consequently, everyone descended from Adam was born with a deadened spirit:

> For if <u>many died</u> through one man's trespass, (Ro.5:15 ESV)

Every person is born physically alive but spiritually dead:

> The widow who lives for pleasure <u>is dead</u> even while she lives.
> (1Ti.5:5-6 NRSV)

Mankind's anomalies are a result of their deadened spirit:

> When you were dead in your sins and in the uncircumcision of your sinful nature, God made you alive with Christ. (Co.2:13 NIV)

The Biblical Concept of Soul

In the Biblical model, God made man a tri-unity like Himself, having a body, soul, and spirit. When Adam sinned, mankind's spirit was deadened, incapable of functioning; hence, man was forced to live by the power of their soul:

> So also it is written, "The first man, Adam, became a living soul." The last Adam became a life-giving spirit. (1Co.15:45 NASB)

Through the fall of Adam, man's spirit died, causing man to operate on a soulical level. Through Christ, we can become spiritual people:

> Humans can reproduce only human life, but the Holy Spirit gives birth to spiritual life. So don't be surprised when I say, "You must be born again."
> (Jn.3:6-7 NLT)

Man's spirit was alive at creation, died in the fall, and can be reborn in Christ. For, only through Christ can man regain tri-unity of body, soul, and spirit:

> May God himself, the God of peace, sanctify you through and through. May your whole spirit, soul and body be kept blameless at the coming of our Lord Jesus Christ. The one who calls you is faithful and he will do it.
> (1Th.5:23-24 NIV)

Our soul distinguishes us from other people and determines who we are. Identical twins share the same DNA but can be very different in their soul through the formation of their personality and preferences which are shaped by their past. Each twin is unique in character because of his experiences: episodes of elation, tragedies exposed to, or frightening experiences from which phobias form. These are not necessarily evil, but they do shape our personality. Likewise, each person has different preferences: a favorite color, music, or food. Most of these preferences are not wrong, just different. Each man is also different in his soul's faculties: intellect, emotion, and will. God has given each of us different strengths: one is intelligent; another is emotionally strong; and another is strong-willed. Animals also have a soul and share these traits and faculties. For instance, animals have intellect similar to that of our soul; that is, there is a difference between a smart or dumb dog. The human intellect allows us to collect and process information on different levels:

- *Mordecai speaketh to send back unto Esther: "**Do not think in thy soul** to be delivered [in] the house of the king, more than all the Jews..."*
 (Es.4:13 Young's Literal Translation)
- *How long shall I **take counsel in my soul**, Having sorrow in my heart all the day? How long will my enemy be exalted over me?* (Ps.13:2 NASB)
- *I will give thanks to Thee, for I am fearfully and wonderfully made; Wonderful are Thy works, **And my soul knows it very well**.*
 (Ps.139:14 NASB)
- *When wisdom entereth into thine heart, and **knowledge is pleasant unto thy soul**...* (Pr 2:10 KJV)
- *As he **hath thought in his soul**, so is he.*
 (Pr.23:7 Young's Literal Translation)

The soul is the center of our emotions and desires. Animals have similar emotions such as happiness or sadness. Human emotions influence our desires and affect what we do:

- *In **bitterness of soul** Hannah wept much and prayed to the LORD.*
 (1Sa.1:10 KJV)
- *But his flesh will be in pain over it, And **his soul will mourn over it**.*
 (Job 14:22 NKJV)
- ***Why are you in despair, O my soul?** And why have you become disturbed within me?* (Ps.42:5 NASB)
- *My soul **longed and even yearned** for the courts of the LORD; My heart and my flesh sing for joy to the living God.* (Ps.84:2 NASB)
- ***Make glad the soul** of Thy servant, For to Thee, O Lord, I lift up my soul.* (Ps.86:4 NASB)

Man's soul also has a will that enacts their thoughts and feelings. An animal, as well, can be either strong-willed or compliant. The human will drives us to action or stagnates with non-action:

- ***Our soul waits** for the LORD; He is our help and our shield.*
 (Ps.33:20 NASB)
- *And **my soul chooseth strangling**, Death rather than my bones.*
 (Job 7:15 KJV)
- *As the deer pants for the water brooks, **so my soul pants for You**, O God.* (Ps.42:1 KJV)
- *The LORD will preserve him and keep him alive, And he will be blessed on the earth; You will not deliver him **to the will** [Soul] of his enemies.*
 (Ps.41:2 NKJV)

- *In the day of my trouble I sought the Lord; In the night my hand was stretched out without weariness; **My soul refused** to be comforted.*
  (Ps.77:2 NASB)

Usually, one of the faculties of the soul is more dominant than another in a person. Dominant characteristics can be observed in soulical Christians (people who attend church but continue to live by the power of their soul and are not born again). If **intellect** is dominant, a person will prefer an evangelical church where knowledge is valued. If **emotion** is dominant, he will prefer a charismatic church which appeals to one's feelings through experiences. Yet, if **will** is dominant, he will prefer a fundamental church which stresses the observance of rules by willpower.

The correlation of our soul's formation and its faculties influence who we are and what we do. The soul is the essence of a person's being. If a body is kept alive by science without the soul, the person is classified as brain-dead—without intellect, emotion, or will. When we die, our bodies remain in the ground and return to dust; but our souls are eternal and experience the spiritual realm:

*When He opened the fifth seal, **I saw** under the altar **the souls of those who had been slain** for the word of God and for the testimony which they held.*
(Re.6:9 NKJV)

The question is not "Will the soul live eternally?" but, rather, "Where will the soul spend eternity?"

*Do not fear those who kill the body **but cannot kill the soul**; rather fear him who can destroy **both soul and body in hell**.* (Mt.10:28 NRSV)

Our soul does not need to go to hell; we can do something proactive:

*My brothers and sisters, if anyone among you wanders from the truth and is brought back by another, you should know that whoever brings back a sinner from wandering **will save the sinner's soul from death** and will cover a multitude of sins.*
(Ja.5:19-20 NRSV)

The death spoken of in the previous verses is an eternal death in the lake of fire. However, if we believe in Jesus and ask Him to save us from our sin, our spirit will live, and God will save our soul from the second death:

*Though now you do not see Him, yet believing, you rejoice with joy inexpressible and full of glory, receiving the end of your faith—**the salvation of your souls**.* (1Pe.1:8-9 NKJV)

Since our soul and spirit both go to heaven while our body remains on the earth, the body and the soul can be separated. However, the spirit and soul are inseparable. Christians learn to discern what is of their soul and what is received by their spirit from God:

> For the word of God is living and active. Sharper than any double-edged sword, *it penetrates even to dividing soul and spirit*, joints and marrow; it judges the thoughts and attitudes of the heart. (He.4:12 NIV)

From our physical birth, our soul was dominant because our spirit was deadened. Paul, in describing his former life under the law, stated that he was unspiritual—without his spirit being operational:

> We know that the law is spiritual; but *I am unspiritual*, sold as a slave to sin. (Ro.7:14 NIV)

Paul was describing his life before his spirit was born again by the Holy Spirit. In the previous verse, Paul's spirit was not in control, and he was still a slave to sin. In Ecclesiastes, Solomon cried out nine times:

> So I hated life, because what is done under the sun was grievous to me; for all is vanity and *a chasing after wind*. (Ec.2:17 NRSV)

Was Solomon merely stating something flippant: "a chasing after the wind"? Or was he stating something profound: "a chasing after the spirit"? The King James Version of the Bible agrees that Solomon was making a profound statement about his spiritual need:

> Therefore I hated life; because the work that is wrought under the sun is grievous unto me: for all is vanity and vexation of *spirit*. (Ec.2:17 KJV)

Solomon sensed that something was missing in his life, that his spirit was in a deadened state. Israel, under the old covenant, also lived by their soul's desire for fulfillment:

> *The fruit for which your soul longed* has gone from you, and *all your dainties* and your splendor are lost to you, never to be found again!" (Re.18:14 NRSV)

In a similar way to Israel, our society lives by the power of the soul and believes that they must nurture their soul both creatively and intellectually. An example of this belief is clearly revealed in the philosophy of education in the eighties. Children were taught that no answer was incorrect. Educational psychologists believed that a child's self-esteem was more important than a child's moral values. In today's society, the self/soul expressed in individuality is very important. The Scriptures disagree:

> *Whoever tries to keep his life* [soul] *will lose it*, and whoever loses his *life* [soul] *will preserve it*. (Lk.17:33 NIV)

Jesus commands that we must not only hate our life controlled by our soul, but we must also die to our soul's control—render it deadened like our spirit:

> *"Truly, truly, I say to you, unless a grain of wheat falls into the earth and dies, it remains alone; but if it dies, it bears much fruit. He **who loves his life** [soul] **loses it**, and **he who hates his life** [soul] in this world will keep it **to life eternal."*** (Jn.12:24-25 NASB)

The Scriptures are not suggesting that we lose who we are but, rather, that our soul must be deadened like our spirit was before rebirth and that our soul must be placed under the control of our spirit. Before we were born again, our spirit still existed but did not function. Once born again, our soul continues to exist with its personality, but the soul is now controlled by God's Spirit through our spirit. We cannot continue to live under the control of our soul because the soul was neither created nor equipped to be master over a person:

> *If anyone comes to Me and does not hate his father and mother, wife and children, brothers and sisters, yes, and his own life [soul] also, he cannot be My disciple.* (Lk.14:26 NKJV)

We must hate our present condition with our soul in control before we will seek to have our spirit come to life again. Therefore, our soul's formation (personality, preferences, and past) and faculties (intellect, emotion, and will) determine who we are as individuals. Our soul must be put in its proper place by being crucified with Christ before our spirit can be born again. All born-again Christians are spirit-controlled.

Man's Distortion of Pleasure

The soul's pursuit of sensuality is only one of the two factors that influence natural man to commit antisocial behavior/sin. If the cause of sin is our soul's quest for sensual fulfillment, then one logical assumption would be that the moment something became unpleasant, we would naturally discontinue the practice. The second assumption would be that we must discontinue our sinful practices by the power of our will. However, both of these assumptions are incorrect! The evidence that opposes these assumptions is found throughout our society and the Old Testament. The Scriptures state that Israel, who had the law, could not bring about the change that God required by the power of their soul's will:

> *"Do not handle! Do not taste! Do not touch!"? These are all destined to perish with use, **because they are based on human commands and teachings**. Such regulations indeed have an appearance of wisdom, with their self-imposed worship, their false humility and their harsh treatment of the body, but they <u>lack any value</u> in restraining sensual indulgence.*
> (Co.2:21-23 TNIV)

Our soul suffered a conflict of interest. The soul's obsession with sensuality cannot be overcome by our soul's resolve to discontinue sensual indulgence. Our soul's resolve will seldom rebel against the very thing in which it finds fulfillment—sensuality. While the death of our spirit enabled the soul to gain control over the body, the sinful nature is another dynamic at work in man. The sinful nature warped the soul's desire to please the body's senses, pushed man's sensuality beyond its natural parameters, and perverted our needs to an evil extreme. Food is not sinful, but gluttony is sinful. Wine is not sinful, but drunkenness is sinful. Sexual intimacy is not sinful, but outside of marriage it is sinful.

The all-consuming perversion of man is clearly seen when we consider man before the fall and immediately after the fall. Before man gained the knowledge of evil, nakedness was not an issue:

> *And **they were both naked**, the man and his wife, and **were not ashamed**.*
> (Ge.2:25 NKJV)

Immediately after eating the fruit, nakedness suddenly became sinful. With their new knowledge of evil, nakedness became a lust, and their senses craved to be satisfied. However, since lust was a new experience, they were uncomfortable and ashamed:

> *Then **the eyes of both of them were opened**, and **they realized they were naked**; so they sewed fig leaves together and made coverings for themselves.*
> (Ge.3:7 TNIV)

The sinful nature perverted natural sensuality to a sinful extreme. The soul seldom stagnates with its pleasures, for it either pursues new pleasures or degenerates in its present pleasures. Sensual enjoyment is not wrong, for God created our senses. However, to make pleasure our purpose for the soul in place of living for the will of God constitutes idolatry or sin.

ADDICTIVE BEHAVIOR

To understand fully the soul's preoccupation with sensuality, we must consider the dynamics of addiction. Addiction is a habitual sin that has taken a person's soul hostage; they hate the addiction but do not want to stop. Habitual sins are referred to as the sins that so easily entangle us:

> Since we have so great a cloud of witnesses surrounding us, let us also lay aside every encumbrance and **the sin which so easily entangles us,** and let us run with endurance the race that is set before us. (He.12:1 NASB)

The sins that so easily entangle us are parasitic sins we discovered by our experimental search for spiritual fulfillment. These parasitic sins captivated and distracted our soul from its intended purpose.

The ability to experience pleasure through the body is dependent upon what happens in the brain. In the pleasure centers of the brain, specific brain cells release dopamine in small amounts which gives a sense of reward. Some natural activities release higher amounts of dopamine than others. However, chemical substances such as endorphins prompt these brain cells to release large bursts of dopamine which grant extreme feelings of reward. Once a person experiences artificial, extreme pleasure, naturally-incurred pleasure will seem insignificant. The introduction of some artificial chemicals into the body will cause the body to cease the production of its own naturally-produced chemicals. The artificial chemical causes an extreme high; however, the body without the drug experiences a depleted low since the body is no longer naturally producing the chemical. This phenomenon increases the strength of the addiction. Thus, without the artificial substance, the body is in a state of depletion, which creates a sense of dependency on the substance to maintain natural levels.

After a period of time, the amount of dopamine released will decrease because of familiarity due to frequency of use. This causes the person to either experiment with other substances/experiences in search of a different high or to continue in the same addictive behavior to unacceptable levels in the hope of obtaining the original sense of elation. An example is sexual predators. They usually start with normal relationships and then descend to abnormal levels of distraction. They are appeased but, through familiarity, become unfulfilled. This in turn causes them to turn to unacceptable means such as pornography to obtain fulfillment. No form of sensuality can remain stagnant:

> Having lost all sensitivity, they have given themselves over **to sensuality** so as **to indulge** in **every kind of impurity,** with a **continual lust for more.**
> (Eph.4: 19 NIV)

Whatever form of sensual fulfillment—sex, mental stimulus, substance abuse, or physical abuse of the body—nothing can replace true spiritual fulfillment. Sensual fulfillment appeases the soul for a time with a sense of reward, for this fulfillment distracts man from his real spiritual need and prevents him from seeking true fulfillment. Many people consider the partial appeasement better than the promise of spiritual fulfillment by God. Man knows what he experiences, but he doubts that what is promised will grant him greater fulfillment in the end. Man's fixation with pleasure is the symptom of a spiritual need—the need of their spirit to be born again:

> But **she who lives in pleasure is dead** while she lives. (1Ti.5:6 NKJV)

The North American church, influenced by Western thinking, seeks fulfillment in the acceptable pleasures of this world. However, to live for the pleasure of anything except God is idolatry:

> But realize this, that in the last days difficult times will come. For men **will be lovers of self,** lovers of money... **lovers of pleasure rather than lovers of God,** holding to a form of godliness, although they have denied its power; Avoid such men as these. (2Ti.3:1-2&4-5 NASB)

The demonic gods of alternative pleasures offer contentment only while a person is under their influence. Apart from the pleasure's influence, the person is empty, oscillating between the highs of influence and the lows of absence. For this reason, these distractions will never quench the need for spiritual fulfillment but, rather, cause a person to continue seeking multiple methods that divert him from his spiritual need. Sensual experiences are never a permanent solution, causing addicts to turn to either an inferior substitute or a temporary distraction. For example, drug addicts usually use sex to fill time between highs.

Solomon best summarized the pursuit of pleasure as a distraction for his soul and a replacement for spiritual fulfillment:

> Whatever my eyes desired <u>I kept not from them</u>, I withheld not my heart from any joy; for my heart rejoiced in all my labor: and this was my portion of all my labor. Then I looked on all the works that my hands had worked, and on the labor that I had labored to do: and, behold, **all was vanity and vexation of spirit**, and there was **no profit under the sun.** (Ecc.2:10-11 KJV)

Like Solomon, our soul is aware of the void created by the death of our spirit and searches continually for pleasures that can fulfill our spiritual need. If we are honest, no earthly pleasure can satisfy our spiritual needs. As spiritual beings, we were meant to experience the fullness of God.

Even though sensuality offered appeasement to our soul, it was a poor substitute:

> So I tell you this, and insist on it in the Lord, that **you must no longer live as the Gentiles do, in the futility of their thinking.** ...Having lost all sensitivity, **they have given themselves <u>over to sensuality</u> so as to indulge in every kind of impurity, with a continual lust for more.**
> (Eph.4:17&19 NIV)

Even in Jesus' day, people lived for sensuality, trying to find fulfillment in the "highs of life":

> Let us behave properly as in the day, not in **carousing** and **drunkenness**, not in **sexual promiscuity** and **sensuality**, not in strife and jealousy.
> (Ro.13:13 NKJV)

The ultimate satisfaction that artificial stimuli can offer is only temporary. Artificial stimuli are only a distraction, a momentary substitute for experiencing God:

> As a result, they do not live the rest of their earthly lives for evil human desires, but rather for the will of God. **For you <u>have spent</u> enough time <u>in the past</u>** doing what pagans choose to do--living in debauchery, lust, drunkenness, orgies, carousing and detestable idolatry. They are surprised that you do not join them **in their reckless, wild living**, and they heap abuse on you.
> (1Pe.4:2-4 TNIV)

Even in the church of Corinth, many church-goers refused to abandon their sensual appeasements:

> I am afraid that when I come again my God may humiliate me before you, and I may mourn over many of those who have sinned in the past and **not repented of the impurity, immorality and sensuality which they have practiced.**
> (2Co.12:21 NASB)

All alternatives to spiritual fulfillment will fail and cause us to suffer a greater emptiness than we had before because the solution to emptiness is to experience true fullness in God. The Bible teaches that everyone has been under sin's illusion of alternative fulfillment to one degree or another:

> We have already made the charge that **Jews and Gentiles alike are all <u>under sin</u>.** As it is written: "There is **no-one** righteous, **not even one**; there is **no-one** who understands, **no-one** who seeks God. **All** have turned away, they have together become worthless; there is **no-one** who does good, **not even one**.
> (Ro.3:9-12 NIV)

Sin's illusion over our life prevented us from approaching God. Notice the all-inclusive words in the previous verses: "all," "no-one," and "not even one." When mankind ate the forbidden fruit, the possibility that other things could be used as an alternative for spiritual fulfillment made sin the master of man:

> Therefore, just **as sin came into the world through one man**, and death came through sin, and so death spread to all because all have sinned.
> (Ro.5:12 NRSV)

The knowledge that sinful indulgences could pacify man's spiritual need in place of God made sin a power over mankind. They now sought a sensual trigger that would produce a chemical release. This release appeased the need for spiritual fulfillment. Man's method of responding to sensual temptation was to yield to the urge. As long as man yielded to the urge for their soulical fix, which was chemically, physically, intellectually, or psychologically met, they were under the illusion that they were in control. Man believed that they determined when to indulge and when to refrain. However, they were deceived because the sin of sensuality really controlled them. The moment that man decided to discontinue indulging in habitual sin, sin's control over them became evident—they were slaves of the substance.

Some people attempt to discontinue addictive behavior for the wrong reasons: a judge's conviction, a doctor's diagnosis, the church's discipline, a wife's ultimatum, or financial ruin. The previous reasons fail because they in themselves have not actually met people's true need for spiritual fulfillment. Because man was created a spiritual being, God intended him to have spiritual fulfillment in intimate communion with Him. God has to initiate within man the desire to seek after Him, which enables a person to stop his addiction by fulfilling the spiritual need. The cause of man's sensuality, which degenerates to unhealthy levels is not because of poor choices but because of an intense longing to commune with God. The cause of unacceptable behavior—sin—is not because of man's soul but because man's spirit is deadened:

> We know that the law is spiritual; but **I am <u>unspiritual</u>, sold as a slave to sin**. I do not understand what I do. For what I want to do I do not do, but what I hate I do. And if I do what I do not want to do, I agree that the law is good. As <u>it is, it is no longer I myself who do it</u>, but **it is sin living in me**.
> (Ro.7:14-17 NIV)

The addictive sin lies to us that it is the real fulfillment for the soul instead of God. These alternative fulfillments become cruel masters which promise fulfillment, but they only pacify the person through continual use. The first time man experiences a source of sensual appeasement, it grants the greatest satisfaction because of its unfamiliarity. Any subsequent exposure will lessen the height of the experience because of the familiarity. (An example is the "first kiss syndrome.") Man continues to seek that same level of stimulus that was experienced in his first exposure, but this level of pleasure will never be achieved again. Therefore, addictive behavior will divert man's attention from the spiritual need of their soul but will always leave them empty the moment they are no longer under the influence of the delusion.

THE BIBLICAL SOLUTION

The soul was designed to submit to man's spirit, but man by himself cannot gain spiritual rebirth. Consequently, the soul readily submits to substitutes which distract from true spiritual need. The Scriptures recognize that man was not just spiritually dead but was, in essence, also a slave to the pleasures of sin:

> When **you** **were** slaves to sin, you **were** free from the control of righteousness. (Ro.6:20 TNIV)

Notice the past tense of the verbs used to describe the experiences of our lives before Christ. Compare the verb tenses in the previous verse with those in the following verses:

> You **have been** set free from sin and **have become** slaves to righteousness. (Ro.6:18 TNIV)

And:

> But now that **you have been** set free from sin and **have become** slaves of God, the benefit you reap leads to holiness, and the result is eternal life. (Ro.6:22 TNIV)

Man was in slavery to sensuality because they were spiritually dead. The soul suffers from a conflict of interests. Consequently, mankind cannot overcome their sensual appetites, for the soul, which seeks sensuality, has to initiate the end of its only fulfillment—sensual thrills. An addict's soul knows intellectually that he is dying. His soul's intellect decides to discontinue the addiction, but the soul's desire for the fulfillment through the addiction is stronger. Christians overcome sensual pleasure by their soul being restored to its rightful place, which is under the direction of their spirit. Once their spirit is born again, their soul is under the control of the Holy Spirit and regains its created purpose of living for God. Our spiritual rebirth by the Holy Spirit frees us from sin's control; and the need for the distraction by pleasure no longer exists because we now experience true fulfillment. In this way, the soul's preoccupation with sin is resolved by the rebirth of our spirit. Overcoming sin is achieved by the indwelling of the Holy Spirit and not by the suppressing of the body's cravings:

> For if you live according to the sinful nature, you will die; but **if by the Spirit you put to death the misdeeds of the body**, you will live.   (Ro.8:13 TNIV)

Only when the Holy Spirit satisfies the need which caused the pursuit of sensuality will we be free. Repentance is not just the turning away from something but also the turning to Someone. We do not overcome our dependence on the pursuit of pleasures by our decision to refrain from indulging but by the receiving of God's Spirit within us. Once our spirit becomes alive in communion with God, our elation from alternative pleasures becomes passé. Thus, the desire for sensual fulfillment will pass away with the greater realization of the Presence of Christ in our life:

> So I say, **live by the Spirit, and you will not gratify the desires of the sinful nature.**   (Ga.5:16 NIV)

Once we experience spiritual life through the indwelling of the Person of Christ, our spirit becomes alive and our soul submits to God. His indwelling frees us from our fixation with sensuality. Thus, we must put an end to the deception that fulfillment can be found in anything other than Christ:

> Even so **consider yourselves to be dead to sin**, but **alive to God in Christ Jesus**. Therefore **do not let sin reign in your mortal body** so that you obey its lusts.   (Ro.6:11-12 NASB)

We do not overcome our sin by the power of our soul's determination, but through our new spiritual life in Christ. This truth can be understood with the example of baby teeth. Baby teeth do not need to be pulled out in order for the new teeth to erupt, but rather, baby teeth are pushed out of the gums by the new adult teeth which displace them. In the same way, our dependency on alternative pleasures is displaced by true spiritual fulfillment that comes from Christ living within us. Christ's indwelling breaks the bondage to the power of sin that controlled us because His Spirit now controls us by His divine nature:

> You, however, **are controlled** <u>**not by the sinful nature**</u> but <u>**by the Spirit,**</u> **if the Spirit of God lives in you.** And if anyone does not have the Spirit of Christ, he does not belong to Christ. (Ro.8:9 NIV)

If the Spirit of Christ lives in us, then we are no longer controlled by the sinful nature. The control by the Holy Spirit's divine nature displaces the control of the sinful nature. Consequently, the change of masters alters the allegiance of our soul and ultimately affects our actions. We do not overcome our sinful actions by our soul's will but by surrendering our soul to the control of the Holy Spirit. He changes our actions:

> For if you live according to the sinful nature, you will die; but **if by the Spirit you put to death the misdeeds of the body**, you will live, because those who are led by the Spirit of God are sons of God. (Ro.9:13-14 NIV)

Placing our soul under the control of the Spirit ends our soul's fixation with its bodily senses:

> And <u>**if** Christ is **in you**</u>, the body is dead because of sin, but **the Spirit is life** because of righteousness. But **if the Spirit of Him** who raised Jesus from the dead **dwells in you**, He who raised Christ from the dead will also **give life to your mortal bodies through His Spirit who dwells in you.** (Ro.8:10-11 NKJV)

If we are going to spend eternity with God, the soul must return to its proper place under the control of our spirit:

> We know **that our old self was crucified** with him **in order that the body of sin might be brought to nothing,** so that we would **no longer be enslaved to sin.** For one who has died has been set free from sin. (Ro.6:6-7 ESV)

Jesus commanded that our mind (intellect), our heart (emotion/desires), and our soul (will) must be given to God. Our soul is God's new Holy Place. Every article in the Holy Place was made from gold or covered with gold (holiness). In the same way, our soul must be placed under the control of the Holy Spirit if we are going to be reconciled to God. In the next three lessons, we will examine the three faculties of our soul in relationship to God. We must stop living by the power of our soul, for we have laid ourselves on the bronze altar of sacrifice and have surrendered our lives to the control of God.

Thinking It Through:

1. Why is it important to treat the cause and not the symptoms of an ailment?

2. In respect to combating sin, what are the primary differences between psychological and Biblical worldviews?

3. Describe the three functions of the soul. How do they relate to each other?

4. Describe the three P's of the soul, which makes each person unique.

5. Compare how the soul functioned before and after the fall.

6. Why do people continue in activities which they find repulsive?

7. Why do some sins form addictions?

8. What is the Scriptural method for overcoming sin?

Pieter Mortier, 1704

The Gold Lampstand

The workers made the lampstand out of pure gold. They hammered out its base and stem. Its buds, blooms and cups branched out from it. Six branches came out from the sides of the lampstand. There were three on one side and three on the other. On one branch there were three cups that were shaped like almond flowers with buds and blooms. There were three on the next branch. There were three on all six branches that came out from the lampstand. On the lampstand there were four cups that were shaped like almond flowers with buds and blooms. One bud was under the first pair of branches that came out from the lampstand. A second bud was under the second pair. And a third bud was under the third pair. There was a total of six branches. The buds and branches came out from the lampstand. The whole lampstand was one piece that was hammered out of pure gold. The workers made its seven lamps out of pure gold. They also made its trays and wick cutters out of pure gold. They used 75 pounds of pure gold to make the lampstand and everything that was used with it. Exodus 37:17-24 NIRV

Lesson 7

The Gold Lampstand

Light

When one entered the tabernacle through the curtained door, his eyes would be drawn to the only source of light: the gold lampstand. The lampstand represented the intellect of our soul, and its light was symbolic of the knowledge which God has given to Christians. The light of the tabernacle was produced by the seven oil lamps on the lampstand which reflected off the golden walls. The lampstand's sole purpose was light:

> ...*the pure gold lampstand* with its row of lamps and all its accessories, and *the oil **for the light**;* (Ex.39:37 NRSV)

Since the lampstand consisted of seven oil lamps, the priests had to tend to them in the morning and in the evening, to prevent them from going out:

> Aaron shall burn fragrant incense on it; **he shall burn it every morning when he trims the lamps. When Aaron trims the lamps at twilight**, he shall burn incense. (Ex.30:7-8 NRSV)

The tending of the lamps occurred at the same time that the incense was to be offered on the gold altar, alluding to a connection between the two. God commanded that the lamps were never to go out:

> Command the Israelites to bring you clear oil of pressed olives for the light **so that the lamps may be kept burning continually.** Outside the curtain of the Testimony in the Tent of Meeting, **Aaron is to tend the lamps before the LORD from evening till morning, continually.** (Le.24:2-3 NIV)

The lamps were to burn continually because God lived in the tabernacle, and He lives only in light:

> God, the blessed and only Ruler, the King of kings and Lord of lords, who alone is immortal and **who lives in unapproachable light.**
> (1Ti.6:15-16 TNIV)

Therefore, the priests had to enter the Holy Place at least twice a day to tend to the lamps, filling them with oil and trimming their wicks.

Purely God

The lampstand represented the intellect of the soul. The lampstand was made from one piece of pure gold. The absence of acacia wood symbolized that spiritual knowledge did not originate from man. The pure gold suggested a work that is entirely of God:

> For God, who said, "Let light shine out of darkness,"**made his light shine in our hearts** to give us **the light of the knowledge** of the God's glory displayed in the face of Christ. But we have this treasure in jars of clay to show **that this all-surpassing power is from God and not from us**.
> (2Co.4:6-7 TNIV)

God made the light of His knowledge shine in our hearts. The whole of humanity lived in darkness, but God has brought light to all men through Jesus. Jesus said:

> **I have come as Light into the world**, so that everyone who believes in Me **will not remain in darkness**. (Jn.12:46 NASB)

Jesus came into the world as light in order to displace man's darkness:

> I will rescue you from your people and from the Gentiles—to whom I am sending you **to open their eyes so that they may turn from darkness to light** and from **the power of Satan to God**, so that they may receive forgiveness of sins and a place among those who are sanctified by faith in me. (Ac.26:17-18 NRSV; Co.1:13-14)

When we come to God through Christ, we no longer live in the darkness of ignorance. Jesus said:

> "**I am the light of the world**. He who **follows Me shall not walk in darkness**, but **have the light of life**." (Jn.8:12 NKJV)

Born-again Christians will never live in darkness again.

The lampstand consisted of a center stem with three branches on either side; each appendage had its own lamp. The lampstand had a total of seven lamps:

> They made the lampstand of pure gold and hammered it out, **base and shaft; its flowerlike cups, buds and blossoms** were of one piece with it. Six branches extended from the sides of the lampstand— **three on one side and three on the other**. **Three cups shaped like almond flowers with buds and blossoms were on one branch**, three on the next branch and the same for all six branches extending from the lampstand. And on the lampstand were four cups shaped like almond flowers with buds and

blossoms. One bud was under the first pair of branches extending from the lampstand, a second bud under the second pair, and a third bud under the third pair—six branches in all. (Ex.37:17-23NIV)

The center branch represented the Holy Spirit, Who is a Christian's source of knowledge. After Jesus arose from the dead, He gave the eleven disciples the Holy Spirit:

> So Jesus said to them again, "Peace be with you; as the Father has sent Me, I also send you." And when He had said this, **He breathed on them and said to them, "Receive the Holy Spirit."** (Jn.20:21-22 NASB)

Before Christ's ascension, the receiving of the Holy Spirit was a different spiritual phenomenon than what happened during Pentecost. Before His ascension, Christ gave the disciples the ability to understand the Scriptures:

> Now He said to them, "These are My words which I spoke to you while I was still with you, that all things which are written about Me in the Law of Moses and the Prophets and the Psalms must be fulfilled." **Then He opened their minds to understand the Scriptures...** (Lk.24:44-45 NASB)

The receiving of the Spirit recorded in John and the receiving of understanding of the Scriptures recorded in Luke are one in the same event. Understanding came by the Holy Spirit. However, the baptism of the Holy Spirit did not occur until after Jesus was glorified—ascended into heaven:

> While he was eating with them, he gave them this command: "Do not leave Jerusalem, but **wait for the gift my Father promised**, which you have heard me speak about. For John baptized with water, but **in a few days you will be baptized with the Holy Spirit.**" (Ac.1:4-5 TNIV)

When the Spirit of God came upon a person in the Old Testament, He supplied everything (strength, miraculous power, knowledge, etc.) that was necessary to accomplish God's work. However, these people did not experience God's Spirit becoming one with man's spirit; rather, God's Spirit came upon them for only the moment. Everyone who lived before the time of John the Baptist was still spiritually dead. Our spirit's rebirth could only take place after Jesus' resurrection.

A vast difference exists between the greatest men of the Old Testament and those who are born-again Christians:

> Among *those born of women* none is greater than John. Yet **the one who is least** in the kingdom of **God is greater than he.**" (Lk.7:28 ESV)

The Christian whom we might consider the least is greater than anyone born under the old covenant because he has been born again by God's Spirit:

> These were all commended for their faith, yet **none of them received** what had been promised. God had planned something better for us so that **only together with us** would they **be made perfect.** (He.11:39-40 NIV)

Everyone who lived before John the Baptist was spiritually dead. However, after Christ rose from the dead, born-again Christians experience the fullness of Christ through the indwelling of His Holy Spirit:

> For in Christ **all the fullness of the Deity** lives in bodily form, and **you have been given fullness in Christ**, who is the Head over every power and authority. (Co.2:9-10 NIV)

The lampstand represented the fullness of the knowledge of God which is given to man through their union with the Holy Spirit. Once God's Spirit lives in us, the light of the knowledge displaces the darkness of ignorance.

Knowledge

The center stem of the lampstand symbolized the Holy Spirit, Who is the source of a Christian's knowledge. Six other branches protruded from the center stem and represented six different forms of knowledge. Isaiah wrote that three couplets describe forms of knowledge:

> A shoot will come up from the stump of Jesse; from his roots a Branch will bear fruit. The **Spirit** of the **LORD** will rest on him—the **Spirit** of **wisdom** and of **understanding**, the Spirit of **counsel** and **of power**, the Spirit of **knowledge** and of the **fear** of the LORD—and he will delight in the fear of the LORD. (Isa.11:1-3 NIV)

Christ's Spirit was the center stem that went from the floor to the height of the other lamps. On the lampstand, each branch had a corresponding branch on the opposite side of the center stem. One of the couplets is knowledge and fear.

Knowledge is information, individual facts that one accumulates through life. If facts remain in our mind, they are of no use to us. Only if the facts are used with the other five forms of knowledge does it have completion. To know the Scriptures thoroughly and not apply them is a tragedy:

> If I had the gift of prophecy, and if I understood all of God's secret plans and **possessed all knowledge**... but didn't love others, **I would be nothing.** (1Co.13:2 NLT)

Knowledge without love (the compassion of God that moves us into action) creates pride, but when knowledge is shared in love, it builds people up:

> We know that we all possess knowledge. **Knowledge puffs up, but love builds up.** (1Co.8:1 NIV)

Knowledge can be like an unmanned fire hose, for knowledge spews facts like a hose that spews water without direction or purpose. For this reason, knowledge needs the other branches of the lampstand to be effective.

Fear is coupled in Scripture with knowledge because fear tempers knowledge to be beneficial. God did not give you knowledge to impress other people with facts. God gave knowledge for a purpose, and He will call you into account for all that He has given you:

> From everyone to whom **much <u>has been given</u>, <u>much will be required</u>**; and from the one **to whom much <u>has been entrusted</u>, <u>even more will be demanded</u>**. (Lk.12:48 NRSV)

Those who are given knowledge and who sense God's calling to teach must carefully consider what they teach, for they will be judged by God more severely:

> Not many of you **should <u>become teachers</u>**, my brothers and sisters, for you know that **we who teach <u>will be judged with greater strictness</u>**. (Ja.3:1 NRSV)

We must fear God because He will judge us for our use of His gift of knowledge.

Wisdom is the application of knowledge. Each couplet is interdependent, for fear also produces wisdom:

> The **<u>fear</u>** of the LORD **is the beginning <u>of wisdom</u>**: and the **<u>knowledge</u>** of the holy **is <u>understanding</u>**. (Pr.9:10 KJV)

Knowledge without application is meaningless:

> Who **is wise** and understanding among you? Show by **your good life** that your **works are done** with gentleness **born of wisdom**. (Ja.3:13 NRSV)

Wisdom is taking the knowledge of the Scriptures and applying it to life. A wise man does not simply know the truth but also readily applies God's truths to his life:

> Therefore **do not be unwise**, but understand what **<u>the will of the Lord</u>** is. (Eph.5:17 NKJV)

Wisdom uses the knowledge of God to transform lives, causing them to become like Him in attitude, behavior, and character:

> It is because of him that you are in Christ Jesus, who has become for us **wisdom from God**—that is, **our righteousness, holiness and redemption.**
> (1Co.1:30 NKJV)

Many people know about God, but born-again Christians know how to take the Scriptures and apply the transforming truths of God to their lives.

Understanding is coupled with wisdom because understanding answers the question "why?" Understanding is the ability to comprehend how the individual facts of truth connect. Understanding places knowledge in context:

> He instructed me and said to me, "Daniel, I have now come **to give you insight and understanding.**"
> (Da.9:22 NIV)

An illustration of understanding is a child's dot-to-dot picture. The dots on the page would be bits of knowledge, but the understanding is represented by the numbers which instruct the order in which a child must connect the dots. Connecting the dots without an order would constitute scribbling, but connecting the dots in the intended order creates a beautiful picture. Knowledge without understanding is useless:

> Think over what I say, for **the Lord will give you <u>understanding in all things</u>**.
> (2Ti.2:7 NRSV)

Understanding takes knowledge and processes it so that wisdom can apply the knowledge:

> My goal is that they may be encouraged in heart and united in love, so **that they may have the full riches of <u>complete</u> understanding**, in order that they may know the mystery of God, namely, Christ, in whom are hidden **all the treasures of wisdom and knowledge.**
> (Co.2:2-3 TNIV)

Without understanding, the Scriptures are just stories. Understanding is the realization of how the stories relate to a person's life.

Counsel is knowledge that is shared with others so that they might know God's will for their lives. God has a specific plan for His people from eternity past. We can be given a diversity of counsel, but God has a specific will for each moment of our lives:

> **The counsel of the LORD stands forever, the plans of His heart** from generation to generation.
> (Ps.33:11 NASB)

When Christians are faced with determining the will of God, they are given discernment, which is the spiritual counsel of God:

> I I did not shrink from **declaring to you the whole counsel of God.**
> (Ac.20:27 ESV)

Counsel is the revelation of specific truths that can be applied to a current situation and reveal the will of God.

Power is a form of discernment. Counsel offers advice; however, sometimes we are called to action. Power produces action. No matter what form of power we discuss, undirected power is dangerous. One day the disciples thought some Samaritans were disrespectful to Jesus and wanted to release the power of God:

> When the disciples James and John saw this, they asked, "**Lord, do you want us to call fire down from heaven to destroy them?**" But Jesus turned and rebuked them. (Lk.9:52-55 NIV)

To access the power of God without discerning the will of God can be counter-productive. Consider healing, which is only one aspect of the power of God. We are not to attempt to heal everyone who asks; for Scriptures command us to use discernment in using God's healing power:

> **Do not be hasty in the laying on of hands**, and do not share in the sins of others. Keep yourself pure. (1Ti.5:22 TNIV)

Sickness could be used for God's glory by miraculous healing, or it could be a form of discipline to bring about repentance, or it could be the time to die—everyone dies. The Bible commands us to wait upon God's direction before we attempt the laying on of hands for healing. Jesus prayed often and was able to use God's power according to God's plan because He took time to discern God's will:

> He replied, "Go tell that fox, 'I will keep on **driving out demons and healing** people <u>today</u> and <u>tomorrow</u>, and on the <u>third day I will reach my goal</u>.'" (Lk.13:32 TNIV)

We need to discern God's will as to when and how to use His power.

THE MIND OF CHRIST

Spiritual knowledge is imparted to man by the Holy Spirit. The Holy Spirit is the One Who gives the ability to comprehend the things of God.

We died with Christ so that Christ might live in us. When Christ lives in us, He controls our mind, or as Scriptures so aptly state:

> **But we have the mind of Christ.** (1Co.2:16 NKJV)

Let me illustrate the significance of receiving the mind of Christ. Suppose my wife and I were in a tragic car accident. My wife's body was crushed, and I was left brain-dead. The surgeons took my wife's unharmed brain and put it into my body. When I got out of the hospital, how would you expect my body to act? Like my wife, of course! Everything about me would be driven by my wife's mind. Hence, a change of mind would cause a change of nature, which would affect a change of behavior:

> Those who live according to the sinful nature **have their minds set** on what **that nature desires**; but those who live in accordance with the Spirit **have their minds set** on what the Spirit desires. (Ro.8:5 NIV)

The Holy Spirit controls our mind, Who changes our thinking from darkness to light. However, the cleansing of our mind is an ongoing process symbolized in the making of the lampstand. We would assume that an elaborate gold lampstand would be made with a mold. The process for making the lampstand could include carving the desired shape from wax, making a mold, and pouring gold into the mold to create the lampstand. However, this was not the process that was commanded by God. Instead, the lampstand was hammered from one piece of gold. This illustrated two things.

First, making the gold lampstand was not an instant or quick process. Second, forethought was required throughout the process as each hammer blow had to be deliberately planned, for mistakes could not be easily corrected. Just like the lampstand was formed one blow at a time, our mind must also be transformed one thought at a time. Our mind must be transformed from the things of this world:

> Their end is destruction; their god is the belly; and their glory is in their shame; **their minds are set on earthly things**. (Php.3:19 NRSV)

Before our life was in Christ, our mind was controlled by sin and, thereby, focused on earthly pleasures. Now that our mind is changed, our focus must be directed from earthly things to the things that are of heaven:

> Therefore if you have been raised up with Christ, **keep seeking the things above**, where Christ is, seated at the right hand of God. **Set your mind on the things above**, not on the things that are on earth. (Co.3:1-2 NASB)

The Scripture teaches that our thought patterns must be changed from being consumed by self-gratification to God-glorification:

> Do not be conformed to this world, but **be transformed <u>by the renewing of your minds</u>**, so that you may discern what is **the will of God**—what is good and acceptable and perfect. (Ro.12: 2 NRSV)

Many Christians will try to change the nature of their thoughts by their own resolve, but they will fail. Only if the Holy Spirit gives birth to our spirit and renews our mind will our individual thoughts to be changed:

> He saved us through **the washing of rebirth** and <u>**renewal**</u> **by the Holy Spirit**. (Ti.3:5 TNIV)

Just as the hammer hit the talent of gold one stroke at a time to form the lampstand, our mind also will be renewed by the Holy Spirit, one thought at a time, over our lifetime. We need to think on the things that reflect God's character:

> Finally, brethren, whatsoever things are **true**, whatsoever things are **honest**, whatsoever things are **just**, whatsoever things are **pure**, whatsoever things are **lovely**, whatsoever things are **of good report**; if there be any virtue, and if there be any praise, **think on these things**. (Php.4:8 KJV)

"The old self is gone, and the new self has come" (2Co.5:17) is an accomplished fact. This affects how we think. Yet, the renewing of the mind with the things of God is a lifelong process:

> Do not lie to each other, since you <u>**have taken off**</u> **your old self** with its practices and <u>**have put on**</u> the **new self**, which is <u>**being renewed in knowledge**</u> in the image of its Creator. (Co.3:9-10 TNIV)

Knowing how God is going to accomplish that which He has promised brings instant freedom from known sin. However, the more I become like Christ, the more I realize I am not like Christ. This understanding creates a desire to know more in order to become more like Christ. An illustration of the renewal process can be seen in marriage. If my wife died after forty years of marriage, and I married another woman, I would habitually try to please my new wife in the same manner that I had pleased my deceased wife. During our new marriage, I would not intentionally try to displease my wife, but the habits that were formed by my relationship with my deceased wife would naturally manifest themselves. Unfortunately, my new wife would have different preferences and, therefore, would tell me when my actions fell short of pleasing her. Even though my first wife was dead, time would be needed to put to death the habits of how I related to her. Time would be needed for the renewal of my mind to develop new habits of how to please my new wife. In the same way, the old self is dead, but the transformation of our old habits will take time, not because of purposeful disobedience but because of habit:

> We demolish arguments and every pretension that sets itself up **against the knowledge of God**, and **we take captive every thought to make it obedient to Christ**. (2Co.10:5 NIV)

Through the Presence of the Holy Spirit, we must address our thinking patterns. As we meditate on the Scriptures, the Holy Spirit convicts us of aspects in our life that are displeasing to God:

> For **the word of God is living and active** and sharper than any two-edged sword, and piercing as far as the division of soul and spirit, of both joints and marrow, and able **to judge the thoughts and intentions of the heart.**
> (He.4:12 NASB)

The Word of God convicts or affirms our heart concerning our actions. The Holy Spirit either convicts us that our actions are sinful or defends us against the accusations from the devil of sin. However, according to God's conviction, we must confess those actions which are sinful:

> **If we confess** our sins, **he** is faithful and just and **will forgive us** our sins and **purify us from all unrighteousness.** (1Jn.1:9 NIV)

The awareness of our acts of sin is only beneficial if we respond in a manner according to the Scriptures. Through our confession of sin, we seek not only forgiveness for our actions but also His grace to purify us from the desire to commit those sins. The Holy Spirit grants us the grace that purifies our life by renewing our thought patterns:

> Paul, a servant of God and an apostle of Jesus Christ for the faith of God's elect and **the knowledge of the truth that leads to godliness**.
> (Ti.1:1 NIV; Jn.8:31-31)

The transformation of the one piece of gold into the lampstand was a long and thought-out process—one hammer blow at a time. The same is true for us. Conviction is the revelation that our actions are displeasing to God. Revelation comes through the Word, but the knowledge is imparted to our mind by the Spirit of God. As we grow in the knowledge of God, we also grow in our understanding of God's holiness:

> ...so that you may lead lives worthy of the Lord, **fully pleasing to him**, as you bear fruit in every good work and **as you grow in the knowledge of God**. (Co.1:10 NRSV)

Many times, the Scriptures teach that we need to grow not only in the grace of God but also in His knowledge:

> ...but **grow in the** grace and **knowledge of our Lord** and Savior Jesus Christ. (2Pe.3:18 NASB)

Being born again is just the beginning of our new life. We need to grow in spiritual knowledge like a newborn infant grows in knowledge:

> Like newborn infants, long for **the pure, spiritual milk**, so **that by it you may grow into salvation**... (1Pe.2:2 NRSV)

God's knowledge is infinite; therefore, we can never mature to the point that we can stop studying His Word to gain understanding:

> And this is my prayer: that your love **may abound more and more in knowledge and depth of insight, so that you may be able to discern what is best** and may be pure and blameless until the day of Christ, filled with the fruit of righteousness that comes through Jesus Christ—to the glory and praise of God. (Php.1:9-11 NIV)

The knowledge of God is like an onion; as we understand one layer, it exposes another layer to be understood. As we understand and apply God's truths, we must be ready to receive a deeper truth which is vital in our relationship with God. God has promised us many things. When we read the Scriptures and become aware of His promises, we simply need to ask for the understanding and the wisdom to apply His Word:

> Now we have received, not the spirit of the world, but **the Spirit who is from God**, so **that we may know the things** freely given to us by God, which things we also speak, not in words taught by human wisdom, but in those **taught by the Spirit, combining spiritual thoughts with spiritual words**.
> (1Co.2:12 NASB)

All born-again Christians are given knowledge by God's Spirit:

> I myself **feel confident about you**, my brothers and sisters, **that you yourselves are** full of goodness, **filled with all knowledge**, and able to instruct one another. (Ro.15:14 NRSV)

Christians will never know everything (omniscient) but will have all the knowledge that they need in order to live the Christian life. The gold lampstand represents truth. Truth is eternal knowledge which is able to free us from sin, self, and Satan. Truth transforms our life to become like Christ.

Darkness

Without the lampstand, the Holy Place would be filled with darkness. Darkness is the absence of light, which is the condition of our world. Only God is holy—a sinless perfection that is void of evil. God's truth is the highest moral standard that has ever existed:

> This is the message we have heard from him and declare to you: **God is light; in him there is no darkness at all.** If we claim to have fellowship with him and **yet walk in the darkness, we lie** and do not live out the truth. But **if we walk in the light, as he is in the light**, we have fellowship with one another, and the blood of Jesus, his Son, **purifies us from all sin.**
> (1Jn.1:5-7 TNIV)

Light and darkness both exist. These represent two forms of wisdom. One originates from finite man—darkness. The other originates from our infinitely perfect God, Who see and knows everything—light:

> **For by Him all things were created, both in the heavens** and on earth, visible **and invisible**, whether thrones or dominions or **rulers or authorities** all things have been created through Him and for Him. He is before all things, and in Him all things hold together. (Co.1:16-17 NASB)

Earthly wisdom is naturally perceived by man through their senses, but man lacks the spiritual faculties to perceive the unseen—they remain in the dark. Satan and his demons offer man an alternative explanation for those things that are of a spiritual nature, for his motive is to keep people from knowing God. Satan cannot be trusted to reveal the things of God. Even though man cannot perceive the spiritual reality, the spiritual realm is real:

> **This wisdom** is not that which comes down from above, but **is earthly, natural, demonic.** For where jealousy and selfish ambition exist, there is disorder and every evil thing. But **the wisdom from above is first pure**, then peaceable, gentle, reasonable, full of mercy and good fruits, unwavering, without hypocrisy. (Ja.3:15-17 NASB)

The spiritual realm is invisible yet interacts with man. The spiritual realm contains a vast array of both good and evil creatures: angels (demons are fallen angels), archangels, cherubim (Satan is a fallen cherubim), and seraphim. God created every creature that exists in the spiritual realm:

> And Ezra said: "You are the LORD, you alone; you have made heaven, **the heaven of heavens, with all their host**, the earth and all that is on it, the seas and all that is in them. **To all of them you give life**, and **the host of heaven worships you.**" (Ne.9:6 NRSV)

Every living creature in the heavenly realm was created for a specific purpose. Angels were created to minister to man:

> Are not all **angels ministering spirits** sent **to serve those who will inherit salvation?** (He.1:14 TNIV)

Every spiritual creature was created good on the sixth day of creation, for God judged all creatures as good:

> God saw <u>**all that he had made**</u>, and it was very good. And there was evening, and there was morning--the sixth day. (Ge.1:31 TNIV)

Even Satan was good in the beginning:

> You were **the model of perfection,** full of wisdom and perfect in beauty. **You were in Eden, the garden of God**... You were **anointed as guardian cherub**, for so I ordained you. You were on the holy mount of God; you walked among the fiery stones. **You were blameless in your ways from the day you were created** till wickedness was found in you. Through your widespread trade you were filled with violence, and you sinned. **So I drove you in disgrace from the mount of God**, and I expelled you, **O guardian cherub**, from among the fiery stones. **Your heart became proud** on account of your beauty, and you corrupted your wisdom because of your splendour. **So I threw you <u>to the earth</u>**; I made a spectacle of you before kings. (Ez.28:12, 14-17 NIV)

Satan was a model of perfection—the guardian cherub of creation. He became proud and rebelled against God; therefore, God banished him to the earth. At some point, Satan conceived a plan to corrupt man. Taking the form of a serpent, Satan tempted Eve, which resulted in Adam and Eve's rebellion toward God. As a result, man was banished from God's garden:

> Therefore **the LORD God sent him out of the garden of Eden** to till the ground from which he was taken. (Ge.3:23 NKJV)

When God banished mankind from His garden, He sent them into the world, which was Satan's realm, and placed them under his authority. The Scriptures teach us that the whole world is part of Satan's kingdom:

> As for you, you were dead in your transgressions and sins, **in which you used to live** when you followed **the ways of <u>this world and of the ruler of the kingdom of the air</u>,** the spirit who is now at work in those who are disobedient. (Eph.2:1-2 TNIV)

Even Jesus recognized Satan as the ruler over this world:

> I will no longer talk much with you, **for the ruler of this world is coming.** He has no power over me... (Jn.14:30 NRSV)

When Adam and Eve left the garden, they were readily received by Satan, who adopted them as his children:

> **Everyone who commits sin is a child of the devil**; *for the devil has been sinning from the beginning. The Son of God was revealed for this purpose, to destroy the works of the devil.* (1Jn.3:8 NRSV)

Through man's fall and subsequent separation from God, Satan received what he sought: lordship over all of mankind. Satan is inferior to God in every way, but Satan is far more powerful than man:

> *Bold and arrogant,* **these men are not afraid to slander celestial beings;** *yet even* **angels, although they are stronger and more powerful**, *do not bring slanderous accusations against such beings in the presence of the Lord.* (2Pe.2:10-1 NIV)

The power of Satan and his demons make them appear like gods to man. In fact, the Scriptures refer to Satan as a finite god:

> *And even if our gospel is veiled, it is veiled to those who are perishing, in whose case* **the god of this world** **has blinded the minds of the unbelieving**, *that they might not see the light of the gospel of the glory of Christ, who is the image of God.* (2Co.4:3-4 NASB)

Satan and his hosts may appear as superior beings to sinful man, but they are only self-proclaimed gods, inferior to the one true God Who created them:

> *For even* **if there are so-called gods, whether in heaven or on earth** *(as indeed there are many "gods" and many "lords")* (1Co.8:5 NIV)

Because of man's fall, all mankind is under the authority of Satan:

> *We know that we are children of God, and that* **the whole world is under the control of the evil one.** (1Jn.5:19 TNIV)

Therefore, all mankind is born under the authority of Satan and are referred to in Scripture as Satan's children.

THE POWER OF DARKNESS

God is omnipresent; however, Satan is limited and can only be in one place at one time. In the temptation of Job, we are given a glimpse of Satan:

> *The LORD said to Satan, "From where do you come?" Then Satan answered the LORD and said,* **"From roaming about on the earth and walking around on it."** (Job 1:7 NASB)

Satan goes to and fro on the earth to maintain control over his demonic forces. Ephesians grants us a glimpse of Satan's authority structure with four types of angelic beings:

> For we do not wrestle against flesh and blood, but against **principalities**, against **powers**, against the **rulers of the darkness** of this age, against **spiritual hosts of wickedness** in the heavenly places. (Eph.6:12 NKJV)

The Bible teaches us that our battle is not against flesh and blood (humans) but against spiritual forces in the heavenly realms. Principalities are spiritual rulers who control people and whose function is defined by geographical location. Powers are spiritual rulers who control people and whose function is defined by religion. Rulers of darkness (as discussed in Lesson 2) are demons who deceive and distract people through the things of this world. The spiritual hosts of wickedness have the sole purpose to manipulate men to sin. While people are enticed by their sensual desires, there is another dynamic, the spiritual hosts of wickedness that are at work to cause people to rebel against God:

> As for you, you were dead in your transgressions and sins, in which you used to live **when you followed** the ways of this world and of **the ruler of the kingdom** of the air, **the spirit** who is now at work in those who are disobedient. (Eph.2:1-2 NIV)

The spiritual force of wickedness has the sole mandate to keep mankind enslaved to sin:

> Perhaps God will change those people's hearts, and **they will learn the truth.** Then they will come to their senses and **escape from the devil's trap. For they have been held captive by him to do whatever he wants.**
> (2Ti.2:25-26 NLT)

The Scriptures refer to Satan as "the tempter":

> Jesus was led up by the Spirit into the wilderness **to be tempted by the devil**... **The tempter came** and said to him... (Mt.4:1&3 NRSV; 6&9)

Satan does not tempt every person but is responsible for tempting people through his "spiritual forces of wickedness." In Jesus' third temptation, we can see how Satan entices people to sin:

> The devil **took** Him to a very high mountain and **showed** Him all the kingdoms of the world and their glory; and he **said** to Him, "All these things I will give You, **if You fall down and worship me**." (Mt.4:8-9 NASB)

Satan not only presented Jesus with an initial complete thought which proposed a course of action, but he also took Jesus to a place of temptation and gave Jesus visualizations. Christ could not see all of the kingdoms of the world from that mountain in Judea, but He could visualize them with their splendor.

Experiencing an initial thought of sin is a temptation. Being taken to a place we should not be is also a part of a temptation. Experiencing visualizations can be a part of the temptation but is still not sin. Jesus experienced all three forms of temptation but did not sin. He was also enticed with satanic worship; obviously there are no limits as to the depth of depravity of thoughts that Satan will place in our mind.

In a fourth temptation, Jesus spoke of His death, and Peter responded that it would never happen. Christ discerned the origin of Peter's thought:

> *Jesus turned and said to Peter, "**Get behind me, Satan!** You are a stumbling block to me; you do not have in mind the concerns of God, but merely human concerns."* (Mt.16:23 TNIV)

Peter spoke from an attitude of loyalty and love for Christ and was unaware of the satanic origin of his thought. Even though it was Peter who said the words, Satan placed the words into Peter's mind in order to tempt Jesus to turn away from death on the cross. Jesus acknowledged that the thought was not of Peter and addressed its author, Satan. In a similar way, Satan and his "spiritual forces of wickedness" place temptations directly into our mind, both in our thoughts while awake or in our dreams while we sleep. The Bible credits Satan for being responsible for all temptations:

> *For this reason, when I could endure it no longer, I also sent to find out about your faith, **for fear that the tempter might have tempted you**, and our labor would be in vain.* (1Th.3:5 NASB)

Satan has ultimate control of all the "spiritual forces of wickedness." They place into our mind temptations to sin against God. Even though Satan can tempt us, God limits how Satan may tempt us:

> *"But reach out and take away everything he has, and he will surely curse you to your face!" "All right, **you may test him**," the LORD said to Satan. "**Do whatever you want with everything he possesses, but don't harm him physically.**"* (Job 1:11-12 NLT)

In fact, Satan needs God's permission before he can tempt anyone:

> And the Lord said, *"Simon, Simon! Indeed, <u>Satan has asked</u> for you, that he may sift you as wheat."* (Lk.22:31 NKJV)

Since Christ was tempted in all the ways that we are, no one is exempt from temptation—not even the mature are exempt:

> Brothers, if someone is caught in a sin, **you who are spiritual** should restore him gently. **But watch yourself, or you also may be tempted.** (Ga.6:1 NIV)

Satan and his demons tempt us by giving thoughts that suggest a course of action, hoping that our sensuality will be enticed and our sinful nature incited to commit an act of sin.

Freedom from Darkness

Christ came not only to forgive us of our sin but to also destroy Satan's work to enslave men in sin:

> Whoever makes a practice of sinning is of the devil, for the devil has been sinning from the beginning. **The reason the Son of God appeared was <u>to destroy the works of the devil</u>.** (1Jn.3:8 ESV)

Many Christians are unaware of their position in Christ. This ignorance leaves them vulnerable. Our knowledge of what Christ accomplished frees us from the power of sin:

> Paul... an apostle of Jesus Christ for the faith of God's elect and **the knowledge of the truth that leads to godliness.** (Ti.1:1 NIV)

Our knowledge of God and His promises teach us of our authority over Satan and his realm. The knowledge prevents us from being bullied by Satan:

> For no matter how **many promises God has made, they are "Yes"** in Christ. And so through him the "Amen" is spoken by us to the glory of God. Now **it is God who makes both us and you stand firm in Christ**.
> (2Co.1:20-21 TNIV)

Christ has provided everything we need to live a holy life:

> **His divine power** has granted to us <u>**all things that pertain to life**</u> and **godliness, <u>through the knowledge of him</u>** who called us to his own glory and excellence, by **which he has granted to us his precious and very great promises,** so that through them you may **become partakers of the divine nature**, having escaped from the corruption that is in the world because of sinful desire. (2Pe.1:1:3-4 ESV)

When the tempter comes, God promises that we will be given the strength to stand. We need to know God's promises of power to access them:

> No temptation has overtaken you that is not common to man. **God is faithful, and <u>he will not let you</u> be tempted beyond your ability**, but with the temptation <u>**he will also provide**</u> **the way of escape**, that you may be able to endure it. (1Co.10:13 ESV)

We were born under the authority of Satan, but Christ delivers us when we are born again:

> Yes, I am sending you to the Gentiles to open their eyes, so they may **turn from darkness to light** and **from the power of Satan to God**. (Ac.26:17-18 NLT)

We no longer have to be bullied by Satan, for we are children of the light:

> For you are all **children of the light** and of the day; **<u>we don't belong to darkness</u>** and night. (1Th.5: NLT)

God promises to give us victory over sin and Satan:

> We know that **anyone born of God <u>does not continue to sin</u>**; the one who was **born of God <u>keeps him safe</u>**, and **the evil one <u>cannot harm him</u>**. (1Jn.5:18 NIV)

When we come to God through Christ, we no longer live in the darkness of wickedness because of ignorance but have the light within us. Jesus said:

> I am the light of the world. He who follows Me **<u>shall not walk in darkness</u>**, but **<u>have the light of life</u>**. (Jn.8:12 NKJV)

When Satan comes to tempt us, we have the authority to respond like Jesus:

> Jesus said to him, "**Away with you, Satan!**" (Mt.4:10 NKJV; Mt.16:23)

The knowledge of what we **can do** and what **to do** enables us to be free from Satan's manipulation and become the light of the world:

> **You are the light of the world**. (Mt.5:14 NKJV)

Christians no longer walk in the darkness of sin and ignorance. Through their knowledge of God, they have overcome sin and Satan. They generate holiness because of Christ in them—the light of God in a world of darkness.

Thinking It Through:

1. What does the lampstand represent?

2. How do darkness and light relate to knowledge?

3. What is the difference between the Holy Spirit coming upon you and the Spirit living in you?

4. What are the different types of knowledge, and how do they relate to each other?

5. Who was the greatest person born prior to Jesus' death, and how can we be greater than he?

6. The lampstand was hammered out of one piece of gold. What does this teach us?

7. What is the mandate of the "spiritual forces of wickedness"?

8. What was Jesus' purpose for coming to earth? Was He successful?

Treasures of the Bible 1894

THE GOLD ALTAR OF INCENSE

Make an altar for burning incense. Make it out of acacia wood. It must be one foot six inches square and three feet high. Make a horn stick out from each of its upper four corners. Cover the top, sides and horns with pure gold. Put a strip of gold around it. Make two gold rings for the altar below the strip. Put the rings across from each other. They will hold the poles that are used to carry it. Make the poles out of acacia wood. Cover them with gold. Put the altar in front of the curtain that hangs in front of the ark where the tablets of the covenant are kept. The ark will have a cover. It will be the place where sin is paid for. There I will meet with you. Aaron must burn sweet-smelling incense on the altar. He must do it every morning when he takes care of the lamps. He must burn incense again when he lights the lamps at sunset. Incense must be burned regularly to me. Do it for all time to come. Do not burn any other incense on the altar. Do not use the altar for burnt offerings or grain offerings. Do not pour drink offerings on it. Once a year Aaron must put the blood of a sin offering on its horns to make it pure. He must do it on the day Israel's sin is paid for. Do it for all time to come. The altar is a very holy place to me."   Exodus 30:1-10 NIrV

Lesson 8

The Gold Altar of Incense

The Structure

The second function of our soul after intellect is our emotions and desires. The gold altar of incense was two cubits high with a base of one cubit square. It was made of acacia wood and overlaid with gold. Acacia wood represented man. Overlaying the wood with gold represented God's work in transforming man's heart with its emotions/desires. How many times have you known the good you ought to do but never did it? Your mind wanted one thing, but your heart desired another. Even though the intellect collects the information gathered by our five senses and logically processes it, we do not make decisions by logic alone. Rather, we do what we desire at the given moment. Someone once said, "The road to hell is paved with good intentions." The desire to do good is an illusion of goodness. Our good intentions mean little if they are left undone.

Since the Holy Place represented our soul with its intellect, emotion/desire, and will, the knowledge of the correct choice required the desire to complete it. In working with youth, a common phrase is, "I don't feel like it!" They know what is right but won't do it. In the world, a spiritual battle exists between a person's intellect and desire. Jesus said that we must love God with our whole being:

> You shall love the Lord your God with **all *your heart***, and with **all your soul**, and with **all *your mind***, and with **all your strength**. (Mk.12:30 NASB)

Our strength represents our body, our mind represents our intellect, our heart represents our emotion/desires, and our soul represents our will. The mind, heart, and soul need to be transformed before the Holy Spirit can indwell us. With man, doing the will of God is not merely a matter of knowing what is right but, rather, a matter of desiring in the heart to do what is right:

> For **as he thinks in his heart**, so is he. (Pr.23:7 NKJV)

Notice that the previous verse does not say that a man thinks in his **mind**; rather, the verse says that a man thinks in his **heart**. Our decisions are not just a cognitive exercise but also a matter of desire. The heart was the issue that led to the destruction of the world through the flood:

> The LORD saw how great man's wickedness on the earth had become, and that **every** inclination of the **thoughts of his heart** was **only evil all the time**. (Ge.6:5 NIV)

The Scriptures do not say that *some* inclinations were *somewhat* evil at *sometimes*. The condition of our heart always controls the moral quality of our actions. Jesus attributed sinful action to the condition of a man's heart:

> Do you not understand that everything that goes into the mouth passes into the stomach, and is eliminated? But the things that proceed out of the mouth **come from the heart**, and **those defile the man**. For **out of the heart come evil thoughts**, murders, adulteries, fornications, thefts, false witness, slanders. These are the things **which defile the man**; (Mt.15:17-19 NASB)

The influence of our heart over our mind can be seen daily in many lives. An example would be my brother. He started smoking cigarettes in high school because he thought it was "cool." He always stated that he was not addicted but that he smoked for enjoyment. He was emphatic that he only smoked when he wanted; hence, he was the one in control. At one point, cigarettes became so expensive that he could no longer justify the pleasure and decided to stop smoking. Suddenly, he was aware that he never determined when to smoke; rather, the sinful addiction controlled when he needed to smoke. His decision to stop smoking started a very long and tough battle against his illusion of choice.

We are controlled by many things, but if we always yield to the desire for sinful gratification, the illusion of choice remains. The decision of when to indulge does not originate from our mind; rather, the desire to indulge originates from our heart. If decisions were strictly made by the mind, then life would be simple. We would only do the things that we desired and would be able to stop the moment that those things became unpleasant or inconvenient. This is not the case. The problem with most people is not that they are ignorant of what they ought to do, but the problem is that their heart does not desire to do it. The Gospel calls these people to purify their heart from their idolatry, to end their double-mindedness:

> **Come near to God and he will come near to you.** Wash your hands, <u>you sinners</u>, and <u>**purify your hearts**</u>, you <u>**double-minded**</u>. Grieve, mourn and wail. Change your laughter to mourning and your joy to gloom. Humble yourselves before the Lord, and he will lift you up. (Ja.4:8-10 TNIV)

Our mind says one thing, but we do another. Our heart controls our mind so that even though we make a decision, we do not carry through on the decision we make. Our heart determines what we do. Rejection of creation and the acceptance of evolution is not a logical decision; rather, our heart did not desire what God had to offer:

> The fool has <u>**said in his heart**</u>, *"There is no God."* (Ps.14:1 NASB; 51:1)

Unbelief comes from man's heart. Our heart desired sin; therefore, it will readily accept any religion or theory other than the true God:

> They are **darkened** <u>**in their understanding**</u> and separated from the life of God because of the ignorance that is in them <u>**due**</u> to <u>**the hardening of their hearts.**</u> (Eph.4:18 NIV)

Our hardened heart is the real reason why people do not accept God. Consequently, God has to draw us to Himself and create in us the desire to turn to Him:

> **No one can come to Me unless the Father who sent Me draws him;** and I will raise him up at the last day. (Jn.6:44 NKJV)

When God draws us to Christ, He actually does a work in our heart. Our heart has to be opened to accept God, which enables our mind to accept the Gospel:

> Now a certain woman named Lydia heard us. She was a seller of purple from the city of Thyatira, who worshiped God. **The Lord <u>opened her heart</u> to heed the things spoken by Paul.** (Ac.16:14 NKJV)

God opens our heart to recognize our sinfulness and our need for a Savior. When the Holy Spirit first came at Pentecost, God performed spiritual heart surgery:

> Now when they heard this, <u>**they were cut to the heart**</u> and said to Peter and to the other apostles, "Brothers, what should we do?" Peter said to them, "**Repent**, and **be baptized** every one of you in the name of Jesus Christ so that **your sins may be forgiven**; and you will **receive the gift of the Holy Spirit.**" (Ac.2:37-38 NRSV)

Just as a surgeon cuts the person to perform physical heart surgery, God had to cut to the people's spiritual heart in order for them to accept the Gospel. In the old covenant, God pleaded with Israel to circumcise their heart:

> **Circumcise** yourselves to the LORD, **circumcise your hearts**, you men of Judah and people of Jerusalem, or **my wrath will break out** and burn like fire **because of the evil you have done**— burn with no-one to quench it.
> (Jer.4:4 NIV; De.10:16)

Since Israel could not answer God's calling to circumcise their heart, He had to constantly deal with Israel's rebellious heart. While Israel wandered in the desert, God promised to one day circumcise Israel's heart for them so that they could live:

> Moreover the LORD your God will **circumcise your heart** and the heart of **your descendants**, to love the LORD your God with all your heart and with all your soul, **so that you may live**.
> (De.30:6 NASB)

Three times God stated that Israel needed to circumcise their heart, and in the Old Testament, God commanded Israel three times to get a new heart:

> **Repent!** Turn away from all your offences; **then sin will not be your downfall**. Rid yourselves of all the offences you have committed, and **get a new heart** and a new spirit. Why will you die, O house of Israel? For **I take no pleasure in the death of anyone**, declares the Sovereign LORD. **Repent and live**!
> (Eze.18:31-32 NIV; 11:19-20)

Since Israel could not obtain a new heart, God promised that one day He would give them a new heart:

> **I will** give you a new heart, and a new spirit **I will** put within you. And **I will** remove the heart of stone from your flesh and give you a heart of flesh. And **I will** put my Spirit within you, and cause you to walk in my statutes and be careful to obey my rules.
> (Eze.36:25-27 ESV)

Notice the number of times God said "I will" in the previous Scripture. The gold placed over the acacia wood symbolized the spiritual transformation that occurs when God circumcises our heart, giving us a new heart:

> A person is not a Jew who is one only outwardly, nor is circumcision merely outward and physical. No, a person is a Jew who is one inwardly; and **circumcision is circumcision of the heart, by the Spirit**, not by the written code.
> (Ro.2:28-29 TNIV)

When the Scripture speaks of circumcising a heart, it is addressing man's need to have the Holy Spirit remove the sinful nature from their heart:

*In him you **were also circumcised**, in the putting off **of the sinful nature**, not with a circumcision done by the hands of men but with the circumcision done by Christ, **having been buried with him in baptism and raised with him** through your faith in the power of God, who raised him from the dead.*
(Co.2:11-12 NIV)

Every born-again Christian has been spiritually circumcised in his heart: that is, he has undergone the removal of the sinful nature by receiving the Holy Spirit.

Circumcision of the Flesh

Every evening and morning, the priest offered incense on the gold altar at the same time that the lamps on the gold lampstand were tended:

Aaron shall burn fragrant incense on it; he shall burn it every morning when he trims the lamps. When Aaron trims the lamps at twilight, he shall burn incense. (Ex.30:7-8 NRSV)

The fact that both the trimming of the lamps and the burning of the incense took place at the same time suggests a direct relationship between man's intellect and man's emotion/desire. Before Christ, mankind's nature was controlled by the desire to sin. From birth, we naturally did what was evil:

*Surely I was sinful at birth, **sinful from the time my mother conceived me**.*
(Ps.51:5 NIV)

A baby cannot sin at birth, but an embryo has a sinful nature at conception. As he gains the knowledge of the world, desire to do evil increases. In the beginning, God commanded Adam and Eve not to eat of the tree of the knowledge of good and evil:

*And the woman said to the serpent, "We may eat the fruit of the trees of the garden; but **of the fruit of the tree which is in the midst of the garden**, God has said, 'You shall not eat it, nor shall you touch it, lest you die.'"*
(Ge.3:2-3 NKJV)

Eve was convinced that to eat of the forbidden fruit would bring death. Still, Eve ate a poisonous fruit because her heart desired what Satan had said could be obtained by eating the fruit:

*When the woman saw that **the tree was good for food**, and that it was **a delight** to the eyes, and that the tree **was desirable** to make one wise, she took from its fruit and ate;* (Ge.3:6 NASB)

Eve's desires were stronger than what her mind knew to be true. Before Eve ate of the fruit, a spiritual change took place; she developed a sinful nature. Satan tempted Eve with the promise that she could become like God:

> **God knows** that in the day you eat from it **your eyes will be opened**, and you will **be like God, knowing good and evil**. (Ge.3:5 NASB)

When Adam and Eve ate the forbidden fruit, they gained the knowledge of evil. After eating the forbidden fruit, God said:

> Then the LORD God said, "Behold, the **man has become like one of us in knowing** good and **evil**." (Ge.3:22 ESV)

Man gained the knowledge of God, the ability to know good from evil. Prior to that point in time, man only did good, for that was all that they knew. However, with the knowledge of evil, Adam and Eve became enslaved to sinful desires for evil—a sinful nature. Six thousand years later, every person descended from Adam is still being born with the desire to do sinful things. No one is exempt; all people are born with a desire for sin:

> **All of us** used to live that way, following **the passionate desires and inclinations** of **our sinful nature**. By **our very nature** we were subject to God's anger, just like everyone else. (Eph.2:3 NLT)

Man's very nature became predisposed to sin. Some people blame Satan for their sin; however, he can only present people with a choice—temptation. When a temptation is presented, the person ultimately makes the choice to sin, and thereby, the person alone is accountable for his actions. Before a person can sin, he has to acquire a desire for sin:

> **Each one is tempted** when, by **his own evil desire**, he is **dragged away and enticed**. Then, **after desire** has conceived, it **gives birth to sin**; and sin, when it is full-grown, gives birth to death. (Ja.1:14-15 NIV)

The previous Scripture states that "his own evil desire" was to blame for his sin. Our old nature was corrupted by our own heart's sinful desires; therefore, the blame rests with us:

> Since you have heard about Jesus and have learned the truth that comes from him, **throw off your old sinful nature** and your **former way of life**, which is **corrupted by lust and deception**. (Eph.4:22 NLT)

Because natural man's heart is predisposed to sin, it deceives them, but Christ can free them from their sinful nature with its deceptive desires:

> For we ourselves **were once** foolish, disobedient, led astray, **slaves to various passions and pleasures**, passing our days in malice and envy, despicable, hating one another. (Ti.3:3 NRSV)

Many people know that their lifestyle is physically killing them; yet, they refuse to change because the sinful desires of their heart overrule what they know with their mind. This was Paul's life before the Holy Spirit lived in Him:

> *I know that <u>nothing good lives in me</u>, that is, in <u>my sinful nature</u>. I want to do what is right, **but I can't**. I want to do what is good, but **I don't**. I don't want to do what is wrong, **but I do it anyway**. But if **I do what I don't want to do**, I am not really the one doing wrong; it is sin living in me that does it.*
> (Ro.7:18-20 NLT)

The sinful nature controlled Paul and forced him to act against that which his mind had decided. Israel was no different. They constantly rebelled against God and lived according to their sinful desires:

> *Nevertheless, God was not pleased with most of them, and they were struck down in the wilderness. Now these things occurred as examples for us, **so that we might <u>not desire evil</u> as they did.*** (1Co.10:5-6 NRSV)

Just as with Israel, our soul was also enslaved by our desire to sin, which prevented us from pleasing God. Through the spiritual circumcision of our heart, we cut away our sinful nature with its desires:

> *As obedient children, do **not conform to the evil desires <u>you had</u>** when you lived in ignorance. But just as he who called you is holy, so be holy in all you do; for it is written: "Be holy, because I am holy."* (1Pe.1:14-16 NRSV)

The previous verses speak of our evil desires in the past tense, referring to our life before Christ. Through faith in Christ, Christians have dealt with the evil desires of their heart, whereby becoming a new creation:

> *In the same way, **count yourselves dead to sin** but alive to God in Christ Jesus. Therefore **do not let sin reign** in your mortal body so **that you obey its evil desires**.* (Ro.6:11-12 TNIV)

Christians are no longer controlled by sinful desires; however, they will still be tempted to fulfill the desires of their past:

> *Dear friends, I urge you, as foreigners and exiles, **to abstain from <u>sinful desires</u>**, which war against your soul.* (1Pe.2:11 TNIV)

You do not need a sinful nature to be tempted. Christ was tempted just as we are, but He did not have a sinful nature:

> *One who **has been tempted in all things as we are, <u>yet without sin</u>**.*
> (He.4:15 NASB)

Born-again Christians have circumcised their heart from the sinful nature, which will enable them to overcome sinful desires.

THE SINFUL NATURE

When Adam and Eve first sinned, the Scriptures state that they became like God, knowing both good and evil. Once they knew good from evil, the sinful nature came into being and enslaved them. We must understand what the sinful nature is in order to know how to gain victory over sinful desires.

The knowledge of evil is not the problem. Consider God. He admitted to having the knowledge of evil:

> Then the LORD God said, "Behold, the **man has become like one of us** in **knowing good and evil**. (Ge.3:22 ESV)

God knows evil. However, another characteristic of God which man did not possess at creation was a holy nature. God was, is, and always will be holy:

> The Rock! His work **is perfect**, for all His ways **are just**; a God of faithfulness and without injustice, righteous and upright is He. (De.32:4 NASB; 2Sa.22:31)

God in His omniscience knows evil; however, God does not do evil because He is holy—absolute moral perfection:

> Your eyes are too pure **to look on evil**; you **cannot tolerate wrong**. (Hab.1:13 NIV)

God cannot dwell with anything evil in His sight. Satan and his angels were banished to the earth. As well, sinners will not enter heaven:

> For You are not a God **who takes pleasure in wickedness**; **No evil dwells with You.** The boastful shall not stand before Your eyes; **You hate all who do iniquity**. (Ps.5:4-5 NASB)

The Scriptures repeatedly support the moral perfection of God:

> Therefore, hear me, you who have sense, **far be it from God that he should do wickedness**, and from **the Almighty that he should do wrong**. (Job 34:10 NRSV)

Even though God has the capacity to know evil, it is impossible for God to do evil. However, man gained the knowledge of God without the nature of God; this produced the sinful nature. The sinful nature is not a thing but the absence of a thing. Consider the example of darkness. Darkness is not a thing; it is the absence of something—the absence of light. We control darkness by controlling light. We cannot force more darkness into a room. We can only control the amount of light to make a room lighter or darker. If darkness is a thing, then we could make a room half dark and half light;

but we cannot separate light and darkness in a room because light displaces darkness. In the same way, the sinful nature is not a thing but the absence of a thing; it is the knowledge of evil with the absence of the divine nature of God. For example, Jesus was human and was tempted like us:

> Since the children have flesh and blood, **he too shared in their humanity**... For this reason **he had to be made like his brothers and sisters in every way**... Because he himself suffered when **he was tempted**, he is able to help those who are being tempted. (He.2:14, 17-18 TNIV)

Jesus was physically a man and in the world. He was tempted with choices to disobey God. However, Jesus was also in nature God:

> **Jesus: Who, being in very nature God**, did not consider **equality with God** something to be grasped, but made himself nothing, taking the very nature of a servant, **being made in human likeness**. And **being found in appearance** as a man, he humbled himself and became obedient to death—even death on a cross! (Php.2:6-8 NIV)

Jesus shared the same faculties of man and was tempted like a man, but He had the holy nature of God:

> For we do not have a high priest who is unable to sympathize with our weaknesses, but one who **in every respect has been tempted as we are**, **yet without sin**. (He.4:15 ESV)

Jesus had the knowledge of evil, but He did not sin because He had the holy nature of God. Man gained the sinful nature when they gained the knowledge of evil, but they did not have a holy nature of God. Because God is holy by nature, He does not sin even though He, in His omniscience, knows evil. Jesus did not sin even though He knew evil and experienced the temptations of a man because He had the holy nature of God. The reason why man commits sin is not because they know evil but because they do not have the holy nature of God. The knowledge of good and evil apart from the holy nature of God produced within man the sinful nature with its evil desires.

EVIL DESIRES

In the tabernacle, the gold altar of incense was dependent upon the bronze altar of sacrifice because the coals from the bronze altar were taken to the gold altar in order to produce heat for its incense. Every evening and morning, Aaron would tend the altar of incense, adding new coals and putting more incense on the altar so that the tabernacle would have a constant fragrance before God:

> **Aaron shall burn fragrant incense** on it; he shall burn it every morning when he trims the lamps. And when Aaron trims the lamps at twilight, he shall burn incense. There **shall be perpetual incense before the LORD** throughout your generations. (Ex.30:7-8 NASB)

The fire on the bronze altar of sacrifice had to constantly burn to produce the coals that continually released the fragrance on the gold altar of incense:

> **The fire on the altar shall be kept burning; it shall not go out.** Every morning the priest shall add wood to it, lay out the burnt offering on it, and turn into smoke the fat pieces of the offerings of well-being. **A perpetual fire shall be kept burning on the altar; it shall not go out.** (Le.6:12-13 NRSV)

Both altars were to burn continually, for the one fueled the other. Only when we are living sacrifices on the bronze altar are our emotions and desires a pleasant fragrance to God. Only when Christ controls our lives will our sinful nature with its desires pass away:

> Those **who belong to Christ** Jesus have **crucified the sinful nature** with its **passions and desires**. Since we live by the Spirit, let us keep in step with the Spirit. (Ga.5:24 NIV)

The Scriptures teach Christians that their sinful nature was crucified once and for all:

> Christ performed a spiritual circumcision—**the cutting away of your sinful nature**. (Co.2:11 NLT)

Christians have had a spiritual circumcision, the cutting away of the sinful nature. The Scriptures speak of the sinful nature in a Christian's life with the past tense:

> For **when** we **were controlled** by our sinful nature the **sinful passions** aroused by the law were at work in us, so that we bore fruit for death. (Ro.7:5 TNIV)

Christians are no longer controlled by the sinful nature:

> But **you are not controlled** by your sinful nature. You are controlled by the Spirit if you have the Spirit of God living in you. (Ro.8:9 NLT)

Obviously the sinful nature (the Greek *sarx*) is no longer alive in Christians. Consequently, we are commanded:

> But put on the Lord Jesus Christ, and **make no provision for the flesh**, to gratify its desires. (Ro.13:14 ESV)

The Scriptures command us not to make provision for the flesh in our theology, our thinking, and, especially, our actions. Christ is the solution to the sinful nature because, by dying on the cross, He paid the penalty for our sin. Then, by rising from the grave, He lives in us, transforming our life:

> When you **were dead** in your sins and in the uncircumcision **of your sinful nature**, God **made you alive** with Christ. He forgave us all our sins, (Co.2:13 NIV)

God did not simply make us alive; He made us alive with Christ. Our hope of overcoming the sinful nature is found with Christ living in us:

> I have been crucified with Christ; **it is no longer I who live**, but **Christ lives in me**. (Ga.2:20 NKJV)

If we have laid our lives on the altar and have died in our baptism, then Christ actually does live in us and imparts His nature in us:

> For **you have died**, and your life is hidden with Christ in God. When **Christ who is your life** appears, then you also will appear with him in glory. (Co.3:3-4 ESV)

Christ is God. Consequently, when Christ lives in us, we receive God's fullness:

> For in him **the whole fullness of deity** dwells bodily, and **you have come to fullness in him**. (Co.2:9-10 NRSV)

Since the sinful nature and Christ cannot abide in the same heart, when the Presence of His Spirit indwells us, the sinful nature must be displaced:

> I pray that out of his glorious riches **he may strengthen you with power through his Spirit** in your inner being, so **that Christ may dwell in your hearts** through faith. (Eph.3:16-17 TNIV)

When Christ lives in a Christian's heart, he receives the divine nature which displaces the sinful nature:

> Thus he has given us, through these things, his precious and very great promises, so that through them you may **escape** from the corruption that is in the world because of lust, and may become participants of **the divine nature**. (2Pe.1: 4 NRSV)

The sinful nature is the knowledge of evil apart from the divine nature. When Christ imparts the holy nature of God through His Spirit in man, the sinful nature is displaced so that we can be tempted and not sin:

> Since you have heard about Jesus and have learned the truth that comes from him, **throw off your old sinful nature** and your **former way of life**, which is **corrupted by lust and deception**. Instead, **let the Spirit renew** your thoughts and **attitudes**. Put on **your new nature**, created to be **like God**—**truly righteous and holy**. (Eph.4:21-24 NLT)

Once we are in Christ, we have His nature, and we will begin to live like Christ because of our new desires:

> No one born of God **makes a practice of sinning**, for **God's seed abides in him**, and he **cannot keep on sinning** because he has been born of God.
> (1Jn.3:9 ESV)

The sinful nature cannot be restrained by man's efforts through the keeping some form of law. But, the sinful nature is eradicated by Christ's Spirit living in us, imparting what was absent in our life—the very nature of God:

> You **who want to be justified** by the law have cut yourselves off from Christ; you have fallen away from grace. For **through the Spirit, by faith, we eagerly wait for the hope of righteousness**. (Ga.5:4-5 NRSV)

Consequently, since Christ lives in us by His Spirit and His Spirit has the nature of God, the Holy Spirit will transform our life:

> Now may the God of peace... equip you with everything good for doing his will, and **may he work in us what is pleasing to him, through Jesus Christ**, to whom be glory for ever and ever. (He.13:20-21 NIV)

Therefore, God's solution to man's sinful nature is to impart the divine nature through the indwelling of His Spirit. Once Christ lives in us, His divine nature displaces the sinful nature of man, which aligns our desires with His. The solution to sin is as simple as light:

> **God is Light**, and in Him there is no darkness at all. If we say that we have fellowship with Him and **yet walk in the darkness, we lie** and do not practice the truth; but **if we walk in the Light as He Himself is in the Light**, we have fellowship with one another, and the blood of **Jesus His Son cleanses us from all sin**. (1Jn.1:5-7 NASB)

A Human Dichotomy

The sinful nature came into existence by man gaining the knowledge of evil without possessing the divine nature. For this reason, the keeping of the law could not enable Israel to overcome the sinful nature because it could not produce that which was missing, the divine nature:

> The law of Moses was unable to save us **because of the weakness of our sinful nature**. So God did what the law could not do. He sent his own Son in a body like the bodies we sinners have. And **in that body God declared an end to sin's control over us** by giving his Son as a sacrifice for our sins. He did this so that the just requirement of the law would be fully satisfied for us, **who no longer follow our sinful nature but instead follow the Spirit**.
> (Ro.8:3-4 NLT)

The previous Scripture makes it obvious that Christians no longer live under the sinful nature but, rather, live by the Spirit. Once the Spirit imparts within man the nature of God, the sinful nature is displaced, and their actions begin to change. Consequently, if the Holy Spirit lives in us, we will not continue to live like we used to by gratifying our old nature:

> I say, **live by the Spirit**, and you **will not** gratify the desires of the sinful **nature**. (Ga.5:16 NIV)

Christians overcome the sinful nature by having the Holy Spirit take control of their life. When Paul found a man living with his stepmother in an immoral relationship, he commanded the Christians to put him out of the church:

> Then you must throw this man out and hand him over to Satan **so that his sinful nature will be destroyed** and **he himself will be saved** on the day the Lord returns. (1Co.5:5 NLT)

If the man's sinful nature remained alive, his spirit would be lost for eternity. But, if his sinful nature was destroyed, he would be saved. Obviously, a Christian is no longer controlled by the sinful nature/flesh with its desires. Even though many Christians deny the concept that their lives are controlled by something or someone, this belief does not alter the Scripture's teaching:

> Those who **are still under** the control of their sinful nature can never please God. But **you are not controlled** by your sinful nature. You **are controlled by the Spirit** if you have **the Spirit of God living in you**. (And remember that those who do not have the Spirit of Christ living in them do not belong to him at all.) (Ro.8:8-9 NLT)

You are either controlled by the sinful nature, or you are controlled by the Spirit. However, **you** are definitely not the one in control:

> For **the sinful nature** [sarx] **desires** what is contrary to the Spirit, and **the Spirit** what is contrary to the sinful nature. They are in conflict with each other, so that **you do not do what you want**. (Ga.5:17 NIV)

A common opinion is that a Christian oscillates between the sinful nature and the Spirit. The Bible does **not** say: "When you are controlled by the sinful nature and when you are controlled by the Spirit"—one person oscillating between two positions. The Scriptures divide mankind into two groups—"**those**" and "**those**":

> *Those who live according to the sinful nature have their minds set on what that nature desires;* **but** *those who live in accordance with the Spirit have their minds set on what the Spirit desires. The mind* **controlled by** *the sinful nature is death, but the mind* **controlled by** *the Spirit is life and peace.* (Ro.8:5-6 TNIV)

There are "those" who remain controlled by their sinful nature, and then there are "those" who are now controlled by the Spirit. The Spirit displaces the sinful nature with His divine nature. Consequently, a person is either of the Spirit or of the sinful nature/flesh. The nature within man determines a person's attitude, behavior, and character:

> **The acts of the sinful nature** *[sarx] are obvious: sexual immorality, impurity and debauchery; idolatry and witchcraft; hatred, discord, jealousy, fits of rage, selfish ambition, dissensions, factions and envy; drunkenness, orgies, and the like.* **I warn you,** *as I did before, that* **those who live like this will not inherit the kingdom of God**. (Ga.5:19-21 NIV)

A person who lives in his sinful nature/flesh will not inherit the Kingdom of God. However, if the Spirit of Christ lives in you, then your nature will reflect His holy Presence, and you will be changed:

> *But* **the Holy Spirit produces** *this kind of fruit in our lives: love, joy, peace, patience, kindness, goodness, faithfulness, gentleness, and self-control. There is no law against these things!* (Ga.5:22-23 NLT)

Church-goers who live in the sinful nature, thinking they are saved, will be shockingly surprised in the next life when they are sent to hell:

> *Therefore, brothers and sisters, we have an obligation—but* **it is not to the sinful nature***, to live according to it. For* **if** *you live according to the sinful nature,* **you will die***; but* **if** *by the Spirit you put to death the misdeeds of the body,* **you will live**. (Ro.8:13-14 TNIV)

The only true sign of a Christian is the evidence of the transforming power of Christ in his life:

> *Do not be deceived: God cannot be mocked. A man reaps what he sows.* **The one who sows to please his sinful nature***, from that nature* **will reap**

destruction; the **one who sows to please the Spirit**, from the Spirit will **reap eternal life**. (Ga.6:7-8 NIV)

Jesus clearly taught the principle that a person's actions are a reflection of a person's spiritual perspective:

Either make the tree good and its fruit good, or make the tree bad and its fruit bad; for **the tree is known by its fruit.** (Mt.12:33 NASB)

Christians live by the Presence of the Holy Spirit, Who imparts the divine nature. This new nature changes our desires and affects our actions:

As obedient children, **do not conform to the evil desires you had when you lived in ignorance**. But just as he who called you is holy, **so be holy in all you do**; for it is written: "Be holy, because I am holy." (1Pe.1:14-16 NIV)

A change of mind will be fruitless without a change of heart, for the heart determines the desires, and the desires ultimately control man's actions. If we have a new heart, we will no longer live for the evil desires of our past:

As a result, they **do not** live **the rest** of their earthly lives **for evil human desires**, but rather **for the will of God**. For you have spent enough time **in the past** doing what pagans choose to do--living in debauchery, lust, drunkenness, orgies, carousing and detestable idolatry. (1Pe.4:2-3 TNIV)

As Christians, we have pure hearts that generate new desires: a genuine love for our fellow man. Agape love is the selfless love of God:

But the goal of our instruction **is love** from **a pure heart** and a good conscience and a sincere faith. (1Ti.1:5 NASB)

Selfless love is not self-generated but comes through the purifying of our heart by the Presence of His Spirit:

And hope does not disappoint us, because **God has poured out his love into our hearts by the Holy Spirit**, whom he has given us. (Ro.5:5 NIV)

The Holy Spirit's Presence changes the heart's focus. Self-gratification and the pleasing of the senses with wickedness are replaced with consideration for others and with pleasing God in holiness:

And **may the Lord make you** increase and **abound in love** for one another and for all, just as we abound in love for you. And may he so **strengthen your hearts in holiness** that you may be blameless before our God and Father at the coming of our Lord Jesus with all his saints. (1Th.3:12-13 NRSV)

Therefore, our new heart has a new nature with new desires which are reflected in our new attitudes, behavior, and character.

Continual Incense

The gold altar of incense symbolized the new heart which we receive through the indwelling of the Holy Spirit. This new heart causes us to desire to please God with the whole of our being—a pleasing fragrance. The golden altar, which was before the Lord, burned only incense that was made of four equal parts:

*Then the LORD said to Moses, "Take for yourself spices, **stacte** and **onycha** and **galbanum**, spices with **pure frankincense**; there shall be an equal part of each. With it you shall make incense, a perfume, the work of a perfumer, salted, pure, and holy. You shall beat some of it very fine, and put part of it before the testimony in the tent of meeting where I will meet with you; it shall be most holy to you."* (Ex.30:34-36 NASB)

The symbolic importance of the fragrance is not its composition (many scholars are unsure of specific ingredients) but, rather, that there were four equal parts to its composition. Again, four symbolizes the four Gospels. The four Gospels use the term "Savior" only three times but the word "Lord" 175 times. Christ cannot be our Savior without being our Lord, for to offer our life/soul on the bronze altar requires that Christ be raised in us through baptism. If we have not died to our soul on the bronze altar, we will not experience the Holy Spirit living in us and changing our desires.

The connection between the two altars is understood because the priest took coals from the bronze altar of sacrifice and placed them on the gold altar of incense to create the heat necessary to offer incense to God. The death of our soul/self on the bronze altar is necessary for us to receive the new heart with a holy nature, symbolized by the gold altar. Our new heart with its new desires enables us to live lives that are pleasing to God:

*Therefore, I urge you, brothers and sisters, in view of God's mercy, to offer your bodies as a **living sacrifice, holy and pleasing to God**--this is true worship.* (Ro.12:1 TNIV)

If we have not died to self and the pleasing of our soulish pleasures, then the altar of incense will be cold and unable to release its fragrance. The Scriptures teach that the true incense that God seeks is the prayers of the saints offered on the gold altar of incense in heaven:

*When He had taken the book, the four living creatures and the twenty-four elders fell down before the Lamb, each one holding a harp and **golden bowls full of incense, which are the prayers of the saints**.* (Re.5:8 NASB)

A Christian's prayers are a sweet smelling fragrance to God and are proof of a surrendered life:

> Another angel with a golden censer came and stood at the altar; he was given a great quantity of incense to offer **with the prayers of all the saints** on **the golden altar** that is before the throne. And **the smoke of the incense, with the prayers of the saints,** rose before God from the hand of the angel. (Re.8:3-4 NRSV)

If we offer prayers without becoming a living sacrifice, our prayers will be nothing but meaningless ritual which go no further than our voices. If we have become living sacrifices but do not pray continually, then we need to consider whether we have received a new heart which is under the control of the Holy Spirit. Just as the incense was to be released continually, God commands that we be devoted to prayer:

> **Devote yourselves to prayer,** being watchful and thankful. (Co.4:2 NIV)

In fact, we are commanded to pray without ceasing:

> **Pray without ceasing.** (1Th.5:17 KJV)

We need to continually pray that our lives will be pleasing to Him. Our prayers are the sweetness of the fragrance:

> And **we pray** this in order that you may live a life worthy of the Lord and **may please him in every way:** bearing fruit **in every** good work, **growing** in the knowledge of God, being **strengthened** with all power according to his glorious might so that you may have **great endurance and patience...**
> (Co.1:10-11 NIV)

Once we are born again, our lives dramatically change; we now seek to please God in every way. Before being born again, we indulged in every impurity with a continual desire for more:

> They are darkened in their understanding and separated from the life of God because of the ignorance that is in them due to the hardening of their hearts. Having lost all sensitivity, **they have given themselves over to sensuality** so as to indulge in **every kind** of impurity, with a **continual lust for more**. (Eph.4:18-19 NIV)

We were predisposed to evil and self-absorbed; now we are God-centered. After going to the altar of sacrifice and dying to self, we can come to the altar of incense to offer a continual sacrifice of praise:

> Through Jesus, therefore, let us **continually offer to God a sacrifice of praise**--the fruit of lips that openly profess his name. (He.13:15 TNIV)

Once our heart is changed, our praise to God is no longer based upon our circumstances. When Paul and Silas were severely beaten and chained in a dungeon, they lifted up songs of praise (Ac.16:25). We must praise God no matter our circumstances. This makes our praises a sacrifice that is pleasing to God. Our praise is based upon who God is and what He has done for us through Christ. Our heart used to be consumed by a sinful nature that was given to wickedness. Now we sing praises to God for all that He is and has done in our lives:

> *Speak to one another with psalms, hymns and spiritual songs. Sing and make music **in your heart** to the Lord, **always** giving thanks to God the Father **for everything**, in the name of our Lord Jesus Christ.* (Eph.5:19-20 NIV)

With the songs of our lips, praise rises up from the goodness in our hearts:

> ***Let the word of Christ richly dwell within you**, with all wisdom teaching and admonishing one another with psalms and hymns and spiritual songs, singing **with thankfulness in your hearts** to God.* (Co.3:16 NASB)

The altar of incense is about a change of heart in its nature and desires. The heart is filled with thanksgiving because of what God has accomplished through the Holy Spirit:

> *Do not worry about **anything**, but in **everything** by prayer and supplication with thanksgiving let your requests be made known to God. And the peace of God, which **surpasses all understanding**, **will guard your hearts** and your minds in Christ Jesus.* (Php.4:6-7 NRSV)

Therefore, just as the fire on the altar of sacrifice and the embers on the altar of incense were never to be extinguished, we too must be living sacrifices whose prayers, a sweet smelling fragrance to God, are never to cease.

Thinking It Through:

1. Why don't people always do what they know is best?

2. What is spiritual circumcision?

3. Which came first: the sinful nature or eating the forbidden fruit?

4. What is the sinful nature?

5. How could Jesus be tempted if He did not have the sinful nature?

6. How does receiving the divine nature release us from our sinful nature?

7. How has humanity become a spiritual dichotomy?

8. What relationship is there between the incense offered on the gold altar of incense and our prayers?

The Gold Table of Showbread

Make a table out of acacia wood. Make it three feet long, one foot six inches wide and two feet three inches high. Cover it with pure gold. Put a strip of gold around it. Also make a rim around it that is three inches wide. Put a strip of gold around the rim. Make four gold rings for the table. Join them to the four corners, where the four legs are. The rings must be close to the rim. They must hold the poles that will be used to carry the table. "Make the poles out of acacia wood. Cover them with gold. Use them to carry the table. "Make its plates and dishes out of pure gold. Also make its pitchers and bowls out of pure gold. Use the pitchers and bowls to pour out drink offerings. "Put the holy bread on the table. It must be near my holy throne on the ark of the covenant at all times.   Exodus 25:23-30 NIrV

Lesson 9

The Gold Table of Showbread

Bread

We have considered the intellect and emotion of the soul with regard to the work that Christ initiates when the Holy Spirit enters a person's life. The gold table of showbread represented the third faculty of a man's soul—the will. The table was made of acacia wood, representing man. It was covered with gold which symbolized a work that God does in transforming man. Every Sabbath, the priests would replace the twelve cakes of bread on the table:

> You must bake twelve loaves of bread from choice flour, <u>using four quarts of flour for each loaf.</u> Place the bread before the LORD on the pure gold table, and arrange the loaves in two rows, with six loaves in each row. Put some pure frankincense near each row to serve as a representative offering, a special gift presented to the LORD. **Every Sabbath day this bread must be laid out before the LORD.** The bread is to be received from the people of Israel as **a requirement of the eternal covenant.** (Le.24:5-8 NLT)

In the previous verse *lechem* means "food," but it is translated "bread" because of the ingredients mentioned. The book of 2 Samuel clearly depicts the dual meaning:

> You therefore, and your sons and your servants, shall work the land for him, and you shall bring in the harvest, that your master's son may have **food** to eat. But Mephibosheth your master's son shall **eat bread** at my table always. (2Sa.9:10 NKJV)

The Hebrew word that is translated "food" and "bread" in the previous verse is the same Hebrew word that is used for the "showbread":

> You shall set the **bread** of the Presence **on the table before Me at all times.** (Ex.25:30 NASB)

Malachi refers to the table as the Lord's table, but he uses the term "food" and not specifically "bread":

> But you profane it when you say that **the Lord's table** is polluted, and **the food** for it may be despised. (Mal.1:12 NRSV)

The reason for the importance of understanding the usage of the Hebrew word *lechem* is because Jesus connected the concept of food with doing the will of God:

> Jesus said to them, "**My food is to do the will of him who sent me** and to complete his work." (Jn.4:34 NRSV)

Christ's food was to do the will of God. Similarly, the food on the gold table of showbread represented man's will being placed on the table, symbolizing our yielding to God in an act of submission.

Unleavened Loaves

God commanded that they use the flour that they had brought from Egypt, something that belonged to them. They physically made the bread according to His command and placed it on the table. God could have commanded that they use the manna He had provided, asking them to collect it and make it into loaves, but He did not. Using their own flour was a cost. The Israelites had to give up the flour that they had saved and give it to God; otherwise, they could not make the bread. Many people are presented with the Gospel message and asked if they would like to receive Jesus as their Savior. However, in the Scriptures, the word "Savior" is seldom used. If we consider the New Testament writings, which discuss Christ after His resurrection (Acts through Revelation), the word "Savior" is used 21 times, while the word "Lord" is used 425 times. The bread that was placed every week on the table of showbread is symbolic of submission to the Lordship of Christ—laying our will before the Lord. For 40 years, Israel lived in the desert eating manna which was miraculously provided by God, and yet, the loaves that were placed before God on the table had to be of flour made by human hands:

> You shall take **fine flour** and bake twelve loaves from it; **two tenths of an ephah shall be in each loaf**. And you shall set them in two piles, six in a pile, on the table of pure gold before the LORD. (Le.24:5-6 ESV)

Imagine the size of the loaf. Even though the loaves were unleavened, they were huge—each was made of sixteen cups of flour. The Scriptures refer to the food on the gold table of showbread as the "bread of the Presence":

> And you shall set **the bread of the Presence on the table before me always**. (Ex.25:30 NRSV; Ex.35:13; Ex.39:36, 1Ki.7:48; 2Ch.4:19)

Since the bread was before God's Presence, it was considered holy; hence Aaron and his sons had to eat the bread that was replaced in the Holy Place:

> Every sabbath day he shall set it in order before the LORD continually; it is an everlasting covenant for the sons of Israel. It shall be for Aaron and his sons, and **they shall eat it in a holy place**; for it is **most holy to him** from the LORD'S **offerings by fire**, his portion forever. (Le.2:8-9 NASB)

The bread on the table was also considered a grain offering made by fire; hence, it could not contain yeast:

> **No grain offering** which you bring to the LORD **shall be made with leaven**, for you shall burn no leaven nor any honey in any offering to the LORD **made by fire**. (Le 2:11 NKJV)

The absence of yeast in the bread symbolized that our will cannot continue to seek after wickedness if we come to God. All of humanity was controlled by sin which was represented by the yeast found in common bread:

> Your boasting is not good. Don't you know that **a little yeast works through the whole batch of dough**? Get rid of the old yeast **that you may be a new batch without yeast**—as you really are. For Christ, our Passover lamb, has been sacrificed. Therefore let us keep the Festival, **not with the old yeast, the yeast of malice and wickedness**, but **with bread without yeast, the bread of sincerity and truth**. (1Co.5:6-8 NIV)

Through Christ, we have become like the showbread, bread without the yeast of malice and wickedness. We are a new loaf, bread without yeast, with sincerity and truth, doing God's will from pure hearts.

THE POWER OF SIN: CHOICE

By creating the tree of the knowledge of good and evil, God gave man the choice to either live for Him or rebel against Him. However, man did not even perceive that they had a choice until Satan taught Eve the concept of evil. Even though Eve was convinced that the forbidden fruit was lethal, she still ate from it. She chose to believe Satan:

> For God knows that when you eat of it your eyes will be opened, and **you will be like God**, knowing good and evil. (Ge.3:5 ESV)

Eve desired to become like God. She did not want to serve God but sought to become His equal. She rejected God as her master and wanted to be the master of her own destiny. The first sin committed by Adam and Eve was an act of rebellion against God. This rebellion was clearly seen again in Israel, as recorded in the Old Testament. While God was performing miracles before Pharaoh, Israel was rebelling against God:

> You **have been rebellious** against the LORD **from the day I knew you.**
> (De.9:24 NASB)

Joshua grew up in Egypt, spent 40 years in the desert, and then conquered the land of Canaan. Before he died, he became critical of Israel:

> Then Joshua warned the people, "**You are not able to serve the LORD**, for he is a holy and jealous God. **He will not forgive your rebellion** and your sins. (Jos.24:19 NLT)

Israel's ultimate rebellion against God was committed when they asked for a king:

> And the LORD said to Samuel, "Obey the voice of the people in all that they say to you, for they **have not rejected you, but they have rejected me from being king over them**". (1Sa.8:7 ESV)

Just like Eve rejected God because she thought that she was wiser than God, Israel also rejected God because they thought that they knew better than He:

> I spread out my hands all the day **to a rebellious people**, who walk in a way that is not good, **following their own devices**; (Isa.65:2 ESV)

All mankind constantly rebels against God. When God told Israel what to do, they refused to listen, for they had their own ideas:

> Oh, **rebellious children**, says the LORD, who carry out a plan, **but not mine**; who make an alliance, **but against my will**, adding sin to sin;
> (Isa.30:1 NRSV)

God considers rebellion against His authority a serious issue. He equates rebellion with the sins of divination and idolatry:

> For **rebellion is as the sin of divination**, and **insubordination** is as iniquity and idolatry. (1Sa.15:23 NASB)

Israel's rebellion is symbolized by the bronze used in the courtyard:

> They are all **stubbornly rebellious**, going about with slanders; **they are bronze** and iron, **all of them act corruptly**. (Jer.6:28 NRSV)

Eve's desire for self-rule has been passed on to her descendants. By nature, mankind seeks to be independent. This results in rebellion against God:

> Even **from birth** the wicked go astray; **from the womb** they are wayward, spreading lies. (Ps.58:3 TNIV)

From birth, mankind seeks to be the masters of their own destiny—to be in control. The Old Testament prophets spoke against Israel's rebellion:

> **All we like sheep have gone astray**; we have **turned every one to his own way;** (Isa.53:6 ESV)

All of mankind refused to submit to God's authority. Eve did not know that her disobedience to God would result in the slavery of all of her descendants to the power of sin and rebellion:

> Jesus replied, "Very truly I tell you, **everyone who sins is a slave to sin.**" (Jn.8:34 TNIV)

The ability to choose enslaved man. Sin is not just an act committed by man; it is a power that is released by the ability to choose. Adam did not just commit a sin, but he also brought the power of sin into the world:

> Just as through **one man sin entered the world**, and death through sin, and thus death spread **to all men, because all sinned.** (Ro.5:12 NKJV)

Christians have attempted to overcome their sins but have failed because they perceive sin as an action and not a power. Many Christians blame their physical body/flesh for their sins because their body actually commits the sin. However, the body is not the cause of sin, but the body's sinful actions are the result of the power of sin:

> Do not **let sin control the way you live**; do not give in to sinful desires. Do not let any part of your body become an instrument of evil to serve sin. Instead, **give yourselves completely to God,** for you were dead, but **now you have new life.** So use your whole body as an instrument **to do what is right for the glory of God.** (Ro.6:12-13 NLT)

The power of sin coupled with man's sinful nature enabled the soul's desire for sensuality to reach an ungodly extreme. Before we were Christians, we always considered temptation as choice—to sin or not to sin. The realization of a choice gives sin the power to seize us, deceive us, and ultimately kill us:

> Once I was alive apart from law; but when the commandment came, **sin sprang to life and I died.** I found that the very commandment that was intended to bring life actually brought death. For sin, **seizing** the opportunity afforded by the commandment, **deceived me,** and through the commandment **put me to death.** (Ro.7:9-10 NIV)

Because Adam and Eve fell, sin was able to take control of our life because we continued to make our own choices. Everyone is born a slave of sin:

> When **you were slaves to sin**, you were **free from the control of righteousness**. (Ro.6:20 TNIV)

The power of sin manipulated our soul, forcing our body to consistently commit sinful actions:

> So **I am not the one doing** wrong; it is <u>sin living in me that does it</u>. (Ro.7:17 NLT; 7:20)

Every time a person is given the choice to either sin or obey God, the power of sin's allurement causes man to rebel against Him.

THE ILLUSION OF SIN

The bread on the table of showbread was twelve large unleavened loaves:

> You shall take fine flour and bake twelve loaves from it; two tenths of an ephah shall be in each loaf. And you **shall set them in two piles, six in a pile, on the table of pure gold** before the LORD. (Le.24:5-6 ESV)

The loaves contained about five pounds of flour, and, according to Josephus, a Jewish historian of Jesus' day, the loaves were unleavened. To use that much flour with leaven would make twelve loaves impossibly huge for the size of the table. Leaven is the active ingredient that makes bread rise. The flour does not rise without living yeast. In the same way, mankind does not commit sin on their own; rather, the power of sin **lives** in them. Many people will argue that they cognitively choose when and how they act. They are unaware of sin's control over their life:

> For sin, **seizing** an opportunity in the commandment, **deceived me** and through it **killed me**. (Ro.7:11 NRSV)

Man is naturally seized and deceived by sin. Those who do not recognize sin's power of allurement over their life are deceived because they think that they make the choice to sin. Sin was the power that mastered Cain through jealousy when he killed his own brother. God warned Cain:

> Then the LORD said to Cain, "Why are you angry? Why is your face downcast? If you do what is right, will you not be accepted? But if you do not do what is right, <u>sin is crouching</u> at your door; <u>it desires</u> to have you, but **you must master it**." (Ge.4:6-7 NIV)

Sin desired to have Cain and was waiting to trap him, but even though God had warned him, Cain could not overcome sin and killed his brother. All of humanity is born captivated by the ability to choose sin:

> The Scriptures declare that **we are all prisoners of sin** (Ga.3:22 NLT)

Sin holds man captive from birth. Its power of allurement forces them to commit acts of sin. A man considers himself good when he compares himself to people who seem less perfect than he. However, when a man continues to commit sin, he proves that the power of sin is his master:

> They promise freedom, but **they themselves are slaves of sin** and corruption. For **you are a slave to whatever controls you.** (2Pe.2:19 NLT)

When Adam sinned, he acquired a spiritual birth defect, the power of sin. This defect has been passed on to the whole of humanity. Everyone born of Adam is under the power of sin—**no exceptions**:

> What then? Are we better than they? Not at all; for we have already charged that **both Jews and Greeks are all under sin**; as it is written, "there is **none** righteous, **not even one**; there is **none** who understands, there is **none** who seeks for God; **all** have turned aside, **together** they have become useless; there is **none** who does good, there is **not even one**." (Ro.3:9-12 NASB)

"All," "none," and "not even one" support the fact that the power of sin took captive of the whole of mankind. Sin existed since the fall of Adam and Eve, but the majority of mankind remains unaware of the power of sin because man is ignorant of His law. The knowledge of sin comes through God's law:

> Before the law was given, sin was in the world. But **sin is not taken into account when there is no law.** (Ro.5:13 NIV)

Until God defined sin through the law, man was unaware that the power of sin existed. Once the law identified actions as sin and man could not stop their sinning, they realized "something" controlled them. Before the law was given, they thought their actions were a product of their own poor choices. However, once the law was given, the power of sin began to thrive. Rather than decreasing disobedience, the law actually increased disobedience. When the law upheld God's standard that was contrary to man's pursuit of sensuality, man was forced to make a choice to obey God or follow their own desires. Because mankind naturally desired self-gratification, they experienced the power of sin's allurement and consistently chose disobedience, for the soul had a fixation with sensuality. Hence, the law did not decrease the possibility for man to sin, but rather, it increased the possibility to sin:

> The law was added so **that the trespass might <u>increase</u>**. (Ro.5:20 NIV)

When Israel's sins increased through the law, they became aware of the power of sin's presence and cried out to God for a solution. The failure of the law due to the power of sin was compounded by God's command for Israel to daily remember the law:

> **You must commit yourselves** wholeheartedly to these commands that I am giving you today. **Repeat them again and again** to your children. Talk about them when you are **at home** and when you are **on the road**, when you are **going to bed** and when you are **getting up**. Tie them to your hands and wear them on your forehead as reminders. Write them **on the doorposts** of your house and **on your gates**. (Du.6:6-9 NLT)

Every time Israel remembered the law, they experienced the power of choice. Consider an analogy of smoking cigarettes. Sam came to realize that cigarettes were harmful to his health and decided to quit. While Sam struggled with his addiction, his coworkers sought to encourage him by asking about his progress. Every time he was encouraged, he was reminded of his desire to smoke and was tempted to have a cigarette. It would have been better if the coworkers had not reminded him through their encouragement. In the same way, the very law that defined God's standard of holiness empowered sin, for it constantly reminded them of what they should not do. This forced man to constantly make the choice to obey or not to obey:

> The sting of death is sin, and **the power of sin is the law**. (1Co.15:56 NRSV)

The power of sin is the law because the law forces man to choose to sin or not to sin. The choice subjects them to sin's power of allurement. For, without the law, man is not forced to make a choice; thus, without the law, the power of sin is rendered dead:

> But sin, **seizing an opportunity** <u>through the commandment</u>, **produced in me all kinds of covetousness**. Apart from the law, **sin lies dead**. I was once alive apart from the law, but when the commandment came, **sin came alive and I died**. (Ro.7:8-9 ESV)

Every time that a new law is made, sin as a power comes to life because man has to choose whether they will obey the law. To illustrate this, imagine a scenario in which a family moved to a house by a creek. In the first summer, their son would play in the slow-moving water. Spring came with the melting of snow and torrential rain. The creek swelled with a raging current. The mother told her young son, "I want you to stay by the house this week and not go near the creek. With the constant rain and melting of snow, the creek has become very deep and dangerous, and I don't want you to fall in and drown." Would the son have been drawn to the creek if he did not know about the flooding? The mother's command gave the son knowledge of the danger which forced the son to choose to obey or disobey, but, at the same time, the command created a sense of curiosity and awakened sin's power of allurement. Through knowledge, the allurement of the creek was increased—the power of sin gained strength. When Paul lived under the law, he could not do the good that he knew but consistently did the evil that he was forbidden to do:

> We know that **the law** is spiritual; but I am unspiritual, **sold as a slave to sin**. I do not understand what I do. For **what I want to do, I do not do**, but **what I hate, I do**. And if I do what I do not want to do, I agree that the law is good. As it is, it is no longer I myself who do it, but <u>it is sin living in me</u>.
> (Ro.7:14-17 NIV)

In essence, the pleasure that sin brought to Paul's body was secondary. He committed sin because sin's power of allurement lived in him and manipulated his life. Paul was a slave of sin, just as Cain had been mastered by sin. Many people deny that sin has power over their lives and believe that they make the choice to sin. However, when they try to stop their sin, their consistent choice to sin proves that they are a slave of sin:

> Don't you know that **when you offer yourselves to someone as obedient slaves**, <u>you are slaves of the one you obey</u>—whether **you are slaves to sin**, which leads to death, **or to obedience**, which leads to righteousness?
> (Ro.6:16 TNIV)

Mankind's denial of the power of sin will not free them any more than a denial of the force of gravity will enable a person to float. The Pharisees, in their legalistic righteousness, denied that they were slaves of sin:

> They answered Him, "We are Abraham's descendants, and **have never been in bondage to anyone**. How can you say, 'You will be made free'?" Jesus answered them, "Most assuredly, I say to you, **whoever commits sin is a slave of sin**." (Jn.8:33-34 NKJV)

Do you consistently commit the same sins? If your answer is "Yes," then you are a slave of sin. A slave is owned and controlled by his master. A slave is different than a hired man. A hired man can choose his employer, but a slave is owned by his master:

> They promise them freedom, but they themselves **are slaves** of corruption; **for people are slaves to whatever masters them**. (2Pe.2:19 NRSV)

When you cannot stop committing a sin, you prove that sin is your master. All of Adam's descendants are conceived in sin and, therefore, are born slaves of sin:

> For **we also once were** foolish ourselves, disobedient, deceived, **enslaved to various lusts and pleasures**, spending our life in malice and envy, hateful, hating one another. (Ti.3:3 NASB)

A person is not enslaved to **all** lusts and pleasures but to **various** lusts and pleasures, for each person is a unique individual, susceptible to different sinful pleasures. Even though natural man can have small victories, permanent victory over the sins in their life eludes them. When a person gains victory over one sin (for example, smoking cigarettes), the power of sin causes him to choose another form of sensual gratification to replace that sin (for example, overeating). This person merely exchanged one sin for another because the power of sin retained its control over him. When we **were** slaves of sin, we were not controlled by righteousness:

> When **you were slaves to sin**, you were **free from the control of righteousness**. What benefit did you reap at that time from the things you are now ashamed of? **Those things result in death**! (Ro.6:20-21 NIV)

The power of sin deceives natural man as long as he yields to its allurement. He is under the illusion that he is in control and that he makes the cognitive decision to indulge in sin. Consider this personal example. I once worked with my friend's brother, Joe. After working with Joe for a week, I realized that he was addicted to alcohol. When I expressed concern about Joe's drinking to my friend, he responded, "My brother is not an alcoholic; he just likes beer." Joe was the one who asked for a beer, but it was the power of sin that influenced his decision. Joe did not control his drinking, but his drinking controlled him. The decision to indulge does not originate from man but from the power of sin to which man has learned to respond.

If decisions were strictly made by the mind, then life would be simple. If man was in control, then he would do only the things that he desired and would stop his sins when they became unpleasant or inconvenient. People confuse their personal choices with sin's deception and manipulation. However, since the power of sin controls man, discontinuing their sins is more complex because the illusion of choice must be broken before natural man will seek freedom from sin's power. The purpose of the law was to break the illusion of choice. A person realizes that an act is not a personal preference but the manipulation of the power of sin, when he attempts to discontinue the act. When a person cannot discontinue a sinful action, he realizes that the power of sin controls him:

> Therefore no-one will be declared righteous in his sight by observing the law; rather, **through the law** we become **conscious** of **sin**. (Ro.3:20 NIV)

THE POWER OF CHRIST

Satan deceived Eve with the possibility of rebelling against God, for she hoped to become like God. She wanted to be the master of her own destiny. The power of sin deceives man into thinking that they are in control, free to choose as they like. I have heard many teach that Christ came to give us a free choice (the freedom to obey or disobey Him) without any effect upon their salvation. These teachers are tempting people with the same temptation as Eve—to be free to do as one likes without consequences:

> They promise freedom, but they themselves **are slaves of sin** and corruption. For **you are a slave to whatever controls you**. And when people escape from the wickedness of the world by knowing our Lord and Savior Jesus Christ and **then get tangled up and enslaved by sin again, they are worse off than before**. It would be better if they had never known the way to righteousness than to know it and **then reject the command they were given to live a holy life**. They prove the truth of this proverb: "A dog returns to its vomit." And another says, "A washed pig returns to the mud."
> (2Pe.2:19-22 NLT)

I have directly asked these teachers for Bible verses that explicitly state that Christians have free choice. So far, not a single teacher has produced even one verse. In fact, one pastor conceded, "There is no Scriptural support for free choice, but we do not need a Scripture to support the doctrine. It is common sense." They are deceived by sin, as every person is either controlled by the sinful nature or the Spirit:

...these [two natures] *are opposed to each other,* **to prevent you from doing what you want.** (Ga.5:17 NRSV)

Man, without the Spirit of God living in them, cannot consistently do the will of God, no matter what they claim. Jesus taught that those who choose to refuse to do God's will are not His Children and will not enter heaven:

Not everyone who says to me, "Lord, Lord," *will enter the kingdom of heaven, but* **only the one** *who does the will of my Father in heaven. On that day many will say to me, "Lord, Lord, did we not prophesy in your name, and cast out demons in your name, and do many deeds of power in your name?" Then I will declare to them,* **"I never knew you; go away from me, you evildoers."** (Mt.7:21-23 NRSV)

The people described in the previous passage were evildoers who performed many miracles for God but did not do the will of God. To call Jesus your Lord but not do His will is incongruent.

When I was seventeen, I joined the army. The moment I swore my allegiance to Canada, I gave up my right to choose and placed myself under the control of my commanding officers. I pledged to carry out my part of a military operation regardless of personal endangerment. I had to have enough courage to accept the most dangerous of missions and enough humility to complete the most insignificant of commands. If I was told to clean the latrine, it would be spotless. If I was told to capture a hill, only death would stop me. My obedience was the result of me signing a contract with the army.

In the same way, we cannot come to the tabernacle without laying our life on the bronze altar of sacrifice, confirming our allegiance to God alone. When we become a Christian, we give up our right to choose by making Christ our Lord. When we are tempted, we no longer consider whether or not we want to obey. We have made Christ Lord of our life and disregard the temptation. Paul no longer considered what he wanted; rather, he only considered Christ's will in the situation:

For to me, to live *is* **Christ**, *and to die* is *gain.* (Php.1:21 NKJV)

Paul gave up his right to choose disobedience when he made Christ his Lord. When a Christian is presented with a choice, we consider no other option but obedience:

> For to this you were called, because Christ also suffered for us, leaving us an example, **that you should follow His steps**: (1Pe.2:21 NKJV)

Christians are Christ's followers. Jesus' sole purpose in life was to do the will of His Father:

> For **I have come down from heaven**, not to do My own will, but **the will of Him who sent Me**. (Jn.6:38 NASB)
>
> I seek **not my own will** but **the will of him who sent me**. (Jn.5:30 ESV)
>
> For I did not speak of my own accord, but the Father who sent me **commanded me what to say and how to say it**. (Jn.12:49 NIV)
>
> I do <u>exactly</u> as the Father commanded Me. (Jn.14:31 NASB)
>
> If you keep my commandments, you will abide in my love, <u>just as</u> I have kept my **Father's commandments** and abide in his love. (Jn.15:10 NRSV)
>
> I have glorified You on the earth. **I have finished the work which You have given Me to do.** (Jn.17:4 NKJV)

Jesus lived for the will of God the Father, and Jesus commands us to follow His example of obedience:

> We know that we have come to know him **if we obey his commands**. The man who says, "I know him," but does not do what he commands is a liar, and the truth is not in him. But if anyone obeys his word, God's love is truly made complete in him. **This is how we know we are in him: Whoever claims to live in him <u>must walk as Jesus did</u>**. (1Jn.2:3-6 NIV)

If we have not given up our will with our right to choose between obedience and disobedience, then we have no part of Him. To Jesus, a rebellious Christian is an oxymoron:

> Why do you call me, **"Lord, Lord," and do not do what I say?**
> (Lk.6:46 TNIV)

Lordship is directly related to our obedience to the will of God. The Scriptures teach that Jesus rose from the dead to live in us and take control of our life. Not only do we die with Christ in our baptism, but Christ also becomes our life:

> **For you have died**, and your life is hidden with Christ in God. **When Christ who is your life appears**, then you also will appear with him in glory.
> (Co.3:3-4 ESV)

When I give Christ my life, that one decision ends my right to rebel against God from that point forward. I do not consider what I feel like doing. When I no longer consider temptation to sin as an option, sin has lost its power over me. We need to give total control of our life to God and believe that the Holy Spirit has taken control of our life. Then we must daily ask God to transform our life as He promised:

> *Christ's love **controls us**. Since we believe that Christ died for all, we also believe that we **have all died to our old life**. He died for everyone so that those who receive his new life will **no longer live for themselves**. Instead, **they will live for Christ**, who died and was raised for them.*
> (2Co.5:14-15 NLT)

Christ's love compels us to live for Him. A born-again Christian has obligated himself to do the will of God:

> *For **whoever does the will of My Father** in heaven **is My brother** and **sister** and **mother**.* (Mt.12:50 NKJV)

You cannot be a Christian and maintain control of your life. Instead, you must give up your life in order to live in submission to God:

> *As a result, he **does not live the rest of his earthly life** for evil human desires, but rather **for the will of God**.* (1Pe.4:2 NIV)

Only those who have placed their life on the bronze altar can come to the table of showbread:

> *And the world and its desire are passing away, but **those who do the will of God** live forever.* (1Jn.2:17 NRSV)

We overcome the power of sin by giving the Holy Spirit control of our life. He sets Christians free from the law of sin:

> *For **the law of the Spirit** of life in Christ Jesus has **set you free** from the **law of sin** and of death.* (Ro.8:2 NRSV)

Romans 6 teaches that born-again Christians cannot continue to sin:

> *What shall we say, then? **Shall we go on sinning**, so that grace may increase? **By no means! We died to sin**; how can we live in it any longer?* (Ro.6:1-2 NIV)

Romans 6 clearly teaches that Christians have died to the power of sin. The verb tense in "we died to sin" is the aorist tense, which is an eternal tense. This tense depicts not past, present, or future, but eternal. Jesus came so that we would die to sin and live to righteousness:

> *He Himself bore our sins in His body on the cross, that **we might die to sin** and live to righteousness; for by His wounds **you were healed**.*
> (1Pe.2:24 NASB)

The power of sin is similar to the vines that grow in the woods. I sometimes find vines at the top of majestic trees, whose weight could break large branches. The vines did not suddenly appear; rather, as the trees grew, the vines also grew. I could try to pull the smaller, more manageable parts of the vines out of the trees to rescue the trees, but these smaller parts would soon grow back because they are nourished by the vines' roots. Or, I could use a chainsaw to cut the vines by their roots at the bottom of the trees to disconnect the roots from the vines. The vines in the trees' branches would die and start to decay, falling from the trees. In the same way, before we were Christians, the power of sin grew in its control of our life as we grew in knowledge of the world. My struggle to hinder the vines' growth is similar to our struggle to conquer our individual acts of sin. Before I was baptized, I could gain victory over some sins by my determination, but the power of sin was still alive in me. The sinful practices undoubtedly returned in my life. To me, all seemed hopeless. To try to overcome our acts of sin without dying to the power of sin (cutting sin off at the root) will only lead to short-term success. However, if we die to the power of sin in our baptism, we will find our sinful actions dying as well:

> We know that our old self was crucified with him in order that **the body of sin might be brought to nothing**, so that we would **no longer** be enslaved to sin. For one who **has died has been set free from sin**. (Ro.6:6-7 ESV)

The Scriptures state that Christians have been set free from sin; sin is no longer their master:

> For **sin shall not be master over you**, for you are not under law, but **under grace**. (Ro.6:14 NASB)

A slave can have only one master at a time. When we were set free from sin, we became slaves of God:

> **Act as free men**, and do not use your freedom **as a covering for evil, but use it as bond slaves of God**. (1Pe.2:16 NASB)

When we were slaves of sin, we could not resist our sinning. Now that we have become slaves of righteousness, we cannot help but do what is right:

> But thanks be to God that **though you were slaves of sin**, you **became** obedient from the heart to that form of teaching to which you were committed, and **having been freed** from sin, you **became** slaves of righteousness. (Ro.6:17-18 NRSV)

The Scriptures speak of our slavery to sin in the past tense but speak of our slavery to righteousness in the present tense:

> I put this in human terms because you are weak in your natural selves. Just as you **used to** offer the parts of your body **in slavery to** impurity and to

*ever-increasing wickedness, so **now** offer them **in slavery to** righteousness leading to holiness.* (Ro.6:19 NIV)

In the same way that sin was once our master with power over us, God is now our new master, with the same level of control over us that sin once had:

*But now that you **have been set free from sin** and **have become slaves to God**, the benefit you reap **leads to holiness**, and the result is eternal life.* (Ro.6:22 NIV)

The Scriptures teach that Jesus came to set us free from the power of sin:

*I say to you, **everyone who commits sin is the slave of sin**... So if the Son makes you free, **you will be free indeed**.* (Jn.8:34&36 NASB)

Jesus not only came to forgive us our sin but also to set mankind free from the power of sin. We are freed from the power of sin's allurement when we give up our right to chose by making Christ Lord of our life.

THE PURE GOLD RIM

Only two articles in the tabernacle had a solid gold rim: the gold altar of incense and the gold table of showbread. Both had the same purpose. On the gold altar of incense, the gold rim kept the coals from falling off the altar. On the gold table of showbread, the rim kept the utensils from falling off the table. The pure gold rim represented God's work in man:

*For **God is working in you**, giving you **the desire** and **the power** to do what pleases him.* (Php.2:13 NLT)

Many Christians try to fulfill God's promises by their own efforts. However, holiness is not their responsibility. Holiness is God's responsibly because He is the One Who promises to transform us:

*He did not waver through unbelief regarding the promise of God, but was strengthened in his faith and gave glory to God, **being fully persuaded that God had power to do what he had promised**.* (Ro.4:20-21 TNIV)

God's Word is truth, and what He has promised is a reality. God states that we are a new creation with a new nature and that He will keep us faithful to Him:

*You shall overlay it with pure gold and **make a gold border around it**. You shall make for it **a rim of a handbreadth** around it; and you shall make a gold border for the rim around it.* (Ex.25:24-25 NASB)

The gold rim symbolized God's promise to keep us from falling. The rim was made of pure gold which teaches us not to rest in our own resolve to do the will of God but in God's faithfulness:

> But **the Lord is faithful**, and **he will strengthen** and protect you from the evil one. We have **confidence in the Lord** that **you are doing and will continue to do the things** we command. (2Th.3:3-4 NASB)

In a similar way to the solid gold rim which ensured that everything would remain on the table of showbread, our confidence is in the Lord. In Him we will persevere. He will protect us and empower us to do His will:

> For no matter how many promises God has made, they are "Yes" in Christ. And so through him the "Amen" is spoken by us to the glory of God. Now **it is God who makes** both us and you stand firm in Christ. He anointed us, set his seal of ownership on us, and put **his Spirit** in our hearts as a deposit, **guaranteeing** what is to come. (2Co.1:20-22 TNIV)

The Holy Spirit living in our heart guarantees that we will continue to live to please God. Through the indwelling of the Holy Spirit, we are empowered to do God's will, instead of being controlled by the power of sin:

> For I am not ashamed of the gospel, **for it is the power of God** for salvation to everyone who believes, (Ro.1:16 ESV)

The Gospel is about power. The power of God's Presence in our life overcomes the power of sin:

> For the kingdom of God **depends** not on talk but **on power.** (1Co.4:20 NRSV)

When I made Christ my Lord, I gave up my right to choose sin, and God took control of my life to accomplish His will for me. I will trust in Him:

> I know whom I have believed, and **am convinced that he is able to guard what I have entrusted to him** for that day... Guard the good deposit that was entrusted to you—**guard it with the help of the Holy Spirit who lives in us.** (2Ti.12&14 TNIV)

The gold border reminds us that our confidence is in God. God, through the Presence of the Holy Spirit, is the One Who initiated the change in our heart; and He is the One Who will overcome the power of sin in our life:

> No-one who is born of God **will continue** to sin, because **God's seed remains in him**; he cannot **go on sinning**, because he has been born of God. (1Jn.3:9 NIV)

I place no confidence in my ability to keep from sin but in God's ability to do as He promised:

> For *I am confident of this very thing, that **He who began** a good work in you **will perfect it** until the day of Christ Jesus.* (Php.1:6 NASB)

A Christian is someone who has surrendered his will to God and has given the Holy Spirit control of his life. Once we are born again, our soul—with its intellect, desires, and will—is controlled by the Holy Spirit. The Scriptures teach that a Christian's mind is controlled by the Holy Spirit:

> *The **mind** of sinful man is death, but the **mind controlled by the Spirit** is life and peace;* (Ro.8:6 TNIV)

The Scriptures teach that a Christian's heart with its emotions/desires is no longer controlled by his sinful nature but by the Holy Spirit:

> *So I say, **live by the Spirit**, and you **will not gratify** the desires of the sinful nature.* (Ga.5:16 NIV)

The Scriptures teach that a Christian's will is enslaved to righteousness, no longer enslaved of the power of sin but controlled by the Holy Spirit:

> *When you **were slaves** to sin, you were free from **the control of righteousness**... But now that you **have been** set free from sin and have become **slaves to God**, the benefit you reap leads to holiness, and the result is eternal life.* (Ro.6:20-22 NIV)

In the previous three lessons, we have seen that the Holy Spirit initiates the change in man's soul, intellect, and emotion. In this lesson, we have discovered that the Holy Spirit controls the will of man, causing us to live to please Him:

> *Now the God of peace... **equip you** in every good thing **to do His will**, **working in us** that which is pleasing in His sight, through Jesus Christ, to whom be the glory forever and ever. Amen.* (He.13:20-21 NASB)

Since our right to choose gives sin its power of allurement, placing our lives under the control of God negates sin's control over our life. We must pray as Jesus taught us to pray:

> *Our Father in heaven, hallowed be your name. Your kingdom come. **Your will be done, on earth** as it is in heaven.* (Mt.6:9-10 NRSV)

Therefore, the table of showbread is about the laying of our will on the table and asking God that His will be done in our life today.

Thinking It Through:

1. Jesus said, "My food is to do the will of Him who sent me" (Jn.4:34). What does this mean?

2. Since the bread of the presence was made with fire, what did the law require it not to have? What does this symbolize for the Christian?

3. What does the Scripture mean when it states that sin came into the world (Ro.5:12)?

4. How can the "power of sin" be the "law"?

5. Does a slave have free choice? Can a slave of sin have free choice?

6. What does it mean to follow in the steps of Christ?

7. What does the pure gold rim around the table represent?

8. What are the implications of making Christ your Lord?

Holman Bible 1890

THE HOLY OF HOLIES

Have them make a chest out of acacia wood. Make it three feet nine inches long and two feet three inches wide and high. Cover it inside and outside with pure gold. Put a strip of gold around it. Make four gold rings for it. Join them to its four bottom corners. Put two rings on one side and two rings on the other. Then make poles out of acacia wood. Cover them with gold. Put the poles through the rings on the sides of the chest to carry it. The poles must remain in the rings of the chest. Do not remove them. I will give you the tablets of the covenant. When I do, put them into the chest. Make its cover out of pure gold. The cover is the place where sin will be paid for. Make it three feet nine inches long and two feet three inches wide. Make two cherubim out of hammered gold at the ends of the cover. Put one cherub on each end of it. Make the cherubim as part of the cover itself. The cherubim must have their wings spread up over the cover. The cherubim must face each other and look toward the cover. Exodus 25:10-20 NIrV

Lesson 10

The Holy of Holies

You Must be Born Again

The courtyard represented the way to God; the tabernacle represented our body; and the Holy Place represented our soul. We must now enter the Holy of Holies, which is represented by our spirit. After we are born again by the Holy Spirit, Christ lives in us. People do not choose to be born again spiritually; God decides to give a person's spirit life:

> He chose to give us birth through **the word of truth**, that we might be a kind of firstfruits of all he created. (Ja.1:18 TNIV; Jn.1:12-13)

In the tabernacle, the Holy of Holies was in the shape of a cube measuring ten cubits. All the walls were of acacia wood covered with gold, but the ceiling consisted of the blue, purple, and scarlet yarn (that represented Christ) with cherubim embroidered into the fabric. The curtain which separated the Holy Place from the Holy of Holies also contained the blue, purple, and scarlet yarn and cherubim:

> You shall make a veil of **blue and purple and scarlet material** and fine twisted linen; it shall be made with **cherubim**, the work of a skillful workman. You shall hang it on four pillars of acacia overlaid with gold, their hooks also being of gold, on four sockets of silver. (Ez.26:31-31 NASB)

The gate to the courtyard and the door to the tabernacle had the blue, purple, and scarlet yarn. Only the curtain separating the Holy Place from the Holy of Holies had cherubim embroidered into the fabric because God actually dwelt behind the curtain. The curtain represented Christ but reminds us that only those who ask Christ to apply His blood as payment for their sins can enter into the Presence of God:

> Therefore, brothers and sisters, since **we have confidence <u>to enter the Most Holy Place by the blood</u> of** Jesus, by a new and living way opened for us through the curtain, that is, his body, (He.10:19-20 TNIV)

The curtain was supported by four columns which represented the four Gospels. The Gospels clearly present that Christ rose from the dead to become our Lord. These columns were supported by silver bases which symbolized redemption. Only Christians, whose souls are redeemed from sin, self, and Satan, are born again in their spirit. Everything made of acacia wood was covered with gold, which is symbolic of Christ living in and controlling us. Shortly before His crucifixion, Jesus encouraged His disciples because He knew that they did not actually understand His approaching death:

> *I will not leave you as orphans; I will come to you. Before long, the world will not see me anymore, but you will see me. Because I live, you also will live. On that day you will realize that **I am in my Father**, and **you are in me, and I am in you**.* (Jn.14:18-20 NIV)

Christ is in the Father, and Christ lives in us by His Spirit. Once the Holy Spirit lives in us, we have become the dwelling place of God—His temple:

> *Do you not know that **you are God's temple** and **that God's Spirit dwells in you**? If anyone destroys God's temple, God will destroy that person. For **God's temple is holy**, and you are that temple.* (1Co.3:16-17 NRSV)

Born-again Christians are the holy temple of God.

A Historic Perspective

The Scriptures teach that the only piece of furniture in the Holy of Holies was the ark of the covenant. God dwelt in the Holy of Holies:

> *The LORD said to Moses: Tell your brother Aaron not to come just at any time **into the sanctuary inside the curtain before the mercy seat that is upon the ark**, or he will die; for **I appear in the cloud upon the mercy seat**.* (Le.16:2 NRSV)

If Aaron, the High Priest, would enter the Holy of Holies at any time other than the Day of Atonement, he would die. The Scriptures teach that God specifically dwelt in a cloud above the mercy seat, which was in the center of the lid of the ark of the covenant:

> *You shall put **the mercy seat** on the top of the ark; and in the ark you shall put the covenant that I shall give you. There **I will meet with you, and from above the mercy seat**, from **between the two cherubim** that are on the ark of the covenant, I will deliver to you all my commands for the Israelites.* (Ex.25:21-22 NRSV; Nu.7:89)

When Moses first set up the tabernacle (1460 BC), God descended on the Holy of Holies. In the Holy of Holies, God's Presence rested between the two pure gold cherubim:

> And he set up the curtain at the entrance of the courtyard. So **at last Moses finished the work**. Then the cloud covered the Tabernacle, and **the glory of the LORD filled the Tabernacle**. (Ex.40:33-34 NLT)

Later, when Solomon's temple was first dedicated (975 BC), God also descended on the Holy of Holies:

> When the priests withdrew from the Holy Place, **the cloud filled the temple of the LORD. And the priests could not perform their service because of the cloud, for the glory of the LORD filled his temple**. (1Ki.8:10-11 NIV)

For 875 years, the ark resided in the Holy of Holies—first in the tabernacle and then in the temple. However, Jeremiah prophesied that the ark would disappear:

> "When your numbers have increased greatly in the land," declares the LORD, "**people will no longer say, 'The ark of the covenant of the LORD.' It will never enter their minds or be remembered; it will not be missed**, nor will another one be made." (Jer.3:16 TNIV)

God declared that the ark of the covenant was never to be replaced but, instead, to be forgotten. Before the Babylonians entered Jerusalem and destroyed the temple (585 BC), the ark of the covenant disappeared:

> God gave them all into the hands of Nebuchadnezzar. He carried to Babylon **all the articles from the temple of God**, both large and small, and the treasures of the LORD's temple and the treasures of the king and his officials. **They set fire to God's temple**. (2Chr.36:17-19 TNIV)

The presence of the ark was not mentioned after the Babylonian destruction of the temple. In Lamentations, Jeremiah prophesied that at the destruction of the temple, God abandoned His earthly dwelling place:

> He has **violently treated His tabernacle** like a garden booth; **He has destroyed His appointed meeting place**. The LORD has caused to be forgotten The appointed feast and sabbath in Zion, And He has despised king and priest In the indignation of His anger. The Lord has **rejected His altar**, He has **abandoned His sanctuary**; (Lam.2:6-7 NASB)

God abandoned the Holy of Holies. After 70 years in exile, Israel returned to the Promised Land and started to rebuild the temple according to God's plans that He gave to Ezekiel. The Scriptures never recorded that the glory of God descended on of Holies of Holies in the temple that Ezra dedicated. The reason was twofold: first, the mercy seat of the ark no longer was within the Holy of Holies, the place where God actually dwelt. Second, without the mercy seat, Israel's sins could not be annually forgiven because the blood on the mercy seat was God's means to forgive Israel's sins. Leviticus states that the Day of Atonement was an eternal sacrament for the forgiveness of Israel's sins:

> This shall be an **everlasting** statute for you, to make atonement for the people of Israel once in the year *for all their sins*. (Le.16:34 NRSV)

According to the commands of God and due to the loss of the ark, Israel has not had their sins forgiven for over 2500 years. In AD 68, Herod renovated Ezra's temple, but the glory of God did not descend on that temple either. Jesus prophesied about the destruction of Herod's temple:

> **As Jesus came out of the temple** and was going away, his disciples came to point out to him the buildings of the temple. Then he asked them, "You see all these, do you not? Truly **I tell you, not one stone will be left here upon another; all will be thrown down."** (Mt.24:1-2 NRSV)

In AD 70, General Titus destroyed the last known temple on the temple mount. For nearly 2000 years, no physical temple has existed in Jerusalem. Jesus prophesied that a new place of worship had come:

> The hour is coming when you will **worship the Father** neither on this mountain **nor in Jerusalem**... But the hour is coming, and **is now here**, when the true worshipers **will worship the Father in spirit** and truth, for the Father seeks such as these to worship him. (Jn.4:21&23 NRSV)

Jesus said that the place of worship would no longer be in Jerusalem; rather, His temple would now be in the spirits of man. When Jesus cleansed the courtyard of the temple, the Pharisees asked Him by Whose authority did He force the buyers and sellers out of the temple:

> Jesus answered them, **"Destroy this temple, and in three days I will raise it up."** The Jews then said, "It has taken forty-six years to build this temple, and will you raise it up in three days?" But **he was speaking about the temple of his body**. (Jn.2:19-21 ESV)

Jesus said that if Herod's temple was destroyed, He would raise up a temple for God in three days—He was referring to His body. When Jesus died on the cross, an important event took place within the temple:

> Jesus cried out with a loud voice, and **breathed His last**. Then **the veil of the temple was torn in two** from top to bottom. (Mk.15:37-38 NKJV)

The tearing of the curtain that separated the Holy Place from the Holy of Holies signified that God would not return to a physical structure. Three days after Jesus died, He rose from the dead, creating the last temple of God—the human body. Ten days after Jesus' ascension, the glory of God descended within His people:

> Suddenly there came from heaven a sound like **a mighty rushing wind**, and it filled the entire house where they were sitting. And divided tongues **as of fire appeared to them and rested on each one** of them. **And they were all filled with the Holy Spirit.** (Ac.2:2-4 ESV)

On Pentecost, the glory of God indwelt His new temple—our body. Our soul became the Holy Place, and our spirit became the Holy of Holies:

> Do you not know **that your body is a temple of the Holy Spirit** within you, whom you have from God? (1Co.6:19 ESV)

Therefore, God dwelt above the mercy seat of the ark until 585 BC. He finally descended on His new temple, the spirit of man, with our heart becoming the new mercy seat.

Spiritual Rebirth

When God created Adam, He placed him in His garden. God was very explicit about the consequences for breaking His command:

> You are free to eat from any tree in the garden; but **you must not eat** from the tree of the knowledge of good and evil, for **when you eat** of it **you will surely die**. (Ge.3:16-17 NIV)

When Adam and Eve ate the forbidden fruit, their penalty was immediate death. Adam and Eve did not suddenly die physically, but lived to have children. Even though Adam and Eve did not die that day, their spirits died when they ate the forbidden fruit:

> For as **in Adam all die**, even so in Christ shall all be made alive. (1Co.15:22 KJV)

Everyone descended from Adam is born spiritually-dead. Jesus referred to those who were not His disciples as being dead:

> But Jesus said to him, "Follow Me, and **let the dead bury their own dead.**" (Mt.8:22 NKJV)

Throughout the Old Testament, God called Israel to turn from their sins and receive a new heart and a new spirit. This new heart and spirit replaced what died in Adam:

> Therefore, house of Israel, **I will judge each of you according to your own ways**, declares the Sovereign LORD. **Repent! Turn away from all your offenses;** then sin will not be your downfall. Rid yourselves of all the offenses you have committed, and <u>get a new heart</u> and <u>a new spirit</u>. Why will you die, house of Israel? **For I take no pleasure in the death of anyone,** declares the Sovereign LORD. **Repent and live!** (Eze.18:30-32 TNIV)

God states the reason for Israel's failure to keep His covenant: Israel's heart was evil, and their spirit was dead. God asked Israel to offer their broken heart and broken spirit as a sacrifice on His altar:

> **You do not desire sacrifice**, or else I would give it; You do not delight in burnt offering. **The sacrifices of God are a <u>broken spirit</u>, A <u>broken and contrite heart</u>**—These, O God, You will not despise. (Ps.51:16-17 NKJV)

When we lay our life on the bronze altar, we are laying our broken spirit and heart before God. For example, as parents, we can remember when our child came to us with a precious toy that was broken and said, "Fix it?" God promises to fix both our spirit and our heart if we come to Him in humility and lay them both on His altar:

> For this is what the high and exalted One says—he who lives forever, whose name is holy: "**I live** in a high and holy place, but also **with those who are contrite and lowly in spirit, <u>to revive the spirit</u>** of the lowly and **<u>to revive the heart</u>** of the contrite. (Isa.57:15 TNIV)

God promised in the Old Testament to revive Israel's heart (a new heart) and to revive Israel's spirit (a new spirit), for theirs were corrupted and deadened because of Adam's sin:

> I will sprinkle clean water on you, and you will be clean... I will **<u>give you a new heart</u>** and **<u>put a new spirit in you</u>**; I will **remove from you your heart of stone** and **give you a heart of flesh**. And **I will <u>put my Spirit in you</u>** and **<u>move you</u> to follow my decrees** and be careful to keep my laws."
> (Eze.36:25-27 NIV; 11:19-20)

In Ezekiel, God promised that He would give mankind a new spirit and a new heart and place His Holy Spirit within them. Jesus reminds us:

> That which is born of the flesh is flesh, and **that which is born of the Spirit is spirit.** Do not marvel that I said to you, "**You must be born again.**"
> (Jn.3:6-7 ESV)

Many Christians are unaware of the new spirit that God has given them:

> God did not **<u>give us</u> <u>a spirit</u>** of cowardice, but rather **<u>a Spirit</u>** of power and of love and of self-discipline. (2Ti.1:7)

When our spirit was dead, our life was consumed by sin, but God has made us alive in Christ:

> When you **were dead** in your sins and in the uncircumcision of your sinful nature, God **made you alive** with Christ. (Co.2:13 NIV)

Once we became alive in our spirit, the body's influence over our soul has ended:

> If Christ is in you, **though the body is dead** because of sin, yet **the spirit is alive** because of righteousness. (Ro.8:10 NASB)

The moment we receive the Holy Spirit, our spirit is given life and our spirit becomes one with God's Spirit:

> But the one who joins himself to the Lord **is one spirit** with Him. (1Co.6:17 NASB)

God's Spirit and our spirit form a relationship through Christ:

> The Spirit Himself **bears witness with our spirit** that we are children of God, (Ro.8:16 NKJV)

Through Christ's death and resurrection, man can once again function as a tri-unity—body, soul, and spirit:

> Now may the God of peace **make you holy in every way**, and may **your whole spirit** and **soul** and **body** be kept blameless until our Lord Jesus Christ comes again. (1Th.5:23 NLT)

Our spirit's new life is affirmed throughout the New Testament. The new life in man's spirit is exemplified with an unmarried believer:

> In the same way, a woman who is no longer married or has never been married **can be devoted to the Lord and holy in body and in spirit**. (1Co.7:34 NLT)

Three times the Scriptures use the greeting "be with your spirit":

> The Lord Jesus Christ **be with your spirit**. (2Ti.4:22 NKJV; Ga.6:18; Phm.1:25)

Jesus taught that the only worship that God would accept would be through our spirit:

> **God is spirit**, and those who worship Him **must worship in spirit** and truth. (Jn.4:24 NASB)

The moment we are born again in our spirit, we begin to function on a spiritual level:

> Otherwise, **if you give thanks with your spirit**... (1Co.14:16 ESV)
>
> I will **pray with the spirit**... (1Co.14:15 NKJV)
>
> I will **sing with the spirit**... (1Co.14:15 NKJV)

Man's born-again spirit can worship God because his spirit has become the new Holy of Holies. Before Christ, God dwelt over the mercy seat of the ark. In the same way that God could not dwell in the Holy of Holies without the ark and the mercy seat, God's Spirit could not dwell in our sinful heart. Just as the blood of the sacrifice on the Day of Atonement was sprinkled on the mercy seat, mankind needed the blood of Christ to be sprinkled on their heart:

> *Therefore, brothers and sisters, since we **have confidence to enter the Most Holy Place by the blood** of Jesus, by a new and living way opened for us **through the curtain, that is, his body**, and since we have a great priest over the house of God, let us draw near to God **with a sincere heart** in full assurance of faith, having **our hearts sprinkled to cleanse us** from a guilty conscience and having our bodies washed with pure water.*
> (He.12:19-22 TNIV)

Jesus' blood was sprinkle on our hearts and cleansed them so that the Holy Spirit could dwell within them:

> *He has commissioned us, and he has identified us as his own **by placing the Holy Spirit in our hearts**,* (2Co.1:22 NLT)

A born-again Christian's heart is the new mercy seat for God:

> *And because you are children, God has **sent the Spirit** of his Son **into our hearts**, crying, "Abba! Father!"* (Ga.4:6 NRSV; Eph.3:16-17)

The term "born-again" refers to the receiving of a new heart and a new spirit—where the Spirit of God dwells:

> *You are controlled by the Spirit **if you have the Spirit of God living in you**. (And remember that **those who do not have the Spirit of Christ** living in them do not belong to him at all.)* (Ro.8:9 NLT)

Your spirit cannot be born again without your life being placed under the Holy Spirit's control. When man's spirit was dead, their spirit still existed but was powerless to influence them. Their soul controlled their life and lived to please their body's senses:

> *But the widow **who lives for pleasure is dead** even while she lives.*
> (1Ti.5:6 NIV)

Through Adam's sin, man's spirit was incapacitated. Under the old covenant, God's Spirit would come upon and control prophets for a time. The Holy Spirit's Presence in someone under the old covenant (one without Christ) can be observed in the life of Simeon:

> It had been **revealed** to him by the Holy Spirit that he would not die before he had seen the Lord's Christ. **Moved** by the Spirit, he went into the temple courts. (Lk.2:26-27 NIV)

Before Pentecost, the Holy Spirit could come upon a person, but his experience was limited. When we become Christians, our soul dies and ceases to control our life, while our spirit becomes alive through the indwelling of the Holy Spirit. Our soul now suffers the same fate that our spirit suffered in the fall. The soul—with its intellect, emotion, and will—is still present but is now incapacitated from controlling our life. The soul is placed under the control of our spirit's faculties that are empowered by the Holy Spirit. We continue to think, but we are not controlled by our thoughts. We make decisions, but the Spirit directs our thought processes:

> But **we have the mind of Christ**. (1Co.2:16 KJV)

We continue to desire but no longer live for the desires of the sinful nature. We have received the divine nature of God by the indwelling of the Holy Spirit. Our new spiritual nature enables us to resist Satan's temptations and to no longer yield to the power of sin's allurement:

> No temptation has overtaken you except what is common to us all. And God is faithful; **he will not let you be tempted beyond what you can bear**. But when you are tempted, **he will also provide a way out so that you can endure it**. (1Co.10:13 TNIV)

We still continue to choose, but with Christ as our Lord, we no longer consider disobedience an option, for God works in us to will and to act according to His purpose:

> For **God is working in you, giving you the desire and the power to do what pleases him**. (Php.2:13 NLT)

A Christian's soul has been relegated to its rightful place, under the control of his spirit. Our soul still exists, but it has been incapacitated. Consequently, our soul is no longer controlled by intellect, emotion, and will. It is now controlled by the spiritual faculties of intuition, conscience, and communion. Since the Holy Spirit controls us, we will see a transformation of behavior because God's Spirit lives within us:

> Those who are **born of God will not** continue to sin, because **God's seed remains in them**; they **cannot go on sinning**, because they have been **born of God**. (1Jn.3:9 TNIV)

Once the Holy Spirit indwells our heart, we have overcome the world:

> For **whatever is <u>born of God</u> overcomes the world**. (1Jn.5:4 NKJV)

The moment we are born of God, we have changed our citizenship and are no longer part of Satan's kingdom. We have become part of the Kingdom of God. Consequently, rebirth relinquishes Satan's right to our life:

> We know that those **who are <u>born of God do not sin</u>**, but the one who was born of God protects them, and **the <u>evil one</u> <u>does not touch them</u>**.
> (1Jn.5:18 NRSV)

The rebirth of our spirit affects more than our attitudes, behavior, and character. It affects who we are, for everything we lost through Adam's fall has been regained through Christ:

> "The first man Adam became a living being." **The last Adam became a life-giving spirit.** (1Co.15:45 NKJV)

THE REALITY OF THE RESURRECTION

The moment that the Holy Spirit gives a person a new heart and a new spirit, his life is empowered by His indwelling:

> I pray that out of his glorious riches **he may <u>strengthen you with power through his Spirit</u>** in your inner being, so that **Christ may dwell in your hearts** through faith. (Eph.3:16-17 NIV)

Christ died to forgive us our sin, but He rose from the dead to indwell and empower us to live for Him:

> I want to know Christ and **the power of his resurrection,** (Php.3:10 NRSV)

The power for living the Christian life rests on Christ's resurrection. Christ's death without His resurrection would only be a sacrifice because His death alone is ineffective to change lives:

> If there is no resurrection of the dead, then not even Christ has been raised. And **if Christ has not been raised**, our **preaching is useless** and **so is your faith**. ...For if the dead are not raised, then Christ has not been raised either. And **if Christ has not been raised**, your **faith is futile**; you **are still in your sins**. Then those also **who have fallen asleep in Christ are lost**.
> (1Co.15:13-18 NIV)

If Christ was not raised, then we are still in our sins and separated from God. Our rebirth rests upon Jesus' resurrection:

> Blessed be the God and Father of our Lord Jesus Christ! By his great mercy **he has given us <u>a new birth</u>** into a living hope **<u>through the resurrection</u> of Jesus Christ** from the dead... (1Pe.1:3 NRSV)

The Gospel focuses on the resurrection of Jesus. To acknowledge the resurrection requires that we acknowledge Christ's death. The Scriptures continue past Christ's death to His resurrection because His resurrection leads to a Spirit-filled life. The apostles preached the resurrection:

> And with great power **the apostles gave witness to the resurrection of the Lord Jesus**. (Ac.4:33 NKJV)

Even in Paul's ministry, the resurrection was emphasized:

> A group of Epicurean and Stoic philosophers began to debate with him. Some of them asked, "What is this babbler trying to say?" Others remarked, "He seems to be advocating foreign gods." They said this because **Paul was preaching the good news about Jesus and the resurrection.** (Ac.17:18 TNIV)

Today most Christians ask people to believe that Christ died for their sins but seldom mention Christ's resurrection. However, the Scriptures teach that Christ's resurrection saves us from hell:

> If you confess with your mouth the Lord Jesus and **believe in your heart that God has raised Him from the dead, you will be saved**. (Ro.10:9 NKJV)

We are saved from our sins through Christ's resurrection. The reality of our baptism is contingent upon of Jesus' resurrection:

> ...this water symbolizes **baptism that now saves you** also—not the removal of dirt from the body but the pledge of a good conscience towards God. **It saves you by the resurrection of Jesus Christ**, who has gone into heaven and is at God's right hand—with angels, authorities and powers in submission to him. (1Pe.3:20-22 NIV)

Baptism will only be a ritual unless Christ gives life to our spirit and takes control of our life by His Spirit. Do not misunderstand. His death is essential, but Christ's resurrection is also of the utmost importance:

> For I handed on to you as **of first importance** what I in turn had received: that **Christ died for our sins** in accordance with the scriptures, **and that he was buried, and that he was raised on the third day** in accordance with the scriptures, (1Co.15:3-5 NRSV)

To end the Gospel presentation with Christ's death makes the Gospel powerless. Christ was raised from the dead so that we can live a new life:

> Therefore we have been buried with Him through baptism into death, so that **as Christ was raised from the dead** through the glory of the Father, **so we too** might walk in newness of life. (Ro.6:4 NASB)

Our new life is a direct result of our life being indwelt and controlled by the living Christ:

> Therefore **if any man be in Christ**, he is **a new creature**: old things are passed away; behold, **all things are become new**. (2Co.5:17 KJV)

Therefore, the resurrection of Christ enables the Holy Spirit to give life to our spirit and to manifest His life in our life.

A Spirit-Controlled Man

God dwelt in the Holy of Holies above the mercy seat. The mercy seat was in the center of the ark's cover, between the two cherubim:

> Then make **the Ark's cover**—the place of atonement—**from pure gold**. It must be 45 inches long and 27 inches wide. Then **make two cherubim from hammered gold**, and place them on the two ends of the atonement cover.
> (Ex.25:17-18 NLT)

The mercy seat/cover was made of pure gold. Pure gold represents God's work of giving us new, pure hearts:

> So **God, who knows the heart**, acknowledged them by **giving them the Holy Spirit**, just as He did to us, and made no distinction between us and them, **purifying their hearts** by faith. (Ac.15:8-8 NKJV)

Once our heart is purified, Christ can live in it by the Presence of His Spirit:

> I pray that, according to the riches of his glory, he may grant that you may be strengthened in **your inner being with power** through his Spirit, and that **Christ may dwell in your hearts** through faith, (Eph.3:16-17 NRSV)

The pure gold symbolized the fullness of God's holy Presence dwelling in man:

> For **in him the whole fullness of deity** dwells bodily, and **you have come to fullness in him**, who is the head of every ruler and authority.
> (Co.2:9-10 NRSV; Eph.3:19)

Just as the pure gold lid was placed over the ark, the power of God's Presence is placed over the lives of man:

> But **we have this treasure in jars of clay** to show that **this all-surpassing power is from God** and not from us. (2Co.4:7 TNIV)

We are like an empty jar of clay, which is similar to the acacia wood box. The acacia wood was overlaid with gold which represents us in our spiritual weakness. God is the One Who empowers us by His Holy Spirit:

> He has said to me, "My grace is sufficient for you, **for power is perfected in weakness.**" *Most gladly, therefore, I will rather boast about my weaknesses, so* **that the power of Christ may dwell in me.** (2Co.12:9 NASB)

Jesus commanded the disciples to go into all the world, but He told them to wait in Jerusalem until they were empowered by the Holy Spirit:

> It is not for you to know the times or dates the Father has set by his own authority. But you **will receive power when the Holy Spirit comes on you;** and you will be my witnesses in Jerusalem, and in all Judea and Samaria, and to the ends of the earth. (Ac.1:7-8 NIV)

Jesus' command to wait teaches us that preaching truth without the power of the Holy Spirit will be ineffective. The power of God that was at work in Paul's life enabled him to minister effectively:

> We want to present them to God, **perfect in their relationship** to Christ. That's why I work and struggle so hard, **depending on Christ's mighty power that works within me.** (Co.1:28-29 NLT)

Paul did not minister by logic alone but relied on the power that came through Christ Who lived in him:

> I came to you in weakness and in fear and in much trembling. My speech and my proclamation were not with plausible words of wisdom, but with **a demonstration of the Spirit and of power**, so that your faith **might rest not on human wisdom but on the power of God.** (1Co.2:3-5 NRSV)

Paul was not a great orator, but, rather, the Holy Spirit empowered his words to impact people's hearts. To have an effective ministry, Christ must minister through us:

> For I will not presume to speak of anything except what **Christ has accomplished through me**, resulting in the obedience of the Gentiles by word and deed, **in the power** of signs and wonders, in **the power of the Spirit;** (Ro.15:18-19 NASB)

If we try to minister by our own abilities, our ministries will come to nothing; but, if we minister by the power which comes from a life yielded to the Holy Spirit, our ministries will bear much fruit:

> **I am the vine**, you are the branches. **He who abides in Me**, and **I in him, bears much fruit;** for **without Me you can do nothing.** (Jn.15:5 NKJV)

The power of God to transform lives only comes through the Holy Spirit:

> I became a minister according to the gift of the grace of God given to me **by the effective working of His power.** (Eph.3:7 NKJV)

The power of God applies to more than just ministry; it also affects all of life:

> *I can do **all things through Christ who strengthens me.*** (Php.4:13 NKJV)

The Presence of God in our life is the source of a Christian's power:

> *I pray that, according to the riches of his glory, **he may grant that you may be strengthened in your inner being with power** through his Spirit, and that Christ may dwell in your hearts through faith...* (Eph.3:16-17 NRSV)

Our dedication or resolve will not transform our life; rather, our humble dependency on God's power within us will change us:

> *With this in mind, we constantly pray for you, that our **God may make you worthy of his calling**, and that **by his power he may** bring to fruition **your every desire for goodness** and **your every deed prompted by faith.*** (2Th.1:11 TNIV)

Today, the church has relegated Christianity to theology; however, the Scriptures teach that the Kingdom of God is actually about power:

> *The **kingdom of God is** not a matter of talk but **of power**.* (1Co.4:20 TNIV)

The Scriptures continually remind us that God will transform our life by His power. This transformation causes us to naturally please Him:

> *We pray this in order that you may live a life worthy of the Lord and may **please him in every way**: bearing fruit in every good work, growing in the knowledge of God, being strengthened with **all power** according to **his glorious might** so that you may have great endurance and patience, and joyfully giving thanks to the Father,* (Co.1:10-12 NIV)

If we surrender our self to His control, God can incredibly affect our life. Unfortunately, our mind is too limited to imagine the possible effects of having the power of God's Presence in our life:

> *Now **to Him who is able to do far more abundantly beyond all that we ask or think, according to the power** that works within us, to Him be the glory in the church and in Christ Jesus to all generations forever and ever. Amen.* (Eph.3:20-21 NASB)

God's power can accomplish immeasurably more than we can imagine. The power of God's Presence gives us everything we need to live the Christian life:

> *His **divine power** has given us **everything needed** for life and **godliness**, through the knowledge of him who called us by his own glory and goodness.* (2Pe.1:3 NRSV)

Our lack of effectiveness is never due to the lack of God's power in our life, but the lack is in our faith, that God will do as He has promised. We need to focus on the promises of God, asking Him to do what we cannot do for our self. If we have been chosen by God, we can be sure that His power will change us:

> For we know, brothers and sisters loved by God, that **he has chosen you, because** our gospel came to you not simply with words but also **with power, with the Holy Spirit** and deep conviction. You know how we lived among you for your sake. (1Th.1:4-5 TNIV)

The Holy Spirit is the power of the Presence of God. He will transform our lives into His holiness and enable us to minister to those we encounter:

> For all of you who were baptized into Christ have **clothed yourselves with Christ**. (Ga.3:27 NASB)

ONE WITH CHRIST

The Christian life can only be lived by Christ indwelling us. The New Testament constantly repeats that Christ lives in us:

> When **Christ who is our life** appears, then you also will appear with Him in glory. (Co.3:3-4 NKJV)

Christ living in us is the essence of the Christian life:

> And the testimony is this, that God has given us eternal life, **and this life is in His Son. He who has the Son** has the life; he who does not have the Son of God **does not have the life**. (1Jn.4:11-12 NASB)

When the Spirit lives in us, we become one with Christ—our spirit is inseparably joined with His Spirit. Consider sexual union. The Scriptures teach that to unite oneself with a prostitute binds the two into one—as soulmates. If we unite ourselves with Christ, we eternally become one with Him through our spirit being joined with His Spirit:

> Do you not know that he **who unites himself with a prostitute is one with her in body**? For it is said, "The two will become one flesh." But whoever is united with the Lord **is one with him** in spirit. (1Co.6:16-17 TNIV)

Once we are spiritually born again, God lives in us, and we are inseparably linked with God. The Scriptures teach that Jesus lives in us:

> I have been crucified with Christ; **it is no longer I who live, but Christ lives in me**; (Ga.2:20 NKJV)

From the moment Christ lives in us, we are raised with Christ. Currently, I am seated with Him in the heavenly realms:

> And God **raised** us up with Christ and seated us with him **in the heavenly realms** in Christ Jesus, in order that **in the coming ages** he might show the incomparable riches of his grace, expressed in his kindness to us in Christ Jesus. (Eph.2:6-7 TNIV)

The foundation of spiritual life is Christ living in Christians and Christians living in Christ. Our spiritual ascension becomes a reality the moment the Holy Spirit indwells us:

> Since, then, you **have been** raised with Christ, set your hearts on things above, where Christ is seated **at the right hand of God**. (Co.3:1 NIV)

Only those who are born again by the Holy Spirit can experience this inseparable union. Our soul must be put to death in the same manner that our spirit died in Adam. In order to experience rebirth of our spirit, the soul must die:

> Whoever seeks **to preserve his life** [psuche, soul] will lose it, but whoever **loses his life** [psuche, soul] will keep it. (Lk.17:33 ESV)

The moment the Holy Spirit lives in us, our spirit is given life, and transformation starts to occur:

> We know that we **have passed from death to life** because **we love one another**. Whoever does not love abides in death. (1Jn.3:14 NRSV)

Christians have passed from death to life. Eternal life is not in the future after physical death; eternal life starts the moment we are born again:

> I tell you the truth, those who listen to my message and believe in God who sent me **have eternal life**. They will never be condemned for their sins, but they **have already** passed **from death into life**. (Jn.5:24 NLT)

You have eternal life because Christ lives in you:

> God has given us **eternal life**, and **this life is in his Son**. He **who has the Son has life**; (1Jn.5:11-12 NIV; 1Jn.5:20; Jn.17:3)

Eternal life is in the Person of Christ:

> We are in him who is true, **in his Son Jesus** Christ. **He is** the true God and eternal life. (1Jn.5:20 NRSV)

The only way we can be in Christ is through the Presence of His Spirit:

> By this we know that we abide **in Him** and He **in us**, because **He has given us of His Spirit**. (1Jn.4:13 NKJV)

Many people in the Old Testament loved God; however, they did not experience life in their spirit. Paul's life as a Jew under the law was an Old Testament example:

> We know that *the law is spiritual; but **I am unspiritual**, sold as a slave to sin. I do not understand what I do. For what I want to do I do not do, but what I hate I do.* (Ro.7:14-15 TNIV)

When Paul lived as a Jew, he was unspiritual. A large part of the Corinthian church remained unspiritual due to the lack of teaching. They were infants in Christ:

> *Brothers, **I could not address you as spiritual but as worldly**— mere **infants in Christ**. I gave you milk, not solid food, for **you were not yet ready for it**. Indeed, you are still not ready. You are still worldly.*
> (1Co.3:1-3 NIV)

Born-again Christians are called to teach truth to the unspiritual (infants) in the church so that the unspiritual might experience freedom from sin:

> *Brothers, if someone is caught in a sin, **you who are spiritual** should restore him gently. But watch yourself, or you also may be tempted.* (Ga.6:1 NIV)

A pastor once commented that he only finds spiritual infants and children in the church and not spiritual young men:

> *I write to you, **children**, because **you know the Father**... I write to you, **young men**, because you **are strong**, the word of God **abides** in you, and you **have overcome** the evil one.* (1Jn.2:14 ESV)

Spiritual infants believe that Christ died for their sins, but the Bible teaches that **in Him**, all who believe will take on His holy character:

> *God made him who had no sin to be sin for us, so that **in him** we might become **the righteousness of God**.* (2Co.5:21 TNIV)

Holiness is produced by God's Spirit of holiness living in us:

> *If you live according to the sinful nature, you will die; but if **by the Spirit** you **put to death the misdeeds of the body**, you will live, because those who are led by the Spirit of God are sons of God.* (Ro.8:13-14 NIV)

The disciples could have started their ministry without the Holy Spirit, but the ministry would have failed when they would be caught in sin:

> *We are always thankful that **God chose you** to be among the first to experience salvation—a salvation that came through **the Spirit who makes you holy** and through your belief in the truth.* (2Th.2:13 NLT)

Since holiness is produced by the indwelling of the Holy Spirit, He is the foundation of a Christian's life. Most of us accept that the triune God lived in the tabernacle and the temple, but many doubt God's Presence in their life. If we live in Christ and Christ lives in God, then we are also in God:

> *"I do not ask on behalf of these alone, but for those also who believe in Me through their word; **that they may all be one**; even as You, Father, are in Me and I in You, that they also **may be <u>in Us</u>**, so that the world may believe that You sent Me."* (Jn.17:20-21 NASB)

Through Jesus, God has removed the formality and distance between man and God. Being in Him means that we can personally know God:

> *Jesus replied, "Anyone who loves me will obey my teaching. My Father will love them, and we will come to them and **make <u>our</u> home with them**.* (Jn.14:23 TNIV)

The plurality of God (Father, Son, and Holy Spirit) lives in man, for the indwelling of His Spirit is our connection to the fullness of God:

> ***Whoever confesses** that Jesus is the Son of God, **<u>God</u> abides <u>in him</u>, and he in God**.* (1Jn.4:15 NKJV; Eph.1:4)

Christianity is set apart from all other religions of the world because our God is not some "thing" that we worship in some "place" up beyond the stars. Our God is alive in us, and we have become His temple. Consequently, Christianity is more than a religious observance because we have an eternal existence **in Him**:

> *For **we are the temple** of the living God; as God said, "**I will live in them and walk among them**, and I will be their God, and they shall be my people."* (2Co.6:16 NRSV)

If we are born again, we have a new spirit and a new heart. We have become the "new" Holy of Holies with our heart becoming the "new" ark where God dwells. Born-again Christians are the temple of God.

Thinking It Through:

1. Where did God actually dwell in the physical tabernacle and temple?

2. Why couldn't God's glory descend into Ezra's and Herod's temples?

3. What does "born again" mean?

4. What is the power of the resurrection, and what are the implications of the resurrection for man?

5. What was the significance of the torn curtain in the temple?

6. What does "becoming one with a prostitute" teach us about our position in Christ?

7. What is the effect of the Holy Spirit living in a Christian?

8. How do we know that we have eternal life?

Aaron's Staff That Budded

Speak to the people of Israel. Get 12 wooden staffs from them. Get one from the leader of each of Israel's tribes. Write the name of each man on his staff. Write Aaron's name on the staff of Levi. There must be one staff for the head of each of Israel's tribes. Put the staffs in the Tent of Meeting. Place them in front of the ark where the tablets of the covenant are kept. That is where I meet with you. The staff that belongs to the man I choose will begin to grow new shoots. The people of Israel are never happy with what you do. I will put an end to what they are saying. So Moses spoke to the people of Israel. Their leaders gave him 12 wooden staffs. They gave one for the leader of each of Israel's tribes. Aaron's staff was among them. Moses put the staffs in front of the LORD in the tent where the tablets of the covenant were kept. The next day Moses entered the tent. He looked at Aaron's staff. It stood for the tribe of Levi. Moses saw that it had not only begun to grow new shoots. It had also produced buds and flowers and almonds

Numbers.17:2-8 NIrV

Holman Bible 1890

Lesson 11

Aaron's Staff that Budded

Born Again

The Scriptures specify that the only piece of furniture in the Holy of Holies was the ark of the covenant. However, inside the ark were three things: Aaron's staff that budded, the two stone tablets of the covenant, and a gold jar of manna:

> Behind the second curtain was a tent called the Holy of Holies. **In it stood the golden altar of incense** and the ark of the covenant overlaid on all sides with gold, in which there were **a golden urn holding the manna**, and **Aaron's rod that budded**, and **the tablets of the covenant...**
>
> (He.9:3-4 NRSV)

All of the articles were supernaturally produced: a dead staff which in one night sprouted leaves, buds, blossoms, and almonds; the stone tablets on which were written the Ten Commandments by the hand of God; and the gold jar that contained the manna, which appeared every morning in the desert to feed the whole nation of Israel. These three articles represented the three faculties of our spirit: intuition, conscience, and communion. In the same way that the three articles were miraculously altered or provided, we miraculously gain the faculties of our spirit. We do not work to gain these faculties, but they come to life when we are born again.

The gold lampstand in the Holy Place symbolized the soul's faculty of intellect, while Aaron's staff symbolized the spiritual faculty of intuition. The gold lampstand was made of pure gold:

> Six branches extended from the sides of the lampstand— three on one side and three on the other. Three cups shaped like **almond flowers with buds and blossoms** were on one branch, three on the next branch and the same for all six branches extending from the lampstand. And on the lampstand **were four cups shaped like almond flowers with buds and blossoms**.
>
> (Ex.37:18-20 NIV)

The pure gold signified a work strictly accomplished by God because no acacia wood was present in the lampstand's structure. God commanded almond buds and blossoms to be incorporated into the gold lampstand's design, but there were no almonds. If we compare the lampstand to Aaron's staff that budded, we would find some similarities. Even though both contained almond buds and blossoms, their structures were significantly different:

> So Moses spoke to the Israelites, and their leaders gave him twelve staffs, one for the leader of each of their ancestral tribes, and Aaron's staff was among them. Moses placed the staffs before the LORD in the Tent of the Testimony. The next day Moses entered the Tent of the Testimony and **saw that Aaron's staff, which represented the house of Levi, had not only sprouted but had budded, blossomed and produced almonds**.
> (Nu.17:6-8 NIV)

Aaron's staff was a dead stick and was no different than the other eleven staffs. In less than twenty-four hours, not only had it sprouted branches, buds, and blossoms, but Aaron's staff had produced almonds as well. The significant difference between the lampstand and the staff was that the lampstand was made of pure gold, symbolizing a work of God. Aaron's staff consisted only of wood. It was natural wood—something that was once alive, died, and returned to life by the power of God. In the same way, the spirit of man was originally **alive** in Adam when he was created, **died** on the day mankind sinned, and was **reborn** when man's spirit was given life by Christ's Spirit:

> Flesh gives birth to flesh, but **the Spirit gives birth to spirit**. You should not be surprised at my saying, "**You must be born again.**" (Jn.3:6-7 NIV)

The almond tree blooms in winter when other plants are without life:

> ...when men are afraid of heights and of dangers in the streets; when the **almond tree blossoms and the grasshopper drags himself along and desire no longer is stirred**. Then man goes to his eternal home and mourners go about the streets. (Ecc.12:5 NIV)

God gives life to a person's spirit while the rest of the world remains dead in their sin:

> **If Christ is in you**, though the body is dead because of sin, yet **the spirit is alive** because of righteousness. (Ro.8:10 NASB; Eph.2:5;Co.2:13)

Just as the almond tree is a sign of life during the dead of winter, born-again Christians are a sign of life in a world deadened by sin.

THE REALITY OR THE PROMISE

In Hebrew, the name for the almond tree is *shâqêd*. The primary root is *shâqad* which means: "to be watchful, alert, on the lookout." This meaning is clearly seen in the vision God granted Jeremiah:

> *The word of the LORD came to me saying, "What do you see, Jeremiah?" And I said, "I see a rod of an almond tree." Then the LORD said to me, "You have seen well, for I am watching over My word to perform it."*
> (Jer.1:11-12 NASB)

Christians are to continually listen for the voice of God and be willing to learn and submit to it. The reason the staff was placed in the Holy Place was because the people of Israel challenged Moses' and Aaron's right to leadership. This challenge occurred after many Israelite people died during three consecutive events. God told Moses:

> *Tell the people of Israel to bring you **twelve wooden staffs, one from each leader of Israel's ancestral tribes**, and inscribe each leader's name on his staff. Inscribe **Aaron's name on the staff of the tribe of Levi**, for there must be one staff for the leader of each ancestral tribe. **Place these staffs in the Tabernacle in front of the Ark** containing the tablets of the Covenant, where I meet with you. **Buds will sprout on the staff belonging to the man I choose**. Then I will finally put an end to the people's murmuring and complaining against you."*
> (Nu.17:2-5 NLT)

The reason for the staffs was to seek knowledge as to whom God had chosen to lead Israel. Aaron's staff budded, proving once and for all that Moses and Aaron were chosen by God to lead Israel. The staff produced branches, leaves, buds, blossoms, and almonds all in one night. The gold lampstand did not have almonds but had lamps that were made in the shape of almond blossoms. These blossoms held the oil that produced the light and illuminated the Holy Place. Blossoms hold the promise of fruit but are not the fruit itself.

The lampstand represented our intellect. The Spirit gave the disciples an understanding of the prophecies of Christ before His ascension. This was given to their intellect in order to accept that Jesus was the true God. This knowledge also enlightens our whole being, leading us to be born again and is the **means of gaining** all that is promised through Christ. However, this knowledge is but the start of all that God has promised. Not only were blossoms (the promise of fruit) present in Aaron's staff, but almonds (the fulfillment of promise) were also present. The almonds symbolized the fulfillment of the promise to **know** God—not to just know about God. Aaron's staff that produced almonds represented the rebirth of our spirit with the faculty of intuition so that we might know God:

> And they shall not teach, each one his neighbor and each one his brother, saying, "Know the Lord," **for they shall <u>all know me</u>, from <u>the least</u> of them to <u>the greatest</u>.** (He.8:11 ESV)

INTUITION

A born-again Christian uses his spirit's intuition instead of using his soul's intellect. By definition *intellect* is "the ability to reason or understand." However, the definition for *intuition* is "the immediate, instinctive knowledge of something—without the conscious use of reasoning." Everyone is born with a different level of intellect; however, we are not born with spiritual intuition. Intuition is given when we are born again by the Holy Spirit Who gives life to our spirit. An excellent example of the effectiveness of intuition is the Ethiopian eunuch:

> And when Philip had run up, he heard him reading Isaiah the prophet, and said, "Do you understand what you are reading?" And he said, **"Well, how could I, unless someone guides me?"** And he invited Philip to come up and sit with him. (Ac.8:30-31 NASB)

When Philip approached, the eunuch could not understand the Scripture by his intellect and asked Philip to teach him. Phillip instructed him about Christ. When they came to water deep enough, he was baptized:

> Then both Philip and the eunuch went down into the water and Philip baptized him. When they came up out of the water, **the Spirit of the Lord <u>suddenly took Philip away</u>**, and the eunuch did not see him again, but went on his way rejoicing. (Ac.8.38-39 TNIV)

We would think that it would be practical for Philip to continue with the eunuch to Ethiopia and to teach him further about Christianity, but the Holy Spirit took Philip away. From God's perspective, the Holy Spirit's gift of intuition was more important than a "physical mentor." The Ethiopian eunuch was but an infant in Christ. When his spirit became one with the Holy Spirit, the eunuch was given spiritual intuition. The Old Testament with spiritual intuition was enough to ensure the eunuch's growth.

The Scriptures speak of spiritual maturity in terms of physical stages of maturity: infants, children, young men, and fathers. Paul used the terms of physical birth to address the process of spiritual rebirth:

> My little children, for whom **I am again in the pain of childbirth until Christ is formed in you**, I wish I were present with you now and could change my tone, for **I am perplexed about you**. (Ga.4:19-20 NRSV)

Paul was perplexed by the Galatians; were they or weren't they saved? Today people have made a commitment to Christ, and yet, they do not seem to grow. To claim to be a Christian and yet not conform to the character of Christ causes one to question whether faith is genuine:

> Brothers, **I could not address you as spiritual** but as worldly—**mere infants in Christ**. *I gave you milk*, not solid food, for you were not yet ready for it. Indeed, you are still not ready. **You are still worldly**. (1Co.3:1-3 NIV)

Many people attend church every Sunday, but their life does not reflect Christ living in them. People cannot reflect something that they do not possess. Two types of people are in the church: born-again Christians who learn from the Spirit and church-goers who are dependent on being spoon-fed from the pulpit. The Scriptures distinguish between the two:

> In fact, though by this time **you ought to be teachers**, you need **someone to teach you the elementary truths** of God's word all over again. You need milk, not solid food! Anyone who lives on milk, **being still an infant, is not acquainted with the teaching about righteousness.** (He.5:12-13 NIV)

It is very difficult to discern an infant in Christ from a religious person who is void of the Holy Spirit. The Scriptures warn that if you continue to live by the intellect of the soul, you do not have the Holy Spirit:

> In the last times there will be scoffers who will follow their own ungodly desires." **These are the men who divide you, who follow mere natural instincts** and **do not have the Spirit**. (Jude 1:18-19 NIV)

Church-goers know what to say to sound spiritual, but they do not reflect Christ in their daily walk. The only way any person will know the transforming truths of God's Word is through the Holy Spirit's revealing of those truths to them:

> But the **natural man does not receive the things of the Spirit of God**, for they are foolishness to him; nor can he know them **because they are spiritually discerned**. (1Co.2:14 NKJV)

Only those who are spiritually born again can discern the deeper things of God that will transform a person's life.

All born-again Christians start as infants but continue to mature to become children:

> *I write to you, dear children, because **your sins have been forgiven on account of his name**... I have written to you, children, because **you know the Father**.* (1Jn.2:12&13 NASB)

Spiritual children know Who their Father in heaven is and have been forgiven by the blood of Jesus. However, a child does not stop growing—he either grows or dies. Spiritual children need to study God's Word so that they can grow spiritually:

> ***Like newborn infants**, long for **the pure spiritual milk**, that **by it you may grow up to salvation**—if indeed you have tasted that the Lord is good.* (1Pe.2:2-3 ESV)

The chief reason why a born-again Christian remains a spiritual child is because he refuses to study God's Word, the Bible:

> *Rather, **you must grow** in the **grace** and **knowledge** of our Lord and Savior Jesus Christ.* (2Pe.3:18 NLT)

As spiritual children study God's Word, they become aware of God's promises and mature into young men.

Young men do not merely study the Scriptures; they have God's living Word within them:

> *I write to you, **young men**, because you are strong, and **the word of God lives in you**, and you have overcome the evil one.* (1Jn.2:14 NIV)

Natural man can read the Scriptures and attempt to understand them, but a spiritual young man has the Word of God living in him. The living Word of God is God's revelation to man by the Holy Spirit, which is far more extensive than what the Old Testament prophets experienced:

> *Above all, you must realize that no prophecy in Scripture ever came from the prophet's own understanding, or from human initiative. No, those prophets were **moved by the Holy Spirit, and they spoke from God**.* (2Pe.1:20-21 NLT)

When Christ lives in us, we have the living Word of God within us:

> *In the beginning was **the Word**, and **the Word** was with God, and **the Word** was God... And **the Word** became flesh and dwelt among us, and we*

have seen his glory, glory as of **the only Son** from the Father, full of grace and truth. (Jn.1:1&14 ESV)

Jesus is the living Word of God, God's interactive revelation to man. The living Word of God speaks to hearts, that we may know God. A person does not become born again because he studies the Scriptures. The Pharisees thought the Scriptures gave life:

> You **study the Scriptures diligently** because you think that **in them you possess eternal life**. (Jn.5:39 TNIV)

Only when the Holy Spirit gives life to our spirit does the living Word of God reveal Himself to our heart:

> You **have been born again**, not of perishable seed, but of imperishable, **through the living and enduring word of God**. (1Pe.1:23 TNIV)

The Spirit gives birth to our spirit; He opens our heart to understand the Gospel. Salvation is not an intellectual realization but a spiritual revelation:

> The gospel came to you **not in word only**, but also **in power** and **in the Holy Spirit** and **with full conviction**; just as you know what kind of persons we proved to be among you for your sake. (1Th.1:5 NRSV)

The Holy Spirit gives life to the Scriptures, empowering them to speak to our spirit. When Jesus lived on earth, He was God's revelation to man. Now that He has ascended into heaven, His Spirit is God's revelation to man. A spiritual young man has learned to discern what comes from his soul's intellect and what is revealed to him by the Holy Spirit through his spirit's intuition:

> For **the word of God is living and active** and sharper than any two-edged sword, and piercing as far as **the division of soul and spirit**, of both joints and marrow, and **able to judge the thoughts and intentions of the heart**.
> (He.4:12 NASB)

Since a spiritual young man has the Word of God living in him, he is taught by the Holy Spirit as he continues to mature to become a father of the faith.

The spiritual fathers are those who are spiritually mature in Christ and who walk with God and know Him:

> I am writing to you, fathers, because **you know Him who has been from the beginning**. (1Jn.2:13 NASB)

The spiritually-mature have come to the realization that the Christian life is more than the accumulation of knowledge. The Christian life includes the intimacy of knowing God. If Christ lives in us, then His Spirit will give us an understanding of His transforming truths:

> We do, however, speak **a message of wisdom among the mature**, but not the wisdom of this age or of the rulers of this age, who are coming to nothing. No, we **speak of God's secret wisdom**, a wisdom that has been hidden and that God **destined for our glory before time began**. (1Co.2:6-7 NIV)

Every born-again Christian has the faculties to access the living Word of God, but many have never been taught how to utilize their intuition. They continue to operate as they did before being born again—by their soul's intellect:

> But solid food is **for the mature**, for those **who have their powers of discernment trained by constant practice** to distinguish good from evil. (He.5:14 ESV)

The fathers of the faith constantly discern truth by their spirit. They know the principles that enable a believer to do what is right. They are equipped to disciple those who are struggling with sin:

> **If someone is caught in a sin**, you who are **spiritual** should restore him gently. But watch yourself, or you also may be tempted. (Ga.6:1 NIV)

Fathers of the faith are not exempt from temptation. Since Jesus was tempted, mature believers will also continue to have temptations and trials. However, they do not fall but instead are trained by their trials. Their intimacy with God enables them to walk through trials and maintain victory:

> My brothers and sisters, **whenever you face trials of any kind, consider it nothing but joy**, because you know that the testing of your faith produces endurance; and let endurance have **its full effect**, so that **you may be mature and complete, lacking in nothing**. (Ja.1:2-4 NRSV)

Christians grow in their ability to be taught by the Spirit and become mature, reflecting the fullness of Christ:

> ... until we all reach unity in the faith and **in the knowledge of the Son of God** and become **mature**, attaining to **the whole measure of the fullness of Christ**. (Eph.4:12-13 TNIV)

Every born-again Christian has the potential to mature to a father of the faith if he is taught by the Holy Spirit through his spirit's intuition.

Spiritual Revelation

A born-again Christian is not omniscient but has the ability to draw from God's omniscience to receive the knowledge he needs. An example of spiritual intuition is seen in evangelism:

> I pray that you may **be active in sharing your faith**, so that you will have **a full understanding of every good thing** we have in Christ. (Phm.1:6 NIV)

The reason evangelism helps us gain a fuller understanding of all that we have in Christ is because people ask questions that we have never considered. Our spiritual intuition needs to reveal the answer. In the same way, Jesus said that what He taught the disciples was just the basics; the Holy Spirit would later reveal all that they needed to know:

> "I have much more to say to you, **more than you can now bear**. But when he, the **Spirit of truth**, comes, **he will guide you into all the truth**. He will not speak on his own; he will speak only what he hears, and he will tell you what is yet to come. **He will glorify me because it is from me that he will receive what he will make known to you**. All that belongs to the Father is mine. That is why I said **the Spirit** will receive from me what **he will make known to you**." (Jn.16:12-15 TNIV)

The Holy Spirit grants us the ability to understand God's truth. A spiritual man has learned to ask God for the wisdom he seeks:

> **If you need wisdom, ask our generous God**, and **he will give it to you**. He will not rebuke you for asking. (Ja.1:5 NLT)

The Bible does not command us to consult other people or commentaries to understand truth but, rather, to ask God. Paul did not encourage the Colossians to ask him questions, but asked God to fill them with knowledge:

> We have not ceased praying for you and **asking** that you may **be filled** with the knowledge of God's will **in all spiritual wisdom and understanding**, so that you may lead lives worthy of the Lord, fully pleasing to him, as you bear fruit in every good work and **as you grow in the knowledge of God**. (Co.1:9-10 NRSV)

Spiritual intuition is more than knowledge; it is knowing God from Whom we receive all needed wisdom:

> "No eye has seen, nor ear heard, **nor the human heart conceived, what God has prepared for those who love him**"—these things **God has revealed to us through the Spirit**; for the Spirit searches everything, even the depths of God. For what human being knows what is truly human except

> the human spirit that is within? So also **no one comprehends** what is truly **God's except the Spirit of God.** Now we have received not the spirit of the world, but **the Spirit that is from God,** so **that we may understand** the gifts bestowed on us by God. And we speak of these things in words not taught by human wisdom but **taught by the Spirit, interpreting** spiritual things to those who are spiritual. (1Co.2:9-12 NRSV)

Our minds are limited in their capacity to understand the things that are spiritual, for these truths cannot be physically observed. Since the spiritual can only be perceived through man's spirit, we need to be born again to have the complete understanding of what we have in Christ:

> My goal is that they may be encouraged in heart and united in love, so that **they may have the full riches of complete understanding**, in order that they may know the mystery of God, **namely, Christ**, in whom are hidden **all the treasures of wisdom and knowledge.** (Co.2:2-3 TNIV)

Intuition offers a complete understanding, for intuition is Christ-based and not knowledge-based. I am not suggesting that we are omniscient but that we will have a complete understanding of the knowledge needed:

> May the God of hope fill you with all joy and peace as you trust in him, so that you may overflow with hope **by the power of the Holy Spirit**. **I myself am convinced**, my brothers, that you yourselves are full of goodness, **complete in knowledge** and **competent to instruct one another**. (Ro.15:13-14 NIV)

Born-again Christians are complete in knowledge because the Holy Spirit is all-knowing. Church-goers continue to use their intellect to study Christianity, in a similar way that one would study geology or history; however, born-again Christians utilize spiritual intuition by asking God to reveal His truth. Born-again Christians will excel in their knowledge of God:

> But **as you excel in everything**—in faith, in speech, **in knowledge**, in all earnestness, and in our love for you—see that you excel in this act of grace also. (2Co.8:7 ESV)

Spiritual knowledge was never based on our intellect but on our humility. We must humbly come to God and talk to Him about the Scriptures:

> At that time Jesus said, "I thank you, Father, Lord of heaven and earth, because you have **hidden these things from the wise** and **the intelligent** and have **revealed** them to infants. (Mt.11:25 NRSV; Lk.10:22)

In fact, having above average intellect can be a hindrance, for the brilliant will try to analyze things rather than come to God. The simple have no choice but to seek God:

> *Not many of you were wise by human standards, not many were powerful, not many were of noble birth. But **God chose what is foolish in the world to shame the wise;*** (1Co.1:26-27 NRSV)

To try to understand the Scriptures by cognitive reasoning is counter-productive because the true knowledge of God comes through revelation:

> *I keep asking that the God of our Lord Jesus Christ, the glorious Father, may **give you the Spirit of wisdom and revelation**, so that you may know him better.* (Eph.1:17 TNIV)

Paul did not tell the Ephesians to be more diligent in studying the Scriptures in order to know about God, but, rather, Paul kept asking God to give the Ephesians the Spirit of wisdom and revelation. A mature Christian knows that his ability to comprehend God's Scriptures is a gift:

> *I always thank my God for you because **of his grace given you** in Christ Jesus. For **in him** you have **been enriched in every way**—with all kinds of speech and with **all knowledge**—God thus confirming our testimony about Christ among you.* (1Co.1:4-6 TNIV)

Shortly after Christ's ascension, the apostles were recognized by the Sanhedrin because of their spiritual intuition:

> *Now when they saw the boldness of Peter and John, and perceived **that they were uneducated and untrained** men, they marvelled. And they realized that **they had been with Jesus**.* (Ac.4:13 NKJV)

Every born-again Christian has spiritual intuition. However, many do not access it because they refuse to spend time with God in His Word. Spiritual growth is not by a cognitive process of the mind but by the revelation of truth though relationship:

> *Those who are **spiritual discern all things**, and they are themselves subject to no one else's scrutiny. For who has known the mind of the Lord so as to instruct him? "But we have **the mind of Christ**."* (1Co.2:15-16 NRSV)

Revelation is based on time spent with Christ. The Scriptures repeatedly state that the Holy Spirit is sufficient to teach His people:

> *But **you have received the Holy Spirit**, and he lives within you, so **you don't need anyone to teach you** what is true. For **the Spirit teaches you everything you need to know**, and what he teaches is true—it is not a lie. So just as he has taught you, **remain in fellowship with Christ**.* (1Jn.2:27 NLT)

Why do people listen to endless Christian programming instead of sitting at the Savior's feet? The Holy Spirit teaches us when we have our Bibles open and are in prayerful conversation with Him. God does not desire people to gain knowledge but to grow in relationship with Him:

> These things I have spoken to you while being present with you. But the Helper, **the Holy Spirit**, whom the Father will send in My name, **He will teach you all things**, and **bring to your remembrance all things that I said to you**. (Jn.14:25-26 NKJV)

The means by which we gain understanding is more important than the knowledge we gain. Christianity is about relationship. The Holy Spirit will remind us of what Jesus taught, and He will teach us all things.

Intuition is heavenly in its origin and holy in nature, which enables us to discern God's truth from Satan's deception:

> But you are not like that, for the Holy One **has given you his Spirit, and all of you know the truth**. So I am writing to you not because you don't know the truth but because **you know the difference between truth and lies**. (1Jn.2:20-21 NLT)

Soulical Christians (church-goers that live by the power of their soul) will always be in the church. They overlook the obvious teachings of the Scriptures and embrace "implied teachings" to support worldly trends:

> For the time is coming when people **will not endure sound teaching**, but having itching ears **they will accumulate for themselves teachers to suit their own passions**, and will turn away from listening to the truth and **wander off into myths**. (2Ti.4:3-4 ESV)

Spiritual Christians take the "explicit truths" and apply them to their lives. They then use the Scriptures to clarify anything implied. The church always experienced differing opinions among its members:

> First, I hear that there are divisions among you when you meet as a church, and to some extent I believe it. But, **of course, there must be divisions among you** so that you who have God's approval will be recognized! (1Co.11:18-19 NLT)

When I was young in the faith, I had been led astray by the "implied truth" taught by soulical teachers, and yet, the Holy Spirit revealed those Scriptures which exposed the heresy:

> Let **those of us then who are mature** be of the same mind; and if **you think differently about anything, this too God will reveal to you**. Only let us hold fast to what we have attained. (Php.3:15-16 NRSV)

God promises to reveal His truth to us, bringing those Scriptures to mind that expressly speak to each issue. God promises to give us the insight which will allow us to know what is truth:

> This is my prayer, that your love may **overflow more and more with knowledge and full insight** to help you **to determine what is best**, so that in the day of Christ **you may be pure and blameless,** (Php.1:9-10 NRSV)

Today, our world is changing with technology, and the issues we encounter are far different than what the disciples faced. Yet, the living Word of God will give us the understanding of God's will for our ever-changing culture:

> Therefore **every teacher** of the law who has been instructed about the kingdom of heaven is like the owner of a house who brings **out of his storeroom new treasures** as well as old. (2Co.11:6 NLT)

We need teachers and preachers who know God (from a depth of relationship) to make God's Word relevant. Today, the church seeks out great orators who know more about our culture than they know about the Scriptures. Paul wasn't an eloquent preacher, but he knew God:

> **I may be unskilled as a speaker**, but **I'm not lacking in knowledge**. We have made this clear to you in every possible way. (2Co.11:6 NLT)

Paul taught the truths that could transform people's lives:

> Paul, a servant of God and an apostle of Jesus Christ for the faith of God's elect and **the knowledge of the truth that leads to godliness**—a faith and knowledge resting on the hope of eternal life, which God, who does not lie, promised before the beginning of time, (Ti.1:1-2 NIV)

A born-again Christian teaches the transforming truths that will empower the people to live holy lives. The goal of knowledge is to be conformed to the character of Christ:

> May grace and peace be multiplied to you in **the knowledge of God** and of Jesus our Lord. His divine power has granted to us all things **that pertain to life and godliness**, through **the knowledge of him** who called us to his own glory and excellence, (2Pe.1:2-3 NASB)

Therefore, spiritual intuition enables us to understand the deeper truths of God, which we can transform us into the likeness of Christ.

THE WRITTEN WORD AND THE REVEALED WORD

I want to be clear. I am not suggesting that God will inspire new Scriptures or add to the canon of Scripture that is found in the New Testament. The inspiration **of** Scripture is totally different than spiritual revelation **through** the Scripture. A Biblical example of revelation is when Jesus asked His disciples who they thought that He was:

> He said to them, "But who do you say that I am?" Simon Peter answered, "**You are the Christ, the Son of the living God.**" And Jesus said to him, "Blessed are you, Simon Barjona, because **flesh and blood did not reveal this to you, but My Father who is in heaven.**" (Mt.16:15-17 NASB)

Peter thought he produced the correct answer, but Jesus was quick to point out that the Spirit revealed this truth to his mind. However, in the next instant when Jesus spoke about His death, Peter again speaks his mind:

> And Peter took him aside and began to rebuke him, saying, "**God forbid it, Lord!** This must never happen to you." But he turned and said to Peter, "**Get behind me, Satan!** You are a stumbling block to me; for **you are setting your mind not on divine things but on human things.**" (Mt.16:22-23 NRSV)

With his limited understanding, Peter spoke from dedication and love for Christ. Again Peter would have claimed that his words originated from himself. Peter did not realize that the thoughts were placed in his mind from an outward source. This time the source of his words was not the Spirit of God but, rather, Satan. Jesus did not address Peter but Satan when He said, "Get behind me, Satan!" Our thoughts can originate from God's Spirit, Satan, or our self. The Holy Spirit can reveal truth to us through our spirits. Satan can place thoughts in our mind such as temptation, fear, and doubt. Or, our thoughts can originate from our self when we use our natural intellect. The Bible teaches that we need to constantly discern the origin of our thoughts through the living Word of God:

> Indeed, **the word of God is living and active**, sharper than any two-edged sword, **piercing until it divides <u>soul from spirit</u>**, joints from marrow; it is **<u>able to judge</u> the <u>thoughts and intentions</u> of the heart**. (He.4:12 NASB)

The written Word of God divides, distinguishing that which is of the soul (natural intellect), that which is of the spirit (spiritual intuition), and that which is of Satan (spiritual deception):

> These people are false apostles. They are **deceitful workers who disguise themselves as apostles** of Christ. But I am not surprised! Even **Satan disguises himself as an angel of light**. So it is no wonder that **his servants also disguise themselves as servants of righteousness**.
> (1Co.11:13-15 NLT)

Satan masquerades as an angel of light to deceive and mislead the church. One day Paul met a slave girl who had spiritual power. She discerned that Paul and Silas were men of God who taught the way of salvation:

> Once when we were going to the place of prayer, we were met by a slave girl who had a spirit by which she predicted the future. She earned a great deal of money for her owners by **fortune-telling**. This girl followed Paul and the rest of us, shouting, "These men are servants of the Most High God, who are telling you the way to be saved." She kept this up for many days. **Finally Paul became so troubled** that he turned round and said to the spirit, "In the name of Jesus Christ I command you to come out of her!" **At that moment the spirit left her.** (Ac.16:16-18 NIV)

The slave girl intuitively identified Paul and Silas, and her proclamation was spiritually-correct. At first glance, one might wonder if the Spirit of God was speaking through this slave girl, for she was declaring a truth and endorsing the Gospel. However, Paul discerned the origin of the girl's knowledge and cast out the evil spirit. While it is true that God spiritually reveals truth to men, we cannot assume that every person who teaches a truth about God is from God. We need to test the spirit of the person:

> Beloved, **do not believe every spirit**, but **test the spirits, whether they are of God;** because many false prophets have gone out into the world.
> (1Jn.4:1 NKJV)

The Living Word of God will never reveal to our heart anything that will contradict the written Word of God—the Bible. All of the words contained within the Scripture are from an eternal, unchangeable God:

> Jesus Christ the **same yesterday**, and **to day**, and **for ever**.
> (He.13:8 KJV; Ja.1:17; He.1:11-12; 1Sa.15:29)

Since God does not change, His words are as applicable to the church today as they were 2000 years ago:

> Heaven and earth will pass away, but **My words will by no means pass away**. (Mt.24:35 NKJV; 1Pe.1:25)

The New Testament was inspired by the Holy Spirit with the authority of our Lord Jesus. The Word of God is for the church across all centuries:

> We **instructed you how to live in order to please God**, as in fact you are living. Now we ask you and urge you in the Lord Jesus to do this more and more. For you **know what <u>instructions we gave you by the authority of the Lord Jesus</u>**... For God did not call us to be impure, but to live a holy life. Therefore, **he who rejects this instruction does not reject man but God, who gives you his Holy Spirit**. (1Th.4:1-2, 7-8 NIV)

Since the Holy Spirit is the source of revelation and the author of the written Word of God, both will always agree because God does not change. Hence, we must stay within the confines of the Scriptures:

> Now, brothers, I have applied these things to myself and Apollos for your benefit, so that you may learn from us the meaning of the saying, "**Do not go beyond what is written.**" **Then you will not take pride in one man over against another.** (1Co.4:6 NIV)

When God reveals truth to our heart through our spirit's intuition, that truth will always align with the written Word of God. Without the written Word, we would not be able to distinguish if a revelation was God-given:

> **All Scripture is God-breathed** and is useful for teaching, rebuking, correcting and training in righteousness, **so that all God's people may be thoroughly equipped for every good work.** (2Ti.3:16-17 TNIV)

The New Testament, the written Word of God, is God's truth for the church. By His Word, we can judge the origin of our thoughts. The importance of having a written account is seen in business. Every business contract of significance is not only agreed to verbally but is also written. Once a contract is written and signed, it takes precedence over anything that might have previously been stated. This illustrates the importance of the written Word of God. The Bible contains the words of God:

> We also constantly give thanks to God for this, that **when you received the word of God that you heard from us**, you accepted it not as a human word **but as what it really is, God's word**, which is also at work in you believers.
> (1Th.2:13 NRSV)

Seldom did the apostles and prophets who wrote down the words of God hear an audible voice; rather, the words of God were revealed by the Spirit to their heart:

> But know this first of all, that **no prophecy of Scripture** is a matter of one's own interpretation, for no prophecy was ever made by an act of human will, **but men moved by the Holy Spirit spoke from God.** (2Pe.1:20-21 NASB)

These individuals who took dictation from God were incredibly aware of the Spirit's leading. They knew what was from God and what was from them. Paul, when answering the Corinthians' specific questions made a point to differentiate between that which came from God and that which originated from himself:

> To the married I give this command **(not I, but the Lord):** A wife must not separate from her husband.... To the rest I say this **(I, not the Lord):** If any

brother has a wife who is not a believer and she is willing to live with him, he must not divorce her. (1Co.7:10-12 NIV)

The writers of the Scriptures were keenly aware of how inspiration differed from their own cognitive processes. The Berean Christians knew that God would never contradict what He had written. Hence, when Paul spoke, they examined the Scriptures in order to discern the authenticity of the message:

> Now the Berean Jews were of more noble character than those in Thessalonica, for they received the message with great eagerness **and examined the Scriptures every day to see if what Paul said was true**.
> (Ac.17:11 TNIV)

Spiritual intuition does not make the Word of God obsolete. Rather, intuition is used to give understanding to the Scriptures. The Scriptures are used as the standard to judge revelation. Both are essential to ensure the authenticity of what was intuitively received.

REVELATION IN THE FACE OF OPPOSITION

We live in the last hours of the last day, and, therefore, Christians are experiencing a greater persecution. God promises to reveal wisdom to us in the face of opposition. Consider the following example. I once entered into a conversation which turned into a debate. As the discussion progressed, the Spirit gave me the Scriptures to defend the Word of God:

> When they bring you before the synagogues and the rulers and the authorities, do not worry about how or what you are to speak in your defense, or what you are to say; **for the Holy Spirit will teach you in that very hour what you ought to say.** (Lk.12:11-12 NASB)

Every time when error was spoken, the Spirit gave me a Scripture to explicitly contradict the argument. In the end, those who were listening knew what the Scripture taught:

> This will result in your being witnesses to them. But make up your mind not to worry beforehand how you will defend yourselves. For **I will give you words and wisdom that none of your adversaries will be able to resist or contradict.** (Lk.21:13-15 NIV)

When we stand up for the Christian faith, God will give us wisdom through our spirit's intuition to enable us to remain firm. Christians do not receive knowledge; rather, when we are born again, we receive Christ. He is the One Who speaks through us with His infinite knowledge:

> *On my account you will be brought before governors and kings as witnesses to them and to the Gentiles. But when they arrest you, **do not worry about what to say or <u>how to say it</u>.** At that time **you will be given what to say,** for it will not be you speaking, **but the Spirit of your Father speaking through you.*** (Mt.10:18-20 TNIV)

A spiritual man is controlled by the Spirit. When Christians are being tried for their faith, their words are not of themselves but are of the Spirit:

> *When they arrest you and hand you over, do not worry beforehand about what you are to say, but **say whatever is given you in that hour; for it is not you who speak, but it is the Holy Spirit."*** (Mk.13:11 NASB)

When persecuted for the faith, far too often we depend on a lawyer to defend us rather than trust God's promises. Consider what the Scriptures record concerning Stephen:

> *Some of those who belonged to the synagogue of the Freedmen (as it was called), Cyrenians, Alexandrians, and others of those from Cilicia and Asia, stood up and argued with Stephen. **But they could not withstand the wisdom and the Spirit with which he spoke.*** (Ac.6:9-10 NRSV)

God promises to give us the words to speak when judged by governments. However, that does not mean we will be set free, but that we will be a witness to them of Christ:

> *Behold, I send you out as **sheep in the midst of wolves**; so be **shrewd as serpents** and **innocent as doves**. But beware of men, for they will hand you over to the courts and scourge you in their synagogues; and you will even be brought before governors and kings for My sake, **as a <u>testimony to them</u> and to the Gentiles**.* (Mt.10:16-18 NASB)

Some of us are destined to go to prison. Some of us are destined to die. However, through the persecution, the Holy Spirit will ensure that Christ is lifted high:

> *If anyone is to be taken captive, **to captivity he goes**; if anyone is to be slain with the sword, **with the sword must he be slain**. **Here is a call for the endurance and faith of the saints.*** (Re.13:10 ESV)

Therefore, God speaks through our spirit's intuition. He will teach us His truth that will not only transform our life but also defend us when we give an account for what we believe.

Thinking It Through:

1. What are the similarities between the gold lampstand and Aaron's staff that budded? What is the significance of these similarities?

2. What are the differences in the stages of spiritual growth in regard to intuition?

3. What is the difference between "omniscience" and "complete in knowledge"?

4. How does a Christian appropriate the fullness of knowledge?

5. In regard to knowledge, what has God promised that the Holy Spirit will accomplish?

6. Why will the revealed Word of God never contradict the written Word of God?

7. What did or did not God promise for Christians who are placed on trial?

8. How have you experienced your spirit's function of intuition?

The Two Stone Tablets

I went up the mountain. I went there to receive the tablets of the covenant. They were made out of stone. It was the covenant the LORD had made with you. I stayed on the mountain for 40 days and 40 nights. I didn't eat any food or drink any water. The LORD gave me two stone tablets. The words on them were written by the finger of God. All of the commandments the LORD gave you were written on the tablets. He announced them to you out of the fire on the mountain. He wrote them on the day you gathered together there. The 40 days and 40 nights came to an end. Then the LORD gave me the two stone tablets. They were the tablets of the covenant.

Deuteronomy 9:9-11 NIrV

F.W. McCleave 1877

LESSON 12

THE TWO STONE TABLETS

THE STONE TABLETS

The two stone tablets that were placed in the ark of the covenant represented God's laws which He writes on the conscience of man's heart. God made a covenant with Israel that, if they would keep the terms of the covenant, God would bless them. God first proclaimed the terms of the covenant audibly to the nation of Israel. Because God wanted to stress the unchanging terms of His covenant with Israel, He personally wrote them in stone. The stones are referred to as the tablets of the covenant:

> The LORD gave me the **two stone tablets** written with the finger of God; on them were **all the words that the LORD** had spoken to you at the mountain out of the fire on the day of the assembly. At the end of forty days and forty nights the LORD gave me the two stone tablets, **the tablets of the covenant.** (De.9:10-11 NRSV)

Many Jews and Christians do not realize that only those things written on the two stone tablets were the terms of the covenant—ten commands:

> And the LORD spoke to you out of the midst of the fire. You heard the sound of the words, but saw no form; you only heard a voice. So He declared to you **His covenant which He commanded you to perform, the Ten Commandments**; and He wrote them on **two tablets of stone.** (De.4:12-13 NASB)

Even though there were many other laws, Israel needed to only keep the Ten Commandments to be considered faithful to God's covenant. God wrote the terms of the covenant in stone, but Israel had to apply them to their life by their own determination. As with most contracts, there is a penalty for violation of the contract; similarly, there was a penalty for breaking God's covenant:

> Thus says the LORD God of Israel: "**Cursed is the man who does not obey the words of this covenant** which I commanded your fathers in the day I brought them out of the land of Egypt, from the iron furnace, saying, 'Obey

*My voice, and **do according to all that I command you**; so shall you be My people, and I will be your God,'"* (Jer.11:3-4 NKJV)

If Israel broke God's covenant, God did not have to honor His promises but could inflict the stated penalty. The Old Testament historical record proved that Israel could not keep God's covenant of law:

*For thus says the Lord GOD, "I **will also do with you as you have done**, you who have despised the oath by **breaking the covenant**."* (Eze.16:59 NASB)

The ten tribes, called Israel, were banished from the Promised Land and were never to return as tribes. The two remaining tribes, called Judah, were sent into exile in Babylon for 70 years, after which they returned to the Promised Land. Because of Israel's and Judah's failure to keep the covenant, God promised to make a new covenant with them. He promised that one day He would give Israel and Judah a new heart and a new spirit:

*"The time is coming," declares the LORD, "when I **will make a new covenant** with the house of Israel and with the house of Judah. It will **not be like the covenant I made with their forefathers** when I took them by the hand to lead them out of Egypt, **because they broke my covenant**, though I was a husband to them," declares the LORD. "This is the covenant that I will make with the house of Israel after that time," declares the LORD. "**I will put my law in their minds and write it on their hearts**. I will be their God, and they will be my people."* (Jer.31:31-33 NIV)

Therefore, God promised a new covenant with His people in which He would write His laws on their heart, making the former covenant obsolete.

COMPARING THE OLD WITH THE NEW

Israel could not keep their covenant with God because their heart was hardened by their sin. To be obedient, Israel needed a new heart. In a previous lesson, we already considered that God purified man's heart:

***God, who knows the heart**, acknowledged them by giving **them the Holy Spirit**, just as He did to us, and made no distinction between us and them, **purifying their hearts by faith**.* (Ac.15:8-9 NKJV)

The giving of a new heart and the purifying of a heart are actually one in the same event. The difference between our experience with a new heart and Israel's experience with an evil heart is so diverse that it required the establishment of a new covenant with new terms which were implemented through Christ:

THE TWO STONE TABLETS LESSON 12

> *But the ministry Jesus has received is as superior to theirs **as the covenant of which he is mediator is superior to the old one**, and it is founded on better promises. For if there had been **nothing wrong with that first covenant**, no place would have been sought for another. But **God found fault with the people** and said: "The time is coming, declares the Lord, when I will make a new covenant with the house of Israel and with the house of Judah. It will **not be like the covenant** I made with their forefathers when I took them by the hand to lead them out of Egypt, because they did not remain faithful to my covenant, and I turned away from them, declares the Lord."* (He.8:6-9 NIV)

The failure of the first covenant was the people of Israel. The law was written on stone and needed to be applied to their heart, but their heart was hardened by their sinful nature. Israel had to apply the law to their life from the outside in. In the new covenant, the Holy Spirit writes God's law on our heart and mind. Consequently, when a Christian looks into his heart to consider an action, he finds God's law written on his heart, which initiates obedience from the inside. The Spirit reveals more than what we should not do; He reveals what God desires us to do:

> *This is the covenant that I will make with them after those days, says the Lord: I will **put my laws in their hearts, and I will write them on their minds**.* (He.10:16 NRSV)

God writes His laws on our mind and, through our intuition, enables us to know His truth. God writes His laws on our new, pure heart and, through our conscience, enables us to know His will. The Jews consistently failed to keep the law because the law only made them aware of their sin:

> *Now we know that **whatever the law says**, it speaks to those who are under the law, so **that every mouth may be silenced, and the whole world may be held accountable to God**. For "no human being will be justified in his sight" by deeds prescribed by the law, **for through the law comes the knowledge of sin**.* (Ro.3:19-20 NRSV)

Before man's spirit was born again, the law exercised their conscience, which enabled them to recognize their disobedience, but the law did nothing to empower them to obey. If a man should break one of God's commands, his conscience would simply respond with a sense of guilt:

> *The law is only a shadow of the good things that are coming— not the realities themselves. For this reason it can never, by the same sacrifices repeated endlessly year after year, make perfect those who draw near to worship. If it could, would they not have stopped being offered? For the*

worshippers would have been cleansed once for all, and **would no longer have felt guilty for their sins.** (He.10:1-2 NIV)

Since Israel's spirit was deadened, man's conscience only sensed guilt instead of utilizing the conscience's original intent. The conscience was meant to function proactively—to reveal God's will. However, man's spirit died, causing separation from God. Hence, a Jew's conscience functioned reactively—sensing guilt when they did not do as God commanded:

> Jesus said, "If you were blind, you would not be guilty of sin; but **now that you claim you can see, your guilt remains."** (Jn.9:41 TNIV)

Without the law, mankind would have never known how depraved their nature was in comparison to the nature of God. The conscience of natural man was referred to as being corrupted because it was only sensitized to God's disapproval as exercised through the law:

> To the pure all things are pure, **but to the corrupt and unbelieving** nothing is pure. **Their very minds and <u>consciences are corrupted</u>**. They profess to know God, but **they deny him by their actions**. They are detestable, disobedient, unfit for any good work. (Ti.1:15 NRSV)

Man's conscience was corrupted, unable to discern the will of God. Only through Christ can our conscience be cleansed of corruption. The Holy Spirit is the only One Who gives life to our spirit and restores the conscience's intended state:

> The blood of goats and bulls and the ashes of a heifer sprinkled on those **<u>who are ceremonially unclean</u>** sanctify them so that they are **outwardly clean**. How much more, then, will **the blood of Christ**, who through the eternal **Spirit** offered himself unblemished to God, **<u>cleanse our consciences</u> from acts that lead to death, so <u>that we may serve the living God</u>!** (He.9:13-14 NIV)

Under the law, mankind's corrupted conscience was merely appeased by the animal sacrifices, for animal sacrifices could only offer a ceremonial cleansing. In fact, by offering the sacrifices to God, mankind was admitting their guilt for sin and their need for God's ultimate sacrifice—Christ:

> For the worshipers would have been cleansed once for all, and **would no longer have <u>felt guilty for their sins</u>**. But those **sacrifices are an annual <u>reminder of sins</u>**. It is impossible for the blood of bulls and goats to take away sins. (He.10:2-4 TNIV)

Animal sacrifices could not restore man's conscience to its original state:

> By this the Holy Spirit indicates that the way into the sanctuary has not yet been disclosed as long as the first tent is still standing. This is a symbol of the present time, **during which gifts and sacrifices are offered that <u>cannot perfect the conscience</u> of the worshiper,** but deal only with food and drink and various baptisms, regulations for the body **imposed until the time comes to set things right.** (He.9:8-10 NRSV)

The conscience could only be restored when the accumulated record of a person's sin was cleansed and when his sinful nature, which sought to rebel against God, was eradicated. Only when we are cleansed from past sin and enabled to live a holy life are we able to enter a relationship with our holy God. This is central to the new covenant, which was given on Pentecost, when God sent the Holy Spirit to give life to man's spirit:

> **Repent,** and each of you **be baptized** in the name of Jesus Christ for the **forgiveness of your sins;** and **you <u>will receive</u> the gift of the Holy Spirit.** For **the promise is for you** and your children and for all who are far off, as many as the Lord our God will call to Himself. (Ac.2:38-39 NASB)

If we turn from our rebellion towards God (repent) and have our sin washed away in baptism, we will receive the Holy Spirit through Whom our conscience will be restored. Our spirit's faculty of conscience was created with the ability to know God's will when our spirit is given life.

For example, the conscience could be compared to a part of the brain. If the brain was injured in an accident, a person could be hindered from seeing. Every part of the eyes could still be fully able to function, but, because of the injury, the brain would not be able to fully interpret the messages from the eyes. All the person could perceive would be a faint, blurry light. In the same way, with man's deadened spirit, the conscience is incapacitated from connecting with God. The conscience is still functional in all its capacity (just as the eye and nerves were), but the problem is man's deadened spirit. Fallen man's conscience only felt the guilt when they sinned; however, the conscience was intended to sense God's will in all situations. In the new covenant, when our heart is purified, our conscience (an aspect of our heart) is also cleansed and restored to its full intent:

> Since we have a great priest over the house of God, let us draw near **with a true heart** in full assurance of faith, **with our hearts sprinkled clean <u>from an evil conscience</u>** and our bodies washed with pure water.
> (He.10:21-22 ESV)

Man's heart was purified and their conscience was made clean to enable them to discern God's will. In the comparison of man to the tabernacle, man's spirit is the Holy of Holies, their heart is the ark over which God dwelt, and their conscience represents the tablets of stone on which God writes His laws. By God writing His laws on our heart, we can know what God's will is through our conscience and have the desire to obey it because we have a new heart with a new nature.

THE PRELIMINARY WORK OF THE HOLY SPIRIT

When Christ came to earth, He was God born as a man. Through His life, we began to see exactly what God was like. It became apparent through Christ's life that God's standard of holiness went far beyond anything that we were called to by the law. Christ went beyond not offending His fellowman. His love and compassion was always manifested in His ministry to mankind. Jesus said:

> *If I had not come and spoken to them, they would not be guilty of sin; but now they have no excuse for their sin. Those who hate me hate my Father as well. If I had not done among them the works no one else did, **they would not be guilty of sin**. As it is, they have seen, and yet they have hated both me and my Father.* (Jn.15:22-24 TNIV)

Christ's teachings and life convict us of our sinfulness in comparison to His holiness. We realize our inadequacy to respond to God's call to imitate Him. Knowing about Christ does not diminish our feelings of guilt. Rather, it increases our guilt, for we are convicted of not possessing the same attitude of love that He had shown toward those around Him. The purpose of Christ's life is the same as the law, to make us aware of our sin and cause us to turn to Him in faith:

> *So **the law was put in charge <u>to lead us to Christ</u>** that we might be justified by faith. Now that faith has come, we **are <u>no longer under</u> the supervision of the law**.* (Ga.3:24-25 NIV)

Once we become aware of our self-centeredness and wickedness, the law becomes obsolete through our faith in Christ, for the law has achieved its intended purpose. A new and better way to live has been provided for us:

> *In the same way, my friends, **you have <u>died to the law</u> through the body of Christ**, so that you may belong to another, to him who has been raised from the dead **in order that we may bear fruit for God**.* (Ro.7:4 NRSV)

The guilt generated by our conscience through the law will never enable us to have a relationship with God. The law only proved that we did not have a relationship, to begin with. The Holy Spirit has replaced the law, giving life to our spirit and restoring our relationship with God. Through the Holy Spirit's union with our spirit, we can discern God's will in every situation through our conscience. In the new covenant, the Holy Spirit replaced the law:

> ...who also made us sufficient as **ministers of the new covenant, not of the letter but of the Spirit**; for the letter kills, **but the Spirit gives life**.
> (2Co.3:6 NKJV)

The Spirit gives life to our spirit, through which our conscience can directly discern the will of God. In this way, we no longer live by the law (what not to do) but by the Spirit, Who reveals what God's will is when we need to make decisions throughout our day:

> For when we were controlled by the sinful nature, the sinful passions aroused by the law were at work in our bodies, so that we bore fruit for death. But now, **by dying to** what once bound us, **we have been released from the law** so that **we serve in the new way of the Spirit**, and not in the old way of the written code.
> (Ro.7:5-6 NIV)

The law did not accomplish the righteousness that God required because it only convicted man after he sinned. The law never taught us the alternative to sin, which is to behave like God. Through the Holy Spirit, we are able to live beyond the standard of the law and to be empowered to attain holiness:

> For what **the law was powerless** to do in that it was weakened by the sinful nature, **God did** by sending his own Son in the likeness of sinful man to be a sin offering. And so he condemned sin in sinful man, **in order that the righteous requirements of the law might be fully met in us**, who do not live according to the sinful nature but **according to the Spirit**.
> (Ro.8:3-4 NIV)

When God displaced our sinful nature with His divine nature by His Spirit, He not only wrote His law on our heart, but He also cleansed our conscience from the desire to commit acts that lead to death. This enabled us to discern the will of God and desire to live lives that are pleasing to Him:

> The blood of goats and bulls and the ashes of a heifer sprinkled on those who are ceremonially unclean **sanctify them so that they are outwardly clean**. How much more, then, will the blood of Christ, who through the eternal Spirit offered himself unblemished to God, **cleanse our consciences from acts that lead to death**, so that **we may serve the living God**! (He.9:13-14 TNIV)

Our spirit's function of conscience works directly with our spirit's intuition. As the Holy Spirit reveals truth by intuition, our conscience discerns direction, and our heart is given the desire to apply that truth. Consider the Gentile believers who never knew the law:

> For when Gentiles who do not have the Law **do instinctively the things of the Law,** these, not having the Law, are a law to themselves, in that they show **the work of the Law written in their hearts, their conscience bearing witness** and their thoughts **alternately accusing or else defending them.** (Ro.2:14-15 NASB)

The Gentiles did not have the law, but once they accepted Christ, the Presence of the Holy Spirit worked in their renewed conscience. Their conscience was then able to discern the will of God, and their new divine nature desired to do the will of God. For this reason, the Gentiles' conscience defended them and gave them the assurance of their obedience to God's will. All born-again Christians walk in the confidence of the Holy Spirit's leading, for our conscience will either affirm that our actions are God's will or convict us of our disobedience. A Christian does not need to strive to make his conscience good. If Christ lives in him, he has already received a good conscience that is able to discern the will of God:

> Now the purpose of the commandment is love from **a pure heart,** from **a good conscience,** and from sincere faith... (1Ti.1:5 NRSV)

The Holy Spirit restores within us a good conscience and a pure heart. Through these two changes, we naturally discern and desire to do God's will. Our conscience senses God's will, and our heart desires to obey His direction:

> This command I entrust to you, Timothy, my son, in accordance with the prophecies previously made concerning you, that by them you fight the good fight, **keeping** faith and **a good conscience...** (1Ti.1:18-19 NASB)

To know what God wants us to do is not enough; we must desire to live according to our conscience. Our intuition's knowledge without the conscience's discernment and the heart's desire is ineffective. The Holy Spirit comes with deep conviction. He does not merely hint at the will of God but speaks clearly—giving one the confidence of His leading:

> For we know, brothers and sisters beloved by God, that he has chosen you, because our message of the gospel came to you not in word only, but also in **power and in the Holy Spirit and with full conviction...** (1Th.1:4-5 NRSV)

Full conviction came as the Spirit spoke to our conscience. Our corrupted conscience first convicted us of sin and our need for Christ. Our conscience is a part of our spiritual heart. Our heart drew us to believe in Christ, and, through Christ, our conscience is cleansed and moved to obedience in baptism:

> ...since we have a great priest over the house of God, let us approach with a true heart in full assurance of faith, **with <u>our hearts</u> sprinkled <u>clean</u> from <u>an evil conscience</u> and our bodies washed with pure water.** (He.10:21 NRSV)

The Holy Spirit's working through our conscience gave us the desire to respond in obedience to the command for baptism. Baptism is the response of a cleansed conscience. Baptism does not give one a good conscience but is the proof that a transformation has occurred from an evil conscience to a good conscience:

> ... this water **<u>symbolizes baptism</u>** that now saves you also--not the removal of dirt from the body but the **<u>pledge of a clear conscience</u>** toward God. (1Pe.3:21 TNIV)

The work of our conscience is not finished the moment we receive Christ. The Holy Spirit continues to work through our conscience to not only convict us of sin but to also reveal God's will, in order that we might live to please Him. The Holy Spirit's interaction with our spirit's conscience is far more perceptive than the law. The Holy Spirit judges not only our action through our conscience but also our thoughts and our attitudes:

> **For the word of God is living and active.** Sharper than any double-edged sword, it penetrates even to dividing soul and spirit, joints and marrow; **it judges the thoughts and attitudes** of the heart. Nothing in all creation is hidden from God's sight. Everything is uncovered and laid bare before the eyes of him to whom we must give account. (He. 4:12-13 NIV)

The law merely convicted us of wrong committed against our fellowman. However, the Holy Spirit convicts us of wrong thoughts, as well as of doing the right things for the wrong reasons—wrong attitudes. Christians do not only know when they have sinned, but they can also discern what is good, acceptable, and perfect through their conscience which is exercised by the Holy Spirit:

> Do not be conformed to this world, but be **transformed by the renewing of your minds**, so that **<u>you may discern what is the will of God</u>—<u>what is good and acceptable and perfect</u>**. (Ro.12:1-2 NRSV)

Therefore, once we are filled with the Holy Spirit, our conscience has been restored, and we no longer live by law. The Holy Spirit through our conscience enables us to discern when we sin, and also reveals to us the perfect will of God as we make decisions throughout our day.

A Good Conscience

Our regenerated conscience now has the ability to discern God's will, and our heart now has the desire to obey. Our spirit not only knows the will of God, but our spirit also grants us the assurance of being in the will of God:

> *Indeed, when Gentiles, who do not have the law, do by nature things required by the law, they are a law for themselves, even though they do not have the law, since they show that the requirements of **the law are written on their hearts, their consciences also bearing witness**, and their thoughts now accusing, now even defending them.* (Ro.2:14-15 NIV)

Our spirit's faculty of conscience will grant us the confidence of having done the will of God. The Spirit speaks through our spiritual faculty of conscience as clearly as the written words of the law on the tablets of stone spoke to Israel:

> *...you are a letter of Christ, cared for by us, written not with ink but **with the Spirit of the living God**, not on tablets of stone but **on tablets of human hearts**.* (2Co.3:3 NASB)

Unlike the ten commands which were written on stone and which Israel had to apply to their heart, God now writes His law on our heart by the Spirit. Born-again Christians internally discern what the will of God is: the good we ought to do or the bad which we ought not to do:

> *...everyone who lives on milk, being still an infant, is unskilled in the word of righteousness. But solid food is for the mature, **for those whose faculties have been trained by practice to distinguish good from evil**.* (He.5:13-14 NRSV)

We need to learn to discern as our conscience interacts with the Holy Spirit. This discernment is not reactive, making us aware that we have sinned. Rather, it is proactive, warning us of possible sin and thus allowing us to avoid it. Paul learned to discern through his conscience:

> *I am telling the truth in Christ, I am not lying, **my conscience testifies with me in the Holy Spirit**, that I have great sorrow and unceasing grief in my heart.* (Ro.9:1-2 NASB)

A born-again Christian lives in constant interaction with the Holy Spirit, and his spirit is always discerning all actions to maintain a clear conscience:

> Always be ready to make your defense to anyone who demands from you an accounting for the hope that is in you; yet do it with gentleness and reverence. **Keep your conscience clear, so that, when you are maligned, those who abuse you for your good conduct in Christ may be put to shame.** (1Pe.3:15-16 NRSV)

We must learn to trust the Spirit's direction by keeping our conscience clear of any violation through disobedience. Paul always lived according to the dictates of his conscience:

> I have the same hope in God as these people themselves have, that there will be a resurrection of both the righteous and the wicked. **So I strive always to keep <u>my conscience clear</u> before God and all people.** (Ac.24:15-16 TNIV)

Through the spiritual faculty of conscience, we can walk in the will of God continually. The Christian does not appease God through rituals, while claiming freedom to follow his own will. Rather, born-again Christians have the divine nature within their heart which desires to please God by following what the Holy Spirit reveals to their conscience:

> So whether we are at home or away, **we make it our aim to please him.** For we must all appear before the judgment seat of Christ, so **that each one may receive what is due for what he has done in the body,** whether good or evil. Therefore, knowing the fear of the Lord, we persuade others. But what we are is known to God, and **I hope it is known also to your conscience.** (2Co.5:9-11 ESV)

Living according to our conscience is God's method of revealing His will to our life. The conscience's purpose is not concerned with perfection, but direction. We strive to live to the dictates of the Holy Spirit, as did Paul:

> I care very little if I am judged by you or by any human court; indeed, I do not even judge myself. **My conscience is clear, but that does not make me innocent.** It is the Lord who judges me. (1Co.4:3-4 NIV)

We are not called to live according to other people's convictions. We are called to strive to keep our conscience clear. No matter our Christian maturity, once we are born again, we have the ability to know God:

> **None of them shall teach his neighbor,** and none his brother, saying, "Know the LORD," **for all shall know Me, from the <u>least</u> of them to the <u>greatest</u> of them.** (He.8:11 NKJV)

Whether we consider our self to be the least of all Christians or the greatest, our conscience is able to know God and discern His will. When we consider what to do in a situation, do we stop and listen to what our conscience discerns? After considering God's Word, we should never go against our conscience. Deacons were commanded to maintain a clear conscience:

> Deacons likewise must be men of dignity, not double-tongued, or addicted to much wine or fond of sordid gain, but **holding to the mystery of the faith with <u>a clear conscience</u>.** (1Ti.3:8-9 NASB)

Many times Paul met opposition from Christians who had good intentions. However, he knew that God was the One Who would judge him, and, consequently, Paul lived faithfully according to what he knew the Holy Spirit was revealing to his conscience:

> Pray for us; for **we are confident that we have a good conscience**, in all things desiring to live honorably. (He.13:18 NKJV)

Paul learned to trust his spiritual faculty of conscience and relied with confidence upon its leading:

> Now this is our boast: **Our conscience testifies that we have conducted ourselves in the world, and especially in our relations with you, in the holiness and sincerity that are from God.** (2Co.1:12 NIV)

Therefore, let us be able to agree with Paul: I strove to please God completely and never strayed from what the Spirit revealed to my conscience:

> While Paul was looking intently at the council he said, "Brothers, up to this day **I have lived my life <u>with a clear conscience</u> before God.**" (Ac.23:1 NRSV)

BORN-AGAIN CHRISTIANS LIVE BY THEIR CONSCIENCE

All Christians are called to obey the Holy Spirit's direction, but not all Christians are alike. Even though we are all on the same journey to become like Jesus in thought and action, we are all unique. We are all called to follow Jesus, but we are not all at the same level of maturity—we grow at different rates and in different areas. The question is not "Where are we when compared to others?" but, "Have we been obedient to the Spirit's direction in our lives?"

> The natural person does not accept **the things of the Spirit of God**, for they are folly to him, and he is not able to understand them because **they are spiritually discerned.** (1Co.2:14 ESV)

A person who does not have the Holy Spirit speaking to his conscience will need someone to tell him what is of God. His conscience, still deadened, will be without the ability to hear God. Not only knowledge is given by the Holy Spirit but also discernment to understand how to act upon the knowledge:

> And this is my prayer: that your love may **abound more and more in** knowledge and **depth of insight**, so that **you may be able to discern what is best** and may be pure and blameless for the day of Christ, filled with the fruit of righteousness that comes through Jesus Christ--to the glory and praise of God. (Php.1:9-11 TNIV)

The **unspiritual man** cannot discern from the Holy Spirit the will of God, and, therefore, he is dependent on preachers for direction. These unspiritual people will be easily deceived, for while they strive to serve God, they constantly rely upon men:

> The Spirit clearly says that in later times some will abandon the faith and **follow deceiving spirits and things taught by demons**. Such teachings come through hypocritical liars, **whose consciences have been seared as with a hot iron.** They forbid people to marry and order them to abstain from certain foods, which God created to be received with thanksgiving by those who believe and who know the truth. (1Ti.4:1-3 NIV)

There are many born-again Christians who remain spiritual infants. They have not been taught to live by their spiritual function of conscience and have not learned to discern. Consequently, these people have a weak conscience. This weakness causes them to follow man and be easily led astray by false teachings:

> Some, through former association with idols, eat food as really offered to an idol, and **their conscience, being weak,** is defiled.... For if anyone sees you who have knowledge eating in an idol's temple, will he not be encouraged, **if his conscience is weak,** to eat food offered to idols? And so by your knowledge this weak person is destroyed, the brother for whom Christ died. Thus, sinning against your brothers and **wounding their conscience when it is weak,** you sin against Christ. (1Co.8:7, 10-12 ESV)

The person described in the previous verse is born again; but, rather than trust in his conscience's leading, he continues to live by the principles of the law. The Holy Spirit working in our conscience is meant to replace the law. If, after studying the written Word of God, our conscience is not exercised concerning sin, we can proceed with complete confidence that our actions are in line with the Scriptures. For, the Holy Spirit has not revealed to us any reason to halt our current course of action:

> Eat anything sold in the meat market **without raising questions of conscience**, for, "The earth is the Lord's, and everything in it." If some unbeliever invites you to a meal and you want to go, **eat whatever is put before you without raising questions of conscience**. But if anyone says to you, "This has been offered in sacrifice," then do not eat it, **both for the sake of the man who told you and for conscience' sake—the other man's conscience, I mean**, not yours. For why should **my freedom be judged by another's conscience?** (1Co.10:25-29 NIV)

Even though as Christians we live by what the Spirit reveals to our conscience, our actions must be tempered by love. If another person's conscience will not permit him to eat certain food, then we must refrain from that act when in his presence; otherwise, we will be encouraging the other person to act against his conscience. The New Testament is not concerned about rules but about a personal relationship with God. Someone may not be allowed to do something due to his conscience, but that does not mean that he is spiritually immature. We cannot assume that we are more spiritually mature than another person. It could be that we have yet to learn something that the Holy Spirit has already taught him. We are called by the Holy Spirit to live up to what He reveals to our conscience:

> **Each of you should test your own actions.** Then you can take pride in yourself, **without comparing yourself to somebody else.** (Ga.6:4 TNIV)

The question is not "Liberal or conservative?" for either could be wrong. The question is "What does the living Word of God say to us as individuals—both the written and the revealed Word of God?" Are we being obedient to what the Holy Spirit is saying to our conscience? Let us be challenged to study God's Word, which equips our spirit to discern through the Holy Spirit what God wills for us in every decision:

> **So whatever you believe about these things keep between yourself and God.** Blessed is the man who does not condemn himself by what he approves. (Ro.14:22 NIV)

We need the Scriptures and should constantly study them so that the Holy Spirit can bring to mind the Scriptural principles that apply to the current situation. The spoken Word of God will always use the written Word of God to confirm the direction of our actions:

> *For everyone who partakes only of milk is not accustomed to the word of righteousness, for he is an infant.* **But solid food is for the mature,** *who because of practice* **have their senses trained to discern good and evil.**
> (He.5:13-14 NASB)

As we considered in our last lesson, the Holy Spirit will not direct us to do something contrary to the written Word of God because He imparts truth through the written Word:

> *And this is my prayer, that your love may overflow more and more with knowledge and* **full insight** *to help you* **to determine what is best...**
> (Php.1:9 NRSV)

As we study the Word of God, we are instilling the truth which will enable us to discern the will of God—our spirit's intuition working with our spirit's conscience. The Holy Spirit brings to mind those things which relate to the situations we face. The knowledge and discernment of God work together so that we can know His will when making a decision. God did not give an explicit list of laws addressing every situation; rather, He gave us principles which the Holy Spirit uses to guide our conscience:

> *Now the purpose of the commandment is love from a pure heart,* **from a good conscience,** *and from sincere faith, from which some, having strayed,* **have turned aside to idle talk...** (1Ti.1:5-6 NKJV)

The actual purpose of the New Testament is to facilitate a relationship with God. Christianity is not about theology—a study of God. It is about the revelation of God alive and active in our lives. Denominations are concerned about everyone agreeing on the same creed—uniformity, but to live by conscience means that even though we will not all respond in the same way, we can trust the Holy Spirit's guiding—unity. Even with differences, there is only one truth. Therefore, we are each accountable to God for our actions:

> *In the first place, I hear that when you come together as a church, there are divisions among you, and to some extent I believe it.* **No doubt there have to be differences among you to show which of you have God's approval.** (1Co.11:18-19 NIV)

Since we live by what the Holy Spirit reveals to our conscience, the Scripture states that some differences are permissible—others are not:

> **The acts of the sinful nature** *are obvious: sexual immorality, impurity and debauchery; idolatry and witchcraft; hatred, discord, jealousy, fits of rage, selfish ambition, dissensions, factions and envy; drunkenness, orgies, and*

the like. I warn you, as I did before, **that those who live like this will not inherit the kingdom of God.** (Ga.5:19-21 NIV)

The sins listed in the previous verses are obvious and have eternal consequences. The Bible warns us to discern through our conscience every action. We must be aware of God's will in everything:

*Test everything that is said. Hold on to **what is good**. Stay away from **every kind of evil**.* (1Th.5:21-22 NLT)

A spiritual man is someone who has learned to discern through his conscience the will of God. We will never be perfect, but we must always strive for perfection, for a born-again Christian maintains a clear conscience:

*In view of this, I also do my best to maintain always a **blameless conscience** both before God and before men.* (Ac.24:16 NASB)

Therefore, our spiritual intuition and our spiritual conscience work together so that we can be complete in knowledge and able to discern the will of God.

WALKING BY THE SPIRIT THROUGH CONSCIENCE

Three definitions for sin are listed in the New Testament. The first definition summarizes the law of Moses:

All wrongdoing is sin... (1Jn.5:17 NRSV)

The law only dealt with sinful actions, and our conscience convicted us of sin. Under the law, if we ceased doing wrong to our fellow man, we fulfilled the law:

Love does no harm to a neighbor; *therefore love is the fulfillment of the law.* (Ro.13:NKJV)

However, love goes beyond the law and the Ten Commandments. The question is not whether we harmed our neighbor, but, rather, did we help our neighbor in their need? In the parable of the Good Samaritan (Lk.10:25-37), both the priest and the Levite kept the law when they walked past their fellow Jew who was hurt. Since they did not harm the man, they could walk past him and feel little remorse. Only the Samaritan loved his neighbor and, thereby, kept the law of Christ:

*A new commandment I give to you, that you **love one another**; as I have loved you, that you also love one another.* (Jn.13:34 NKJV)

The command of the new covenant is to love. This forms the second definition of sin:

> So then, if you **know the good you ought to do** and **don't do it, you sin.**
> (Ja.4:17 TNIV)

If we know what the Bible is asking but do not do it, we sin. The New Testament instructs us to do many good things, but we can only be in one place at a time. If I am visiting the sick, I am not feeding the hungry. If I am feeding the hungry, I am not sharing the Gospel. Christ said:

> "Then he will say to those on his left, '**Depart from me, you who are cursed, into the eternal fire prepared for the devil and his angels**. For I was hungry and you gave me nothing to eat, I was thirsty and you gave me nothing to drink, I was a stranger and you did not invite me in, I needed clothes and you did not clothe me, I was sick and in prison and you did not look after me.'" (Mt.25:41-43 NIV)

Since we can only do one thing at one time, it is important to know which one thing God wants us to do. Sometimes I know of three urgent needs; which do I do first? We need to discern through our conscience God's perfect will for our life in every situation. God's perfect will is to do only one of the many things in any given moment. This takes us to a third definition of sin:

> ... **whatever is not from faith is sin.** (Ro.14:23 NASB)

No matter what we want to accomplish for God, unless we have faith in the confidence of His leading in our conscience, it is sin. For example, I may know of two good things to be done, a hospital visitation (John) and visiting an unsaved neighbor (Sam). After choosing Sam, some people might question why I didn't visit John. In truth I could respond that God revealed that I should share the Gospel with Sam. Christians need to discern what God's will is specifically for them at any given moment. This goes beyond the big decisions of careers, marriage, and children, and encompasses all of the decisions of daily life. We could refer to this as walking by faith through the leading of our conscience:

> For in the gospel a righteousness from God is revealed, a righteousness that is by faith from first to last, just as it is written: "**The righteous will live by faith.**" (Ro.1:17 NRSV; Ga.3:11; He.10:38)

Some interpret this verse as "the righteous receive life by faith"; however, the verse states that we will live by faith, walking in the confidence of His leading through our conscience:

> We remember before our God and Father **your work produced by faith**, your labor prompted by love, and your endurance inspired by hope in our Lord Jesus Christ. (1Th.1:3 TNIV)

Christians should never act out of doubt or fear. God's purpose for all our life will always come with the confidence of His leading. God gives the faith to know what He desires:

> Such things promote controversial speculations rather than advancing **God's work—which is by faith**. (1Ti.1:4 TNIV)

Since Christ is the perfector of our faith (He.12), faith is the check and balance to the Scripture by which God directs His specific will for our life. We must not go beyond faith; rather, we must keep in step with faith:

> We have different gifts, according to the grace given us. If a man's gift is prophesying, **let him use it in proportion to his faith**. (Ro.12:6 NIV)

Without the surety of faith in His leading, even becoming a pastor or missionary is sin. If God desires anyone to act in any decision, He will grant him the faith to proceed. In this way, God uses faith as the means to direct our paths:

> With this in mind, we constantly pray for you, that our God may make you worthy of his calling, and that by his power he may bring to fruition your every desire for goodness **and your every deed prompted by faith**.
> (2Th.1:11 TNIV)

As we are prompted by our faith in our conscience to proceed, we also use our spiritual intuition to confirm this leading which agrees with the previous New Testament verses. If there is agreement, then we must acknowledge our actions as the will of God:

> Trust in the LORD with all your heart, and **do not rely on your own insight**. In all your ways acknowledge him, and he will make straight your paths.
> (Pr.3:5-6 NRSV)

God wants us to believe that He has a specific purpose for our life. We must trust that He will reveal that purpose as we listen to our conscience and follow its discernment. In conclusion, our spiritual function of intuition will teach us what we need to know, but the spiritual function of conscience will enable us to discern what God's will is in every situation.

Thinking It Through:

1. What do we know about the two stone tablets given to Moses?

2. How does the Holy Spirit replace the law?

3. What were the conditions of our conscience before and after being born again?

4. What can we learn from the fact that baptism is the pledge of a clear conscience?

5. What does it mean "to keep a clear conscience"?

6. How can there be differences among Christians with each still keeping a clear conscience?

7. What is the relationship between our faith and our conscience?

8. Since our intuition gives knowledge, what does our conscience give?

The Gold Jar of Manna

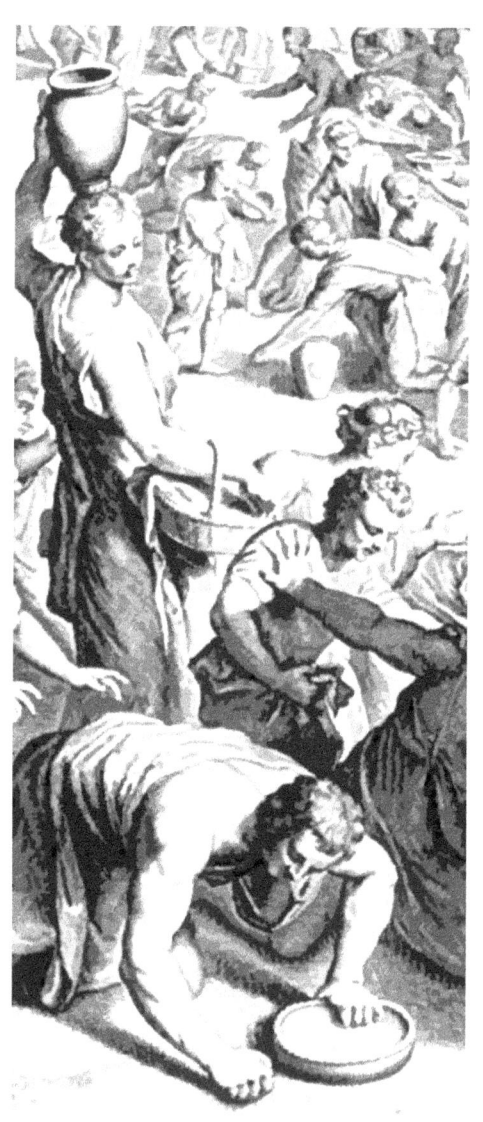

The people of Israel called the bread manna. It was white like coriander seeds. It tasted like wafers that were made with honey. Moses said, "Here is what the LORD has commanded. He has said, 'Get two quarts of manna. Keep it for all time to come. Then those who live after you will see the bread I gave you to eat in the desert. I gave it to you when I brought you out of Egypt.' " So Moses said to Aaron, "Get a jar. Put two quarts of manna in it. Then place it in front of the Lord. Keep it there for all time to come." Aaron did exactly as the LORD had commanded Moses. He put the manna in front of the tablets of the covenant. He put it there so it would be kept for all time to come. The people of Israel ate manna for 40 years. They ate it until they came to a land that was settled. They ate it until they reached the border of Canaan.

Exodus 16:31-35 NIrV

Figures de la Bible 1728

Lesson 13

The Gold Jar of Manna

What is it?

The final article in the tabernacle that we will be considering is the gold jar containing manna. During Israel's exodus from Egypt and shortly after crossing the Red Sea, the Israelites were in need of food:

> In the desert the whole community grumbled against Moses and Aaron. The Israelites said to them, "If only we had died by the LORD's hand in Egypt! **There we sat round pots of meat and ate all the food we wanted,** but you have brought us out into this desert to starve this entire assembly to death." Then the LORD said to Moses, "**I will rain down bread from heaven for you. The people are to go out each day and gather enough for that day.** In this way I will test them and see whether they will follow my instructions. **On the sixth day** they are to prepare what they bring in, and that is to be **twice as much as they gather on the other days.**" (Ex.16:2-5 NIV)

When the Israelites saw the flakes of bread on the ground, they asked, "What is it?" *Manna*, in a direct translation from Hebrew, means "what is it?" For six days a week, until they entered the Promised Land, manna was found on the ground. This food was sufficient to feed the entire nation of Israel. However, the bread that came down from heaven provided physical nourishment but had little spiritual effect on the people who ate it:

> For I do not want you to be ignorant of the fact, brothers, that our forefathers were all under the cloud and that they all passed through the sea. They were **all baptized into Moses** in the cloud and in the sea. They all ate **the same spiritual food and drank the same spiritual drink**; for they drank from the spiritual rock that accompanied them, and that rock was Christ. Nevertheless, **God was not pleased with most of them; their bodies were scattered over the desert.** (1Co.10:1-5 NIV)

Even though God was not pleased with the majority of the Israelites, He still provided for them. God commanded Moses to collect and keep a gold jar filled with manna in the ark as a reminder of His faithfulness, for He provided for the needs of His people:

> Moses said, "This is what the LORD has commanded: 'Take an omer of manna and **keep it for the generations to come**, so they can see the bread I gave you to eat in the wilderness when I brought you out of Egypt.'" So Moses said to Aaron, "**Take a jar and put an omer of manna in it. Then place it before the LORD** to be kept for the generations to come." As the LORD commanded Moses, Aaron put the manna with the tablets of the covenant law, so that it might be preserved. **The Israelites ate manna forty years**, until they came to a land that was settled; they ate manna until they reached the border of Canaan. (Ex.16:32-35 TNIV)

The manna in a pure gold jar reminded Israel of God's provision.

THE BREAD OF HEAVEN

Twelve cakes of unleavened bread were on the gold table in the Holy of Holies. Every week, the priests were commanded by God to replace the loaves with fresh ones; hence, they did the work. The changing of the bread by the priests represented the Old Testament relationship with God, in which Israel would serve God by their determination to keep God's law. On the other hand, the manna came down from heaven every morning six days a week for 40 years; hence, God did the work. Every morning the manna left on the ground would melt away with the rising sun. The daily provision of bread represented the New Testament relationship with God. The manna was physical food that sustained physical life. It represented Jesus as the living bread that gives spiritual life to men:

> **I am the bread of life.** Your ancestors ate the manna in the wilderness, and they died. This is the bread that comes down from heaven, so that one may eat of it and not die. I am **the living bread** *that came down from heaven. Whoever* **eats of this bread** **will live forever**; and the bread that I will give for the life of the world is my flesh. (Jn.6:48-51 NRSV)

Unlike the manna which physically fed the people of Israel, Jesus is the living bread—spiritual food for a spiritual person. Those who partake of Him are spiritually born again and will live forever:

> As the living Father sent Me, and I live because of the Father, **so he who eats Me, he also will live because of Me**. This is the bread which came down out of heaven; not as the fathers ate and died; **he who eats this bread will live forever**. (Jn.6:57-58 NASB)

When Jesus said that we must eat His body and drink His blood, He did not mean His actual physical body and blood. Jesus was referring to the Lord's Supper which He later was going to initiate:

> While they were eating, Jesus took bread, and when he had given thanks, he broke it and gave it to his disciples, saying, **"Take and eat; this is my body."** Then he took the cup, and when he had given thanks, he gave it to them, saying, **"Drink from it, all of you. This is my blood of the covenant,** which is poured out for many for the forgiveness of sins."
> (Mt.26:26-28 TNIV)

In the Lord's Supper, we partake of the unleavened bread and the wine, symbolic of the body and blood of Christ. Each piece of bread that is taken from the one loaf symbolizes our participation in the life and body of Christ—symbolic of His Presence within us:

> Is not the cup of blessing which we bless **a sharing in the blood of Christ?** Is not the bread which we break **a sharing in the body of Christ?** Since there is one bread, we who are many **are one body; for we all partake of the one bread.** (1Co.10:16-17 NASB)

The bread at communion is more than a mere ritual commemorating His death. The eaten bread is a reminder of the reality that Christ is living in us. When Moses took some of the manna and filled a gold jar, it did not melt away:

> ...the ark of the covenant overlaid on all sides with gold, **in which** were the **golden pot that had the manna**, Aaron's rod that budded, and the tablets of the covenant; and above it were the cherubim of glory overshadowing the mercy seat. (He.9:4-5 NKJV)

Even though the manna stopped being supplied once Israel reached the Promised Land, the manna in the gold jar lasted forever.

Before Jesus died on the cross, He tried to console His disciples about His departure by making a promise:

> **I will not leave you as orphans; I will come to you.** After a little while the world will no longer see Me, but **you will see Me;** because **I live,** you will live also. In that day you will know that **I am in My Father,** and **you in Me, and I in you.** (Jn.14:18-20 NASB)

Jesus promised to be with them by living in them. Just as Moses placed the jar of manna in the ark in the Holy of Holies, Christ sent His Spirit into our heart. Jesus is the bread that came down from heaven. Jesus lives permanently in the heart of born-again Christians:

*I pray that out of his glorious riches he may **strengthen you with power through his Spirit** in your inner being, so that **Christ may dwell in your hearts** through faith.* (Eph.3:16-17 TNIV)

The manna was placed in the gold jar which symbolized our purified heart:

*All of you who were baptized into Christ **have clothed yourselves with Christ**. There is neither Jew nor Gentile, neither slave nor free, neither male nor female, for **you are all one in Christ Jesus**.* (Ga.3:27-28 TNIV)

Once the Spirit came at Pentecost, the world became a dichotomy: those who are physically born of Adam and those who are spiritually born again by Christ:

*And so it is written, "The **first man Adam became a living being**." The last **Adam became a life-giving spirit**.* (1Co.15:45 NKJV)

Just as the manna in the gold jar came down from heaven, Jesus is the bread that came down from heaven. He gives us a new heart and a new spirit so that we will participate in His life.

HOLINESS BY COMMUNION

In the second chapter, we considered that the tabernacle was Holy. God warned that if anyone should enter the tabernacle in any way other than what was commanded by Him, the person would die. The first violation was committed by Aaron's two sons, who, as priests, offered incense to God in an unauthorized manner. Fire came from the Holy of Holies and killed them instantly. This is a warning for us. Since born-again Christians are the temple of God, we too are called to be holy:

*Do you not know **that you are a temple of God** and that the Spirit of God dwells in you? If any man destroys the temple of God, God will destroy him, for **the temple of God is holy**, and that is what you are.*
(1Co.3:16-17 NASB)

You cannot become the temple of God without becoming holy:

*Make every effort to live in peace with everyone and to be holy; **without holiness** no-one will see the Lord.* (He.12:14 TNIV)

We will never be perfect in this life, but we will always be in the process of progressive sanctification—the constant conforming to God's character:

*For by that one offering he **forever made perfect** those **who are being made holy**.* (He.10:14 NLT)

In the old covenant, Israel tried to live up to ten commands but consistently failed. They failed because they were trying to fulfill the law from the goodness within them. However, the jar that held the manna was made of pure gold, indicating that our holiness is a work of God:

> Don't you realize that **those who do wrong will not inherit the Kingdom of God**? Don't fool yourselves. **Those who indulge in** sexual sin, or who worship idols, or commit adultery, or are male prostitutes, or practice homosexuality, or are thieves, or greedy people, or drunkards, or are abusive, or cheat people—**none of these will inherit the Kingdom of God**. Some of you **were once** like that. But you **were cleansed**; you **were made holy**; you **were made right with God** by calling on the name of the Lord Jesus Christ and **by the Spirit** of our God. (1Co.6:9-11 NLT)

Who you were before accepting Christ does not matter; all that matters is that you were cleansed of your sin, made right with God, and are being made holy. All this is accomplished by the Spirit of God.

Possessed

The ability of a spirit to control a person and alter his attitude, behavior, and character is clearly seen in demonic possession:

> When Jesus got out of the boat, **a man with an evil spirit** came from the tombs to meet him. This **man lived in the tombs**, and no one could bind him anymore, not even with a chain. For he had often been chained hand and foot, but **he tore the chains apart and broke the irons** on his feet. **No one was strong enough to subdue him**. Night and day among the tombs and in the hills he would **cry out and cut himself with stones**.
> (Mk.5:2-5 TNIV)

This man's whole being was affected by the presence of demons. However, an extreme change took place when Jesus cast out the demons:

> Then they came to Jesus, and saw the one who had been demon-possessed and had the legion, **sitting and clothed and in his right mind**. And they were afraid. (Mk.5:15 NKJV)

Removing the evil spirits that controlled him altered every aspect of his life and brought instant and complete change. In the same way, if the Holy Spirit enters us, He will control us and move us to be changed in all areas of our life—we become holy like Him. Every born-again Christian has the Holy Spirit because God promised that His Spirit would be given if we come to Him as He commanded in the new covenant:

*"Repent and be baptised, every one of you, in the name of Jesus Christ for the forgiveness of your sins. And **you will** receive the gift of the Holy Spirit. The promise is for you and your children and for all who are far off— for all whom the Lord our God will call."* (Ac.2:38-39 NIV)

If we believe on God and come to Him in repentance and are baptized in obedience, God promises that we will receive the Holy Spirit. Before we believe on Christ, our sin separated us from God:

*Your iniquities have made a **separation** between you and your God, and **your sins have hidden his face from you** so that he does not hear.* (Isa.59:2 ESV)

A heresy is being taught today that God is within everyone. However, the Scriptures teach that the whole of humanity is born void of God:

*And remember that **those who do not have the Spirit** of Christ living in them do not belong to him at all.* (Ro.8:9 NLT)

If a person continues to live solely by his intellect, emotion, and will, he obviously does not have the Holy Spirit:

*These are the people who divide you, **who follow mere natural instincts** and **do not have the Spirit**.* (Jude 1:19 NKJV)

Once a person is born-again, Christ's Spirit enters him:

*And because you are children, God has sent **the Spirit of his Son into our hearts**, crying, "Abba! Father!"* (Ga.4:6 NRSV)

Many Scriptures support the fact that God has sent the Holy Spirit to live in every born-again Christian:

*Do you not know that **you are a temple of God** and that **the Spirit of God dwells in you**?* (1Co.3:16 NASB; Ro.8:11; 1Co.6:19; 2Ti.1:14; 1Jn.3:24; Jude 1:19)

Once we receive the Holy Spirit, God lives in us and we become His temple.

Our only hope of living eternally with God is dependent upon Christ living in us and controlling our life:

*To them God willed to make known what are the riches of the glory of this mystery among the Gentiles: which is **Christ in you, the hope of glory**.* (Co.1:27 NKJV)

The essence of Christianity is that Christ lives in us. The fact that Jesus was the fullness of God in human likeness is a tenet of the Christian faith:

*For God was pleased to have **all his fulness dwell in him**,* (Co.1:19 TNIV)

When we are born again, Christ's Spirit lives in us and becomes one with our spirit, and we receive all the fullness of Christ. Some people believe that Christ enters into a person in increments; however, the Holy Spirit is a Person. He is either in you, or He is not. If the Holy Spirit lives in you, you are full of His Presence. You cannot have a partial filling of His Spirit:

> For **in Christ all the fulness of the Deity lives** in bodily form, and **you have been given fulness in Christ,** who is the Head over every power and authority. (Co.2:9-10 NIV)

The question is never, "To what extent has the Holy Spirit filled you?" but rather, "Are you born again by the Holy Spirit living in you?" The goal of our spiritual growth is not the accumulation of knowledge. The goal is to become mature and display the full measure of Christ in our life:

> ...until we all reach unity in the faith and in the knowledge of the Son of God and **become mature, attaining to the whole measure of the fulness** of Christ. (Eph.4:12-14 TNIV)

Christian maturity is when we become all that Christ was. Someone said that it is not about **perfection** but **direction**—becoming like Christ. For example, the Scriptures teach that God is love. Since God lives in us, and He is love, we will love because He controls us:

> **God is love,** and the **one who abides in love abides in God,** and God abides in him. (1Jn.4:16 NASB)

If we display the agape love of God in our life, then we can be assured that we will have the other attributes of God's fullness as well:

> ...**to know the love of Christ** which passes knowledge; **that you may be filled with all the fullness of God.** (Eph.3:19 NKJV)

Many Christians desire to have God's fullness but want no part of His control. Since the fullness of God is contingent on the union of our spirit with God's Spirit, you cannot have fullness without the surrender of control. Again, consider love:

> **For the love of Christ controls us,** having concluded this, that one died for all, therefore all died; and He died for all, so that **they who live might no longer live for themselves, but for Him who died** and rose again on their behalf. (2Co.5:14-15 NASB)

When the Holy Spirit lives in us, we are empowered with the fullness of God because the fullness of God controls us:

> You have been set free from sin and **have become slaves** to righteousness... When you were slaves to sin, **you** were free from the control of righteousness... But now that you have been set free from sin and **have become slaves to God**, the benefit you reap leads to holiness, and the result is eternal life. (Ro.6:18,20,22 TNIV)

A born-again Christian willingly becomes a slave of God. Our first forefather, Adam, sold us into slavery to sin. Jesus came to save us from sin to enable us to live for God. You are either controlled by sin or God. Do not be deceived; you never did what you wanted:

> So I say, **live by the Spirit**, and you **will not** gratify the desires of the sinful nature. For the sinful nature desires what is contrary to the Spirit, and the Spirit what is contrary to the sinful nature. They are in conflict with each other, **so that you do not do what you want**. (Ga.5:16-17 NIV)

The only way that the Holy Spirit will live in us is if we lay our life on the altar by giving Him control of our life. Born-again Christians have willingly placed their lives under the control of the Holy Spirit:

> You **are controlled** by the Spirit **if** you have **the Spirit of God living in you**. (Ro.8:9 NLT)

If you do not have the Holy Spirit controlling you, then the Holy Spirit does not live in you. You cannot become a Christian without giving Christ ultimate control of your life:

> For you died, and **your life is hidden with Christ in God**. When **Christ who is our life** appears, then you also will appear with Him in glory. (Co.3:3-4 NKJV)

Christ's control is best summarized when we read:

> For "**In him** we **live** and **move** and have our being." (Ac.17:28 NRSV)

Born-again Christians know the key to living the Christian life. We live for God because He lives in us and controls us.

One of the gravest mistakes that a Christian can make is to think that he must change his life into God's holy character by his own determination. The Scriptures state that the same way that we became a Christian is the same way that we are to grow to become like Christ:

> So then, **just as you received Christ** Jesus as Lord, **continue to live in him**, (Co.2:6 NIV)

How did we receive Christ? By the Holy Spirit working in our life:

> *I would like to learn just one thing from you:* **Did you receive the Spirit by observing the law,** *or by believing what you heard? Are you so foolish? After* **beginning with the Spirit**, *are you now trying to finish by human effort?* (Ga.2:2-3 TNIV)

How are we going to transform our life? We are not! Just as we are saved by the Holy Spirit, we are also transformed by His control:

> *We are always thankful* **that God chose you** *to be among the first to experience salvation—a salvation that came* **through the Spirit who makes you holy** *and through your belief in the truth.* (2Th.2:13 NLT)

The Scriptural concept of predestination makes it obvious that God is the One Who makes us holy, for we were predestined to take on the character of Christ before we were born:

> *For whom He foreknew,* **He also predestined to be conformed to the image of His Son**, *that He might be the firstborn among many brethren.* (Ro.8:29 NKJV)

If we are predestined to be conformed to the likeness of Christ, then we must conclude two things: there is no salvation apart from our sanctification, and we did not transform our life to the holiness of Christ. Both were already pre-determined by God before the foundation of the world:

> **He chose us in him** *before the foundation of the world,* **that we should be holy** *and blameless before him.* (Eph.1:4 ESV)

Since God chose us before creation to be holy, our transformation is an act of God rather than an act of man's will. We became born again by the Holy Spirit giving life to our spirit. Through the bond of our spirit with God's Spirit, our life is transformed:

> *God the Father* **knew you and chose you long ago,** *and* **his Spirit has made you holy**. *As a result, you have obeyed him and have been cleansed by the blood of Jesus Christ.* (1Pe.1:2 NLT)

The Scriptures clearly state that the originator of the transformation of our character from wickedness to holiness is the Holy Spirit:

> *I bring you the Good News so that I might present you as an acceptable offering to God,* **made holy by the Holy Spirit**. (Ro.15:16 NLT)

Since the Holy Spirit is the One Who makes us holy, our responsibility is to humbly ask Him to do as He has promised:

> *Some of you were once like that. But you* **were** *cleansed;* **you were made holy**; *you* **were** *made right with God by calling on the name of the Lord Jesus Christ and* **by the Spirit** *of our God.* (1Co.6:11 NLT)

The past tense used in the previous Scripture makes the actions listed as an accomplished fact in the life of the believer. Born-again Christians gave control of their life to the Holy Spirit, and He overcame our sin:

> For if you live according to the sinful nature, you will die; but **if by the Spirit you put to death the misdeeds of the body**, you will live, because **those who are led by the Spirit of God** are sons of God. (Ro.8:13-14 NIV)

Let me state it simply: we become holy because the Holy Spirit controls us, and He is holy:

> As He who called you is holy, **you also be holy in all your conduct**, because it is written, "**Be holy, for I am holy**." (1Pe.1:15-16 NKJV)

From the moment we are born again, the Holy Spirit begins to manifest His character in our life—transforming us to be like Christ:

> My little children, for whom I am again in the pain of childbirth **until Christ is formed in you**, (Ga.4:19 NRSV)

Everyone who is born again has Christ being united with his life. Throughout the New Testament, the Scriptures refer to our lives as being "in Him":

> God made **him who had no sin** to be sin for us, so that **in him** we might become the righteousness of God. (2Co.5:21 TNIV)

Christ's Presence in our life is the power that transforms our life:

> You know that he appeared **to take away sins**, and **in him** there is no sin. No one **who abides in him** keeps on sinning; no one **who keeps on sinning** has either seen him or known him. (1Jn.3:5-6 ESV)

John states it simply:

> No-one **who is born of God will continue to sin, because** God's seed remains **in him**; he **cannot go on sinning, because** he has been born of God. (1Jn.3:9 NIV)

Through Christ living in us, we have received a new nature which changes our actions from our former sinful nature:

> Thus he has given us, through these things, his precious and very great promises, so that through them **you may escape from the corruption that is in the world** because of lust, and **may become participants of the divine nature**. (2Pe.1:4 NRSV)

Rather than bear the fruit of the sinful nature, we now have the fruit of our new divine nature, which is revealed in our character:

> But **the fruit of the Spirit** is love, joy, peace, patience, kindness, goodness, faithfulness, gentleness, and self-control. Against such things there is no law. Those who belong to Christ Jesus have crucified the sinful nature with its passions and desires. **Since we live by the Spirit, let us keep in step with the Spirit.** (Ga.5:22-25 TNIV)

If the Holy Spirit lives in us, then we will bear the fruit of righteousness:

> For you were once darkness, but now **you are light in the Lord**. Walk as children of light (for **the fruit of the Spirit is in all goodness, righteousness**, and truth), (Eph.5:8-9 NKJV)

God is the One Who will accomplish the transformation of our life:

> Now **may the God** of peace **make you holy in every way**, and may your whole **spirit** and **soul** and **body** be kept blameless until our Lord Jesus Christ comes again. **God will make this happen, for he who calls you is faithful.** (1Th.5:23-24 NLT)

No matter what temptation you face, God has promised to either protect you from being tempted or give you the strength to overcome:

> No temptation has overtaken you that is not common to man. **God is faithful, and he will not let you** be tempted beyond your ability, but with the temptation **he will also provide the way** of escape, that you may be able to endure it. (1Co.10:13 ESV)

God's promises are not erratic—to only strengthen us some of the time. He promises to strengthen us all of the time, until we die:

> He will also **strengthen you to the end**, so that you may be blameless on the day of our Lord Jesus Christ. **God is faithful**; by him you were called into the fellowship of his Son, Jesus Christ our Lord. (1Co.1:8-9 NRSV)

Therefore, our holiness is contingent on God's faithfulness. He controls us, and through His control, we begin to manifest His character:

> God is love. Whoever lives in love **lives in God, and God in them**. This is how love is made complete among us so that we will have confidence on the day of judgment: **In this world we are like Jesus.** (1Jn.4:16-17 TNIV)

A Christian has responsibility to walk in holiness. Walking in the Spirit is no different than walking on water. Consider the narrative of Jesus walking on water. The disciples had been in a boat rowing against a strong wind for hours when Jesus was about to pass by them, walking on the rough sea:

> And when the disciples saw Him walking on the sea, they were troubled, saying, "It is a ghost!" And they cried out for fear. But immediately Jesus

*spoke to them, saying, "Be of good cheer! It is I; do not be afraid." And Peter answered Him and said, "**Lord, if it is You, command me to come to You on the water.**" So He said, "**Come.**" And when Peter had come down out of the boat, **he walked on the water to go to Jesus.** But when he saw that the wind was boisterous, **he was afraid; and beginning to sink he cried out, saying, "Lord, save me!**" And immediately Jesus stretched out His hand and caught him, and said to him, "O you of little faith, why did you doubt?"*
(Mt.14:26-21 NKJV)

The wind and waves were raging when Jesus told Peter to come to Him on the water. Up to that point, no one had ever walked on water. Peter had to believe in Jesus and step out of the boat. In the same way, we might not know of anyone who lived a holy life, but the Scriptures clearly teach us that His Holy Spirit will make us holy. We need to step out each day, asking God to sustain us by His Spirit and enable us to live a holy life. Like Peter, some of us will take our eyes off of Jesus. Some of us will look at other Christians and see them sinking into sin. This could cause us to experience fear and doubt or to try to achieve what was promised by our own determination. If we try to live a holy life by our own effort, we will begin to sink into sin just like Peter sank into the water:

*You who want to be justified by the law **have cut yourselves off from Christ**; you **have fallen away from grace**. For **through the Spirit**, by faith, we eagerly **wait for the hope of righteousness**.* (Ga.5:4-5 NRSV)

To try to achieve a holy life isolates us from not only Christ but also His grace. Instead of trying, we need to rely on God's promises and call out to Jesus every day. He taught us to pray:

*And <u>**do not lead us**</u> into temptation, but <u>**deliver us**</u> from the evil one.*
(Mt.6:13 NKJV)

The normal Christian life is not to sin, but, if we are convicted by the Holy Spirit of sin, Jesus' death will cleanse us:

*My dear children, I write this to you **so that you will not sin.** But <u>**if anybody does sin**</u>, we have an advocate with the Father—Jesus Christ, the Righteous One.* (1Jn.2:1 TNIV)

When we are convicted of sin in our lives, we do not need to try harder or read our Bibles more often; rather, we confess our sin to God:

***If we confess** our sins, <u>**he** </u>is **faithful** and just <u>**to forgive**</u> us our sins and <u>**to cleanse**</u> us from **all unrighteousness**.* (1Jn.1:9 NKJV)

Man's responsibility is to come honestly before God and admit that we have sinned. God promises that He will forgive us our sin (forgiveness which is reactive), and He promises that He will cleanse us from all unrighteousness (removing our desire to sin which is proactive). Mercy deals with the past; while grace empowers us for the future:

> Let us then with confidence draw near to the throne of grace, that **we may receive mercy** and **find grace to help in time of need**. (He.4:16 ESV)

The question is not whether we can live a holy life, but, rather, is God faithful? For example, I once went to Texas for ministry. A friend offered me a stay at his house during my time in Texas. After confirming my plans, did I go on the internet to find which hotels could accommodate me and make reservations? Of course not! I believed that my friend would do as he promised. Jesus promised that His Holy Spirit will transform my life, and I walk daily in the confidence that He will do just that. We need to walk in the confidence that the Holy Spirit lives in us and will empower us not to sin:

> Now to **him who is able to keep you from falling**, and **to make you stand without blemish** in the presence of his glory with rejoicing, to the only God our Savior, through Jesus Christ our Lord (Jude 1:24-25 NASB)

A Christian's responsibility in overcoming sin is to humbly come to God and ask Him to do all that He has promised.

THE POWER OF COMMUNION

In the Old Testament, the priest had to enter the Holy Place once a week to change the twelve cakes of bread on the gold table. Born-again Christians have Jesus, the bread that came down from heaven. Like the manna in the gold jar, a Christian's living bread—Jesus—never has to be changed but will last forever. The difference between the table of showbread and the gold jar of manna is the *one* who does the work. The bread of the Presence had to be baked and then physically changed by the priests—a work of man. This represented that the law was attained by man's efforts:

> I gave them my decrees and made known to them my laws, **for the man who obeys them will live by them**. (Eze.20:11 NIV)

The manna that was put in the pure gold jar came down from God; it was received by Moses and then preserved by God forever—a work of God:

I will give you a new heart and put a new spirit in you; I will remove from you your heart of stone and give you a heart of flesh. And I will put <u>my Spirit in you and move you</u> to follow My decrees and be careful to keep my laws. (Eze.36:26 TNIV)

God promised to put His Spirit within man, Who would move them to keep His commands. This promise is not to just stop sinning. It is about doing what is right—the will of God. To understand how God's Spirit can move Christians to walk in obedience to the will of God is best understood in the relationship Jesus had with His Father:

Jesus said to them, "My food <u>is to do the will of Him</u> who sent Me, and to finish His work." (Jn.4:34 NKJV)

Jesus came to earth to do the will of His heavenly Father; however, we need to consider how He accomplished God's will. Jesus taught:

Anyone who has seen me has seen the Father. How can you say, "Show us the Father"? Don't you believe that I am in the Father, and that the Father is in me? The words I say to you I do not speak on my own authority. Rather, it is <u>the Father, living in me, who is doing his work</u>. (Jn.14:9-10 TNIV)

The Father, Who was living in Christ, was doing His work through Christ. Christ could do nothing on His own, for the Father worked through Him:

<u>I can of Myself do nothing</u>. As I hear, I judge; and My judgment is righteous, because I do not seek My own will but the will of the Father who sent Me. (Jn.5:30 NKJV)

Christians minimize the oneness of Christ with the Father and the Spirit, but there is an actual connection that existed because They are One Being. The absurdity of Jesus doing something apart from the Father's involvement could be seen in the statement, "My body decided to sleep longer than usual this morning." My body does not decide anything apart from my soul's involvement. In the same way, Jesus could do nothing apart from His Father's involvement:

Jesus said to them, "Very truly, I tell you, the Son <u>can do nothing on his own</u>, but only what he sees the Father doing; for whatever the Father does, the Son does likewise. (Jn.5:19 NRSV)

Jesus said multiple times that He lives in the Father:

On that day you will know that <u>I am in my Father</u>, and you in me, and I in you. (Jn.14:20 NRSV)

Jesus stressed the oneness between God the Father and Himself:

I and My Father are one. (Jn.10:30 NKJV)

You cannot separate Jesus from the fullness of God because They are One:

*For in Christ lives **all the fullness of God** in a human body.* (Co.2:9 NLT)

The fullness of God was in Jesus. Everything Jesus did was a reflection of the union Christ shared with His Father:

*Jesus said, "When you have lifted up the Son of Man, then you will realize that I am he, and **that I do nothing on my own**, but I speak these things as the Father instructed me. And the one who sent me **is with me**; he has not left me alone, for I always do what is pleasing to him."* (Jn.8:28-29 NRSV)

The Father was in the Son, but the Spirit was the connection between the two. Jesus, in quoting a prophecy of the Messiah, said of Himself:

*For **the one whom God has sent** speaks the words of God, for **God gives the Spirit without limit**.* (Jn.3:34 TNIV)

God the Father gave Jesus the Holy Spirit without limit. The Holy Spirit descended on Jesus when He was baptized by John the Baptist:

*When He had been baptized, Jesus came up immediately from the water; and behold, the heavens were opened to Him, and **He saw the Spirit of God descending** like a dove and alighting upon Him.* (Mt.3:16 NKJV)

Once the Spirit descended on Jesus, the Spirit controlled Him:

*Then **Jesus was led up by the Spirit** into the wilderness to be tempted by the devil.* (Mt.4:1 NKJV)

The Holy Spirit did not just lead Jesus but also empowered Jesus to do miracles:

*How **God** anointed **Jesus** of Nazareth **with the Holy Spirit and power**, and how he went around doing good and healing all who were under the power of the devil, because **God was with him**.* (Ac.10:38 TNIV; Ro.1:4)

Jesus' entire ministry proceeded from the Holy Spirit within Him:

*But **if I cast out devils by the Spirit of God**, then the kingdom of God is come unto you.* (Mt.12:28 KJV)

The Holy Spirit was the Person of God Who implemented the power of God in Jesus:

*One day He was teaching; and there were some Pharisees and teachers of the law sitting there, who had come from every village of Galilee and Judea and from Jerusalem; and **the power of the Lord was present** for Him to perform healing.* (Lk.5:17 NASB)

The Father revealed His will to Jesus, but the Spirit worked His power through Jesus. All Three were working to do the will of God:

> For I have come down from heaven, **not to do my own will but the will of him who sent me.** (Jn.6:38 ESV)

In the same way that our body is controlled by our soul, Jesus responded to the will of God with instant, absolute obedience:

> He comes so **that the world may learn** that I love the Father and **do exactly what my Father has commanded me.** (Jn.14:31 TNIV)

Jesus did not enjoy the concept of pain, but He lived to please His Father. In the Garden of Gethsemane, Jesus said:

> "**My soul is deeply grieved**, to the point of death; remain here and keep watch with Me." (Mt.26:38 NASB)

Jesus' soul agonized concerning what He was about to suffer, and yet His Spirit sought to do the will of the Father:

> He knelt down and began to pray, saying, "Father, **if You are willing, remove this cup** from Me; **yet not My will, but Yours be done.**" (Lk.22:41-42 NKJV)

Jesus lived for the glory of God. Days before His arrest, Jesus spoke of His death and stated His reason for enduring the cross:

> "**Now my soul is deeply troubled.** Should I pray, 'Father, save me from this hour'? But **this is the very reason I came!** Father, <u>**bring glory to your name.**</u>" (Jn.12:27-28 NLT)

Jesus brought glory to God by dying on the cross:

> **I brought glory to you here on earth by completing the work you gave me to do.** (Jn.17:5 NLT)

Therefore, even though Jesus lived His life on earth, He did not cease being one with the Father and the Spirit. Jesus' sole purpose in life on the earth was to bring glory to the Father by accomplishing the Father's will.

The effect of the Father being one with Jesus caused Jesus to share in the Father's will. When Jesus' Spirit lives in us, we also become one in the Father:

> As you, **Father, are in me** and **I am in you**, may they also <u>**be in us**</u>, so that the world may believe that you have sent me. (Jn.17:21 NRSV)

In a similar way that the Father was in Christ, the Father is connected with us through the Spirit:

Jesus answered him, "If anyone loves me, he will keep my word, and **my Father** will love him, and **we will come** to him and **make our home** with him." (Jn.14:23 ESV)

Christians are so apt to divide the three Persons of God without recognizing that the Three are in reality One Being. If the Holy Spirit lives in us, then God lives in us. If Jesus lives in us, then God lives in us. To have the One indwelling us is to have the Three living in us:

You are controlled by the Spirit if you have **the Spirit of God** *living in you. (And remember that those who do not* have **the Spirit of Christ** *living in them do not belong to him at all.)* (Ro.8:9 NLT)

Once the Holy Spirit lives in us, we have the fullness of God living in us:

For **in Christ all the fullness of the Deity lives** *in bodily form, and* **you have been given fullness in Christ**, *who is the Head over every power and authority.* (Co.2:9-10 NIV)

John repeats the truth that the three Persons of God live in us because God (Father, Son, and Spirit) Who lives in man is the central point of Christianity:

Whoever confesses that Jesus is the Son of God, **God abides** *in him, and he* **in God**. (1Jn.4:15 NKJV)

God lives in born-again Christians. Christianity is the Trinity of God living in man. Each of the Persons of God plays a role in man's salvation:

Peter, an apostle of Jesus Christ, To God's elect... who have been chosen according to **the foreknowledge of God** *the Father, through the* **sanctifying work of the Spirit**, *for* **obedience to Jesus Christ** *and sprinkling by his blood: Grace and peace be yours in abundance.* (1Pe.1:1-2 NIV)

Each Person of the Godhead plays a role in a Christian's life:

The **grace of the Lord Jesus** *Christ, and the* **love of God**, *and the* **fellowship of the Holy Spirit**, *be with you all.* (2Co.13:14 NASB)

Jesus lived for the glory of God. Now that He controls our life, we will also live for the glory of God. The purpose of man is to bring glory to God:

Bring my sons from afar and my daughters from the end of the earth, everyone who is called by my name, whom **I created for my glory**, *whom I formed and made."* (Isa.43:6-7 ESV)

The fullness of God works in us so that God will be glorified through our life.

YOUR WILL BE DONE

The way born-again Christians bring glory to God is by living to fulfill His will for their life. God has a purpose for every Christian's life, and by living to please Him, God is glorified:

> In Him *also we have obtained an inheritance,* **being predestined according** *to* **the purpose of Him** *who works all things* **according to the counsel of His will,** *that we who first trusted in Christ should be* **to the praise of His glory**. (Eph.1:11-12 NKJV)

Born-again Christians live their life through Christ's control:

> *Who has first given to him that it might be paid back to him again? For* **from Him** *and* **through Him** *and* **to Him are all things.** *To* **Him be the glory forever.** *Amen.* (Ro.11:35-36 NASB)

Recognizing the sovereignty of God in our life causes two effects. First, we acknowledge that God has a will for our life in every situation. Second, if we are going to thrive in life, we will have to live through Him:

> *For us there is one God, the Father,* **from whom are all things** *and* **for whom we exist,** *and one Lord, Jesus Christ,* **through whom are all things** *and* **through whom we exist.** (1Co.8:6 NRSV)

A Christian lives for God. We have learned to thrive by living through Jesus' Spirit indwelling us. Jesus humbles us when He said:

> *I am the vine, you are the branches. Those who* **abide in me and I in them** *bear much fruit, because* **apart from me you can do nothing.** (Jn.15:5 NRSV)

For me to abide in Jesus and Jesus to abide in me requires that both of us share the same purpose. The prophet Amos so aptly states it:

> *Can* **two walk** *together,* **unless they are agreed**? (Am.3:3 NKJV)

Through the Lord's Prayer, Jesus tried to help His disciples grasp the concept that the purpose of man is to live for the will of God:

> *Your kingdom come.* **Your will be done on earth** *as it is in heaven.* (Mt.6:10 NKJV)

In the Lord's Prayer, we are asking God to accomplish His will for our life just as His will is accomplished in heaven. One day, Jesus' mother and brothers came to see Him. He said:

> *"For* **whoever does the will of my Father** *in heaven is my brother and sister and mother."* (Mt.12:50 NRSV)

Only those who live for God's will are in the family of God. Luke records the same incident; however, rather than referring to the will of God, He tells us what God's will is:

> But He answered and said to them, "My mother and My brothers **are these who hear the word of God and do it.**" (Lk.8:21 NKJV)

To do the will of God for a period of time is good; however, if a person stops serving God, this is an indication that the Spirit did not control his life:

> **You need to persevere** so that **when you have done the will of God**, you will receive what he has promised. (He.10:36 TNIV)

Jesus died in the will of God. If He lives in us controlling our life, we too will persevere in doing God's will until death. The only way that we can be assured of heaven is for us to live for the will of God:

> And the world and its desire are passing away, **but those who do the will of God live forever**. (1Jn.2:17 NRSV)

Every Christian lives in the acknowledgement that God has a specific will for his life. We know that in every situation God has something specific He seeks to accomplish:

> For **we are God's workmanship**, created in Christ Jesus **to do good works**, which God **prepared in advance for us to do**. (Eph.2:10 NIV)

Since our good works have been decided before the world began, we do not decide what to do, but, instead, God produces the work in us just as He did in Christ. God saved us with a specific purpose for our life:

> **God, who has saved us** and called us to a holy life—not because of anything we have done but **because of his own purpose** and grace. (2Ti.1:9 NIV)

God saved us because we are a strategic part of His plan. When the Scriptures use the word "predestined," they acknowledge that God controls us and accomplishes His specific purpose for our life:

> We know that **all things work together for good** for those who love God, who are called according to his purpose. For those whom **he foreknew he also predestined**, (Ro.8:28-29 NRSV)

The fact that we are predestined implies that fulfilling God's purpose for our life is a work of God. This work is not of man because the work was predetermined prior to our birth. The Scripture clearly supports God's control of man:

*For **God is working in you**, giving you **the desire and the power to do what pleases him**.* (Php.2:13 NLT)

The Christian life is God living and working within man, shaping his desires to fulfill God's purpose:

*In him we were also chosen, **having been predestined** according to the plan of him **who works out everything** in conformity **with the purpose of his will**,* (Eph.1:11 NIV)

The Scriptures are undeniably clear that God is responsible for all the good that we do. The reason why born-again Christians do what they do is because of God's effective control of their life:

*But **by the grace of God I am what I am**, and his grace toward me has not been in vain. On the contrary, **I worked harder than any of them**—though it was not I, but **the grace of God that is with me**.* (1Co.15:10 NRSV)

Christ fulfilling God's purpose in our life is the only way we will ever fulfill the purpose of God. He works His will through man:

*Now may the God of peace... **equip you with everything good for doing his will**, and **may he work in us what is pleasing to him**, through Jesus Christ, to whom be glory for ever and ever.* (He.13:19-20 TNIV)

The Christian life is not about our dedication or determination but about our resting on Christ Who lives in us. This was a martyr's source of strength:

*No, in **all these things** we are more than conquerors **through him** who loved us.* (Ro.8:37 NRSV)

In the context of all that Paul suffered, his focus was on God's purpose because his strength was in Christ Who was within him:

*I can do **all things through Christ** who strengthens me.* (Php.4:13 NKJV)

The reason why many Christians live a mediocre life is because they have not submitted their life to God's control. If we give God control, God promises a fruitful ministry:

*And God is able to bless you abundantly, so that in **all things** at **all times**, having **all that you need**, you **will abound** in every good work.* (2Co.9:8 TNIV)

I attended one church for thirteen years and reminded them many times of the sufficiency of Christ living in them. All I heard in reply were excuses, such as: "We are only human; what can we do?" But God said in the Scriptures:

> And my **God will supply all your needs** according to His riches in glory **in Christ Jesus**. (Php.4:19 NIV)

The Holy Spirit enables us from within to do the will of God by the power of God to the glory of God, but the church has yet to realize their full potential. God said in the Scriptures:

> Now you **have every spiritual gift you need as you eagerly wait** for the return of our Lord Jesus Christ. (1Co.1:7 NLT)

And God said in the Scriptures:

> Very truly, I tell you, the one who believes in me **will also do the works that I do** and, **in fact, will do greater works than these**, because I am going to the Father. I will do whatever you ask in my name, so that the Father may be glorified in the Son. (Jn.14:12-13 NRSV)

Then God said in the Scriptures:

> Now to **Him who is able to do far more abundantly beyond all that we ask or think,** according **to the power that works within us**, to Him be the glory in the church and in Christ Jesus to all generations forever and ever. Amen. (Eph.3:20-21 NASB)

The Scriptures teach that God has a specific plan for our life and has empowered us to complete His plan.

LORDSHIP

Some who are reading this can't comprehend how Biblical truths can apply to our everyday life. Let me simply state the cause and its effect. Since the Holy Spirit lives in us and controls our actions, we will begin to act like Christ. Sin is disobedience. When the Holy Spirit lives in us, He moves us to be obedient:

> To God's elect... who <u>**have been chosen**</u> according to the foreknowledge of God **the Father,** through <u>**the sanctifying work of the Spirit**</u>, to **be <u>obedient to</u> Jesus Christ** and sprinkled with his blood: (1Pe.1:2 TNIV)

We are not saved by our obedience but by Christ's Spirit living in us. He moves us to obey:

> Now he who <u>**keeps His commandments**</u> abides <u>**in Him**</u>, and **He in him.** And **by this we know** that He abides in us, **by the Spirit** whom He has given us. (1Jn.3:24 NKJV)

Our obedience to God is the evidence of the Holy Spirit living in us:

> *And we are witnesses to these things, and **so is the Holy Spirit**, whom **God has given to those who obey him**.* (Ac 5:32 ESV)

Born-again Christians are saved by the Spirit Who controls them and causes them to live out the will of God.

The lesson we learn from the courtyard of the physical tabernacle is that we cannot become the temple of God without laying our life on the bronze altar, which is making Christ our Lord, and without washing in the bronze basin, which is dying to self in baptism. These acts do not earn salvation but authenticate our faith:

> *The revelation of the mystery that was kept secret for long ages but has now been disclosed and through the prophetic writings has been made known to all nations, according to the command of the eternal God, to **bring about the obedience of faith**—* (Ro.16:25-26 ESV)

You cannot become the temple of God without His control:

> *I will not venture to speak of anything except what Christ has accomplished through me **in leading the Gentiles to obey God** by what I have said and done—* (Ro.15:18 NIV)

Since Jesus was obedient to God in everything and He controls us, we will be obedient through Christ to everything the Spirit reveals to us. Jesus asked:

> *"Why do you call Me, 'Lord, Lord,' and **do not do what I say**?"* (Lk.6:46 NASB)

We cannot separate obedience to Christ from Christ living in us:

> *Although he was a Son, he learned obedience through what he suffered; and having been made perfect, **he became the source of eternal salvation for all who obey him**...* (He.5:8-9 NRSV)

If Jesus lives in us, then we will live as He did—for the will of God:

> *We know that **we have come to know him if we keep his commands**. Those who say, "I know him," but do not do what he commands are liars, and the truth is not in them. But if anyone obeys his word, love for God is truly made complete in them. **This is how we know we are in him**: Whoever claims **to live in him** must live as Jesus did.* (1Jn.2:3-6 TNIV)

The church-goer must consider the relationship between belief and obedience, for the connection is undeniable. You can tell me that you believe in Christ, but I can tell what you believe by your actions.

Believing in the truth always alters one's actions in an appropriate response:

> Through him and for his name's sake, we received grace and apostleship to call people from among all the Gentiles **to the obedience that comes from faith**. (Ro.1:5 NIV)

To say that people believe in Christ or to say that they became obedient to Christ is the same—a saving faith produces obedience to God:

> So the word of God spread. The number of disciples in Jerusalem increased rapidly, and **a large number of priests became obedient to the faith**. (Ac.6:5 NASB)

Obedience is the only appropriate response to a saving faith in Christ. Laying our lives on the altar and being baptized is the start of a lifelong obedience of living for Christ. If we are not doing the will of God, then we are simply not saved. Many people would say, "But you don't understand. We love Jesus." Can we love our parents and not obey them? Our obedience is a true gauge of our love for God:

> If anyone loves me, **he will obey** my teaching. My Father will love him, and we will come to him and make our home with him. He who does not love me will not obey my teaching. (1Jn.14:23-24 NIV)

Many verses tie our love for God to an appropriate response of obedience to Him:

> For this is the love of God, that we keep His commandments. And His commandments are not burdensome. (1Jn.5:3 NKJV)

If anything keeps us from obeying the Scriptures, then we love that "thing" more than we love God. To love something more than Christ is idolatry!

> And **this is love: that we walk in obedience to his commands**. As you have heard from the beginning, **his command is that you walk in love**. (2Jn.1:6 TNIV)

You cannot separate the fact that Christ lives in born-again Christians from the resulting effect of a life lived to please God.

MIRACULOUSLY PRESERVED

The bread on the gold table in the Holy Place was called the Bread of the Presence and was to be placed before God:

> Place **the Bread of the Presence** on the table to remain **before me at all times**. (Ex.25:30 NLT)

In the Old Testament, the priests had to physically change the Bread of the Presence every week, for the bread would spoil. The bread (manna) that came down from heaven, which was placed in the pure gold jar, was preserved forever. The manna represents Christ in us. Once Christ's Spirit controls us, we are secure in Him forever:

> I will ask the Father, and He will give you **another Helper, that He may be with you forever**; that is the Spirit of truth, whom the world cannot receive, because it does not see Him or know Him, but you know Him because He abides with you and will be in you. (Jn.14:16-17 NASB)

Like the manna in the gold jar that was preserved **forever**, the Holy Spirit will remain in us **forever**. This is different from the Old Testament experience. In the Old Testament, the Spirit would come upon a prophet for a period of time and then leave. For a Christian, the Holy Spirit takes residence and possession of the individual **forever**:

> The elder to the elect lady and her children, whom I love in the truth, and not only I but also all who know the truth, because of **the truth that abides in us** and **will be with us forever**: (2Jn.1:1-2 NRSV)

Some teach that we control the Holy Spirit and, like a guest, that we determine if He comes or stays and for how long. This concept is contrary to the Scriptures which teach that if the Holy Spirit lives in us, He will be in us forever. Jesus promised to be with us always:

> "Go therefore and make disciples of all nations, **baptizing** them in the name of the Father and of the Son and of the Holy Spirit, and teaching them **to obey everything** that I have commanded you. And remember, **I am with you always**, to the end of the age." (Mt.28:19-20 NRSV)

Always is a very long time! The only reason why Jesus can make the promise to be with us forever is because when He moves in, He takes control of the individual and, consequently, stays forever:

> **You, however, are controlled** not by the sinful nature but by **the Spirit**, **if the Spirit of God lives in you**. And **if** anyone does not have the **Spirit of Christ**, he does not belong to Christ. (Ro.8:9 NIV)

The omnipotent God says that His Spirit will never leave:

> He Himself has said, "**I will never desert you, nor will I ever forsake you**," so that we confidently say, "the LORD is my helper, I will not be afraid. what will man do to me?" (He.13:5-6 NASB)

God has placed the Holy Spirit in our heart, altering our being and guaranteeing that we will inherit eternal life:

*And you also were included in Christ when you heard the word of truth, the gospel of your salvation. Having believed, you were **marked in him with a seal, the promised Holy Spirit, who is a deposit guaranteeing our inheritance** until the redemption of those who are God's possession—to the praise of his glory.* (Eph.1:13-14 NIV)

The concept of a guarantee means that God ensures that it will occur. **Only** the manna in the gold jar was preserved forever, while all the other manna dissolved with the morning sun. And, **only** if the Holy Spirit lives in us can we be assured of eternity with Christ:

*Now it is God who makes both us and you stand firm in Christ. He anointed us, set his seal of ownership on us, and **put his Spirit in our hearts as a deposit, guaranteeing what is to come.*** (2Co.1:21-22 TNIV)

The guarantee is based on the Holy Spirit's control. If we remain in control of our life, then the Holy Spirit does not live in us. God repeats many times in the New Testament that the Holy Spirit's Presence in our life forms our guarantee:

*Now it is God who has made us for this very purpose and has **given us the Spirit as a deposit, guaranteeing what is to come.*** (2Co.5:5 NIV)

A guarantee is only as good as the person who offers it. Once I bought something with a good warranty; however, because the company closed, the warranty was reduced to a useless piece of paper. In Christianity, our **eternal, immutable** God is the One Who guarantees what is to come. His Holy Spirit guards our life:

*Guard the good deposit that was entrusted to you—**guard it with the help of the Holy Spirit who lives in us**.* (2Ti.1:14 NIV)

Once God's Spirit lives in us and controls our life, no one can negate that life because God is the One in control:

*I give them eternal life, and they will never perish. **No one will snatch them out of my hand.** What my Father has given me is greater than all else, and **no one can snatch it out of the Father's hand**.* (Jn.10:28-29 NRSV)

Since no one can snatch a Christian from God's hand, those who leave Christianity and return to their life of sin did not lose their salvation but simply prove that they were never in the hand of God:

*Anyone who hates his brother is a murderer, and **you know that no murderer has eternal life in him**. .* (1Jn.3:15 NIV)

We do not lose our salvation by hating or committing murder; we simply prove that we never had eternal life. If the Holy Spirit lives in us, our old sinful habits will be changed. However, if we do not continue to be changed, our actions prove that we are not born again and will not inherit heaven:

> **The acts of the sinful nature are obvious**: sexual immorality, impurity and debauchery; idolatry and witchcraft; hatred, discord, jealousy, fits of rage, selfish ambition, dissensions, factions and envy; drunkenness, orgies, and the like. I warn you, as I did before, **that those who live like this will not inherit the kingdom of God.** (Ga.5:19-21 NIV)

A term I have often heard is *backslider*: someone who claimed to be a Christian but returned to a life of sin. Since the Holy Spirit guards the good deposit which guarantees our salvation, someone who leaves Christ and returns to a life of sin proves that he was never indwelt by the Holy Spirit:

> They went out from us, but they were not of us; for if they had been of us, they would have continued with us; but **they went out** that they might be made manifest, that **none of them were of us**. (1Jn.2:19 NKJV)

People who leave the faith may have made Jesus their Savior, but they obviously did not make Christ their Lord. For, if the Holy Spirit lived in them and controlled their life, then He would have ensured that they remained faithful to Him:

> ...being confident of this very thing, that **He who has begun a good work in you will complete** it until the day of Jesus Christ. (Php.1:6 NKJV)

The Scriptures clearly teach that we are the temple of God in which the Holy Spirit dwells—the power and holiness of God's Presence within us. Since God's Spirit lives in us, He controls and keeps us faithful:

> Now **the Lord is the Spirit**, and where the Spirit of the Lord is, there is freedom. And we all, with unveiled face, beholding the glory of the Lord, **are being** transformed into the same image from one degree of glory to another. For **this comes from the Lord** who is **the Spirit**. (2Co.3:17-18 ESV)

We will never be perfect, but we will become more like Him every day. Our Christian walk is not about attaining perfection but about maintaining direction. Are we living for the will of God by the power of God for the glory of God? If we can answer "yes," then we can be assured of our salvation:

> **He who has the Son has life**; he who **does not have the Son of God does not have life**. (1Jn.5:12 NKJV)

Thinking It Through:

1. Manna came down from heaven. What does this symbolize?

2. What is the importance of knowing that the Holy Spirit is a Person?

3. How does the Holy Spirit transform our life?

4. What is the significance of the verse, "Be holy, for I am holy" (1Pe.1:16)?

5. What is the Christian responsibility in becoming like Christ?

6. What is the purpose of a Christian's life, and how is it accomplished?

7. How does a person persevere as a Christian?

8. What is the test of a true Christian? Did you pass?

Epilogue

The Christian life is a journey! Will we ever be fully yielded and controlled by God? Nearing the end of his life, Paul wrote about his walk:

> Not that I have already obtained all this, or have already been made perfect, but **I press on** to take hold of that for which **Christ Jesus took hold of me**. Brothers, I do not consider myself yet to have taken hold of it. But one thing I do: Forgetting what is behind and straining towards what is ahead, I press on towards the goal to win the prize for which God has called me heavenwards in Christ Jesus. **All of us who are mature should take such a view of things.** And if on some point you think differently, that too God will make clear to you. **Only let us live up to what we have already attained.**
> (Php.3:12-16 NIV)

The Christian life is about being born again and then maturing and growing in Christ. Just as a newborn does not come from the womb one day and then run a marathon the next, when we are born again, we have new life, but there is a process of maturing. John writes:

> I write to you, **dear children**, because you have **known the Father**. I write to you, **fathers**, because you have **known him who is from the beginning**. I write to you, **young men**, because you **are strong, and the word of God lives in you, and you have overcome the evil one.** (1Jn.2:13-14 NIV)

Children know their Daddy; young men walk by the Spirit; but fathers know the Father in depth. No matter which stage you are in, you must persevere to become spiritual men and women. The Scripture warns:

> My **dear children**, for whom I am again in the **pains of childbirth until Christ is formed in you**, how I wish I could be with you now and change my tone, because **I am perplexed about you!** (Ga.4:19-20 NIV)

Christ died and arose from the dead so that we could live in Him and have Him control our lives. If Christ is not manifesting His attitudes, behavior, and character in our lives, then the question should be raised as to whether we are saved. This was the concern we find in Paul's letter to the Corinthians:

> And so, brothers and sisters, I could not speak to you **as spiritual people**, but rather as **people of the flesh, as infants in Christ**. I fed you with milk, not solid food, for you were not ready for solid food. Even now you are still not ready, **for you are still of the flesh.** For as long as there is jealousy and

quarrelling among you, **are you not of the flesh, and behaving according to human inclinations***?* (1Co.3:1-3 NRSV)

Christ died so that we could stop living by the soul's obsession with the body's senses and could start living by the Spirit to please the Father. This transformation is not something that we accomplish; it is something that happens when we are born again: our spirits are made alive by the indwelling of the Spirit of the living God. The Hebrews were also infants in Christ, not knowing the way of righteousness, and unable to discern between good and evil:

> *In fact, though by this time you ought to be teachers,* **you need someone to teach you the elementary truths of God's word all over again***. You need milk, not solid food! Anyone who lives on milk, being* **still an infant, is not acquainted with the teaching about righteousness***. But solid food is for the mature,* **who by constant use have trained themselves to distinguish good from evil***.* (He.5:12-14 NIV)

Christ died so that we might become mature, having Him fully manifested in our lives. Church is not an organization to orchestrate our times of dedication for Christ; it is an organism that should enable people to become mature:

> *It was he who gave some to be apostles, some to be prophets, some to be evangelists, and some to be pastors and teachers,* **to prepare God's people for works of service***, so that the body of Christ may be built up until we all reach unity in the faith and in the knowledge of the Son of God and* **become mature, attaining to the whole measure of the fullness of Christ***.* (Eph.4:11-13 NIV)

The Christian life is about living in the fullness of God, not that we become God but, rather, that we learn to draw on the power of His Presence for our current situation. The Christian life is a life of humility and dependence:

> *I pray that out of* **his** *glorious riches* **he may strengthen you with power through his Spirit in your inner being,** *so* **that Christ may dwell in your hearts through faith***… that you may be filled to the measure of all the fullness of God. Now to him who is able to do immeasurably more than all we ask or imagine, according* **to his power that is at work within us***, to him be glory in the church and in Christ Jesus throughout all generations, for ever and ever! Amen.* (Eph.3:16-21 NIV)

My hope is that at the end of this study you will not be content to live the status quo Christian life, and that you will believe that there is more to life than that which is experienced by an average person who attends church. God desires all His people to mature:

> My brothers and sisters, **whenever you face trials of any kind, consider it nothing but joy**, because you know that the testing of your faith produces endurance; and let endurance have its full effect, so **that you may be mature** and **complete, lacking in nothing**. (Ja.1:2-4 NRSV)

Mature, complete, lacking nothing—this is God's will for your life. It is my hope that you have developed a better understanding of all that God has promised us in Christ through this study.

Appendix

I Am's

When I was young in the faith, a battle raged within me for the control of my mind. I would read verses such as:

> You are witnesses, and God also, **how holy and righteous and blameless was our conduct** toward you believers. (1Th.2:10 ESV)

I would strive to live the Christian life but was told: "You cannot live a holy life. Look at David. He had a heart after God, yet he committed adultery and murder." Other times respected Christians would say, "Do you think that you are better than Paul? He consistently sinned":

> And I know that **nothing good lives in me**, that is, in my sinful nature. I want to do what is right, **but I can't**. I want to do what is good, **but I don't**. I don't want to do what is wrong, **but I do it anyway**. But **if I do what I don't want to do,** I am not really the one doing wrong; it is sin living in me that does it. (Ro.7:18-20 NLT)

These people interpreted Romans 7 out of its context. God consistently drew me back with a call to holiness through the conviction of the Scriptures:

> Now may the God of peace **make you holy in every way**, and may **your whole spirit and soul and body** be kept blameless until our Lord Jesus Christ comes again. (1Th.5:23 NLT)

However, at the same time that I was searching, friends would provide excuses for me to continue in sin, such as: "We're only human, no one is perfect." My life fluctuated between victory and defeat, depending upon what I believed. I found that my thoughts directly affected my effectiveness in overcoming sin. The Scriptures teach:

> For **as he thinks** within himself, **so he is**. (Pr.23:7 NASB)

Our thinking dictates who we are. Consider the example of a boy who is an exceptional soccer player. Even though he is gifted in the skills of soccer, he does not have confidence in and of himself. Even though he has great skill, he never achieves his potential on the field because he does not believe in himself. Christians also need to believe in order to achieve. If we think of ourselves as sinners, we will continue to sin, but if we think of ourselves as saints, our lives will begin to change:

> **For we walk by faith**, not by sight. (2Co.5:7 ESV)

Therefore, as the body of Christ, we must perceive ourselves from God's perspective and not base our beliefs on common opinions.

Over the centuries, Satan has been involved in an aggressive campaign of propaganda, for he knows the power of perception. He and his workers masquerade as Biblical scholars to teach doctrines which ensure that Christians will continue in sin. The Bible warns:

> For such men **are false apostles**, deceitful workmen, **masquerading as apostles of Christ**. And no wonder, for **Satan himself masquerades as an angel of light**. It is not surprising, then, if his servants masquerade as servants of righteousness. (2Co.11:13-15 NIV)

Satan uses church-goers and false teachings to negate the New Testament promises by using Old Testament experiences:

> All these, though commended through their faith, **did not receive what was promised**, since God had provided something better for us, (He.11:39-40 ESV)

If Satan can convince us to believe the lie that our lives have not changed through Christ, Satan will have a foothold by which he will tempt us and cause us to fall. For this reason, God gave us the written Word:

> **All scripture is inspired by God** and is useful for teaching, for reproof, **for correction**, and **for training in righteousness**, so that everyone who belongs to God may be proficient, equipped for every good work.
> (2Ti.3:16-17 NRSV)

We are all that the Bible claims we are. The written Word of God enables us to discern if something is truth. Jesus taught:

> If you **abide in my word**, you are truly my disciples, and **you will know the truth**, and **the truth will set you free**. (Jn.8:31-32 ESV)

If God's truth shall set us free, then Satan's lies will keep us bound by sin. If we believe Satan, we will doubt God; and if we believe God, we will doubt Satan. Who are we going to believe, the father of lies or the Father Who cannot lie? As we meditate on what God states about us and what He promises to do for us, our lives will be freed from the lies that Satan has taught us over the years. This booklet, a collection of promises from the New Testament, is divided into seven perspectives or days. As we meditate on God's truth each day, we claim what God states about us as truth for our lives. God knows us better than we know ourselves, and if He states something has been accomplished, we can accept this as truth. My hope is that we will not only know all that God has promised but that our lives will also be transformed by God's revelation of who we are through Christ.

APPENDIX   I AM'S

FORGETTING MY PAST   SUNDAY

- **I am forgiven:**

    *I am writing to you who are God's children because **your sins have been forgiven** through Jesus.*   (1Jn.2:12 NLT)

- **I am washed:**

    *And now why are you waiting? Arise and **be baptized, and wash away your sins**, calling on the name of the Lord.*   (Ac.22:16 NKJV; 1Co.6:11)

- **I am justified by Christ:**

    *Since **we have now been justified** by His blood, how much more shall we be saved from God's wrath through Him!*   (Ro.5:9 NIV)

- **I am reconciled to God:**

    *While we were enemies **we were reconciled to** God through the death of His Son.*   (Ro.5:10 NASB)

- **I am freed from condemnation:**

    *Therefore **there is now no condemnation** for those who are in Christ Jesus.*   (Ro.8:1 NASB)

- **I am freed from Satan's accusations:**

    *But now He has reconciled you by Christ's physical body through death to present you holy in His sight, without blemish and **free from accusation—if you continue in your faith**.*   (Co.1:22-23 NIV)

- **I am freed from my slavery to sin:**

    *Now **you are free from your slavery to sin**, and you have become slaves to righteous living.*   (Ro.6:18 NLT; Ro.6:22)

- **I am redeemed from wickedness:**

    *Jesus Christ, Who gave himself for us **to redeem us from all** wickedness and to purify for Himself a people that are His very own, eager to do what is good.*   (2Ti.2:14 NIV)

- **I am delivered from the kingdom of Satan:**

    *He **has delivered us from the domain of darkness** and transferred us to the kingdom of His beloved Son.*   (Co.1:13 ESV; Ga.6:14)

- **I have died with Christ:**

    I have been crucified with Christ and I no longer live, but Christ lives in me.
    (Ga.2:20 NIV)

- **I have died to the law and now live by the Spirit:**

    So, my brothers, you also died to the law through the body of Christ, that you might belong to another, to him who was raised from the dead, in order that we might bear fruit to God. (Ro.7:4 NIV; Ro.6:14)

- **I have died to the principles of the world—self-righteousness:**

    Since you died with Christ to the basic principles of this world, why, as though you still belonged to it, do you submit to its rules: "Do not handle! Do not taste! Do not touch!"? (Co.2:20-21 NIV)

- **I have died to the power of sin through Christ:**

    Shall we go on sinning, so that grace may increase? By no means! We died to sin; how can we live in it any longer? Or don't you know that all of us who were baptized into Christ Jesus were baptized into His death? We were therefore buried with him through baptism into death. (Ro.6:1-4 NIV)

- **I have died with Christ to self-centeredness:**

    We know that our old self was crucified with him in order that the body of sin might be brought to nothing, so that we would no longer be enslaved to sin. (Ro.6:6 ESV)

- **I have died with Christ to my sinful nature/flesh:**

    Those who belong to Christ Jesus have crucified the sinful nature with its passions and desires. Since we live by the Spirit, let us keep in step with the Spirit. (Ga.5:24-25 NIV; Co.2:11-12)

- **I have died with Christ to the world:**

    May I never boast of anything except the cross of our Lord Jesus Christ, by which the world has been crucified to me, and I to the world.
    (Ga.6:14 NRSV)

- **I have died to what I was, and Christ is the new me:**

    So if anyone is in Christ, there is a new creation: everything old has passed away; see, everything has become new! (2Co.5:17 ESV)

I Am Special

Monday

- **I am loved by God:**

  The Father himself loves you because you have loved Me and have believed that I came from God. (Jn.16:27 NIV)

- **I am chosen by God:**

  For *He chose us in Him* before the creation of the world to be holy and blameless in His sight. (Eph.1:4 NIV; Jn.15:16)

- **I am called by God:**

  And you also are among those Gentiles *who are called* to belong to Jesus Christ. (Ro.1:6 TNIV)

- **I am accepted by Christ:**

  Therefore, accept each other just *as Christ has accepted you* so that God will be given glory. (Ro.15:7 NLT)

- **I am victorious through Christ:**

  Thanks be to *God, Who gives us the victory* through our Lord Jesus Christ. (1Co.15:57 NASB)

- **I am perfect through Christ:**

  By one sacrifice *He has made perfect for ever* those who are being made holy. (He.10:14 NIV)

- **I am predestined through Christ:**

  He predestined us for adoption through Jesus Christ, according to the purpose of His will, (Eph.1:5 ESV)

- **I am reunited with God through Christ:**

  For Christ also suffered for sins once for all, the righteous for the unrighteous, in order *to bring you to God*. (1Pe.3:18 NRSV)

- **I am one in spirit with Christ:**

  But anyone united to the Lord *becomes one spirit with Him*. (1Co.6:17 NRSV)

- **I am born again through Christ:**

  In His great mercy *He has given us new birth* into a living hope through the resurrection of Jesus Christ from the dead. (1Pe.1:3 NIV)

Realizing Who I Am   Tuesday

- **I am a child of God:**

    How great is the love the Father has lavished on us, that we should be **called children of God! And that is what we are!** (1Jn.3:1 NIV)

- **I am Jesus' brother:**

    Both the One who makes men holy and those who are made holy are of the same family. So **Jesus is not ashamed to call them brothers**.
    (He.2:11 NIV)

- **I am Jesus' disciple:**

    Jesus said to the people who believed in Him, "You **are truly my disciples** if you remain faithful to My teachings. (Jn.8:31 NLT)

- **I am a new creation:**

    Therefore, if anyone is in Christ, **he is a new creation**; old things have passed away; behold, all things have become new. (2Co.5:17 NKJV)

- **I am a saint:**

    Paul, an apostle of Jesus Christ by the will of God, **To the saints** who are in Ephesus, and faithful in Christ Jesus: (Eph.1:1 NKJV)

- **I am a conqueror:**

    Yet in all these things **we are more than conquerors** through Him who loved us. (Ro.8:37 NKJV)

- **I am an ambassador of Christ:**

    So **we are Christ's ambassadors;** God is making His appeal through us.
    (2Co.5:20 NLT)

- **I am the temple of God:**

    Do you not know that **you are God's temple** and that **God's Spirit dwells in you**? (1Co.3:16 ESV, 1Co.6:19)

- **I am the body of Christ:**

    Now **you are the body of Christ** and individually members of it.
    (1Co.12:27 NRSV)

- **I am alive with Christ:**

    Then **God made you alive with Christ**, for He forgave all our sins.
    (Co.2:13 NLT)

I Am Empowered — Wednesday

- **I have grace through Christ:**

  But **to each one of us grace has been given** as Christ apportioned it.
  (Eph.4:7 NIV)

- **I have faith through Christ:**

  Let us fix our eyes on **Jesus, the author and perfecter of our faith**.
  (He.12:2 NIV)

- **I have a pure heart:**

  He did not discriminate between us and them, for **He purified their hearts by faith**. (Ac.15:9 TNIV)

- **I have a new nature:**

  He has granted to us His precious and magnificent promises, so that by them **you may become partakers of the divine nature**. (2Pe.1:4 NASB)

- **I have a new life:**

  "Go, stand in the temple courts," he said, "and tell the people **the full message of this new life**." (Ac.5:20 NIV; Ro.6:3-4)

- **I have a new character:**

  But **the fruit of the Spirit is** love, joy, peace, patience, kindness, goodness, faithfulness, gentleness and self-control. (Ga.5:22-23 NIV)

- **I have a new mind:**

  But **we have the mind of Christ**. (1Co.2:16 NKJV)

- **I have gifts for service:**

  A spiritual gift is given to each of us so we can help each other.
  (1Co.12:7 NLT)

- **I have access to God through Christ:**

  For through Him we both have access in one Spirit **to the Father**.
  (Eph.2:18 ESV)

- **I have His Holy Spirit living in me:**

  Repent, and each of you be baptized in the name of Jesus Christ for the forgiveness of your sins; and **you will receive the gift of the Holy Spirit**.
  (Ac.2:38 NASB)

I Will Succeed THURSDAY

- **I am transformed by Christ:**
  We will have confidence on the day of judgment, because **in this world we are like him.** (1Jn.4:17 NIV)

- **I am empowered by Christ:**
  I can do all things through Him who strengthens me. (Php.4:13 NRSV)

- **I am godly through Christ:**
  His divine power has **given us everything needed for life and godliness,** through the knowledge of Him. (2Pe.1:3 NRSV)

- **I am fruitful through Christ:**
  If a man remains in Me and I in him, **he will bear much fruit;** apart from Me you can do nothing. (Jn.15:5 NIV)

- **I am equipped to minister to people through Christ:**
  I tell you the truth, **anyone who has faith in Me will do what I have been doing.** He will do **even greater things than these,** because I am going to the Father. (Jn.14:12 NIV)

- **I am taught by the Spirit:**
  The Holy Spirit, whom the Father will send in My name, **will teach you all things** and will **remind you of everything** I have said to you. (Jn.14:26; NIV; Ro.15:14)

- **I am provided with everything that I need by God:**
  And God is able to bless you abundantly, so that in **all things** at **all times,** having **all that you need,** you **will abound in every good work.** (2Co.9:8 TNIV)

- **I am swayed by Christ:**
  May the God of peace... **equip you with everything** good for doing His will, and **may He work in us what is pleasing to Him,** through Jesus Christ. (He.13:20-31 NIV)

- **I am possessed by Christ:**
  For you died, and your life is hidden with Christ in God. When **Christ Who is our life appears,** then you also will appear with Him in glory. (Co.3:3-4 NKJV)

THINGS WILL CHANGE: FRIDAY

- **I will find rest because of Christ:**

  Take My yoke upon you. *Let me teach you, because I am humble and gentle at heart, and **you will find rest for your souls**.* (Mt.11:29 NLT)

- **I will have peace because of Christ:**

  And the peace of God, which surpasses all understanding, **will guard your hearts and your minds** in Christ Jesus. (Php.4:7 NRSV)

- **I will be restored because of Christ:**

  And *after you have suffered a little while*, the God of all grace, Who has called you to his eternal glory in Christ, **will himself restore, confirm, strengthen, and establish you.** (1Pe.5:10 ESV)

- **I will stand against sin because of Christ:**

  To his own master he stands or falls; **and he will stand, for the Lord is able to make him stand.** (Ro.14:4 NASB)

- **I will be filled because of Christ:**

  To know the love of Christ that surpasses knowledge, that **you may be filled with all the fullness of God.** (Eph.3:19 NIV; Co.2:10)

- **I will become holy because of Christ:**

  Now may the God of peace **make you holy in every way**, and may your whole spirit and soul and body be kept blameless until our Lord Jesus Christ comes again. **God will make this happen.** (2Th.5:23-24 NLT)

- **I will become mature because of Christ:**

  Let endurance have its full effect, so **that you may be mature and complete**, lacking in nothing. (Ja.1:4 NRSV; Eph.4:13)

- **I will overcome Satan's realm because of Christ:**

  You are from God, little children, and **have overcome them**; because greater is He who is in you than he who is in the world. (1Jn.4:4 NASB)

- **I will change because Jesus is alive:**

  He is **able to save completely** those who come to God through Him, because He always lives to intercede for them. (He.7:25 TNIV)

PROMISES FOR TOMORROW: Saturday

- **All God's promises are for Me:**

  For no matter how many promises God has made, **they are "Yes" in Christ.**
  (2Co.1:20 TNIV)

- **God promises to be with me:**

  For God has said, "I will never fail you. **I will never abandon you."**
  (He.13:5 NASB)

- **God promises to work in me:**

  For **God is working in you**, giving you <u>the desire and the power</u> to do what pleases Him. (Php.2:13 NLT; He.13:20-21)

- **God promises to give me endurance:**

  I am certain **that God**, who began the good work within you, **will continue His work until it is finally finished** on the day when Christ Jesus returns.
  (Php.1:6 NLT; 2Ti.1:12)

- **God promises to give me strength when tempted:**

  And God is faithful; **He will not let you be tempted beyond what** you can bear. But when you are tempted, **He will also provide a way out so that you can stand up under it.** (1Co.10:31 NIV)

- **God promises to give me wisdom when tried:**

  So don't worry in advance about how to answer the charges against you, for **I will give you the right words and such wisdom** that none of your opponents will be able to reply or refute you! (Lk.21:14-15 NLT)

- **God promises to give protection when opposed:**

  But the Lord is faithful, and He **will strengthen and protect you from the evil one.** (2Th.3:3 NKJV; 1Jn.5:18)

- **God promises to do more than what I can imagine:**

  Now to Him who is able to do **immeasurably more than all we ask or imagine,** according to His power that is at work within us. (Eph.3:20 NIV)

- **God promises that everything will be for my good:**

  We know that **all things work together for good** for those who love God, who are called according to His purpose. (Ro.8:28 NRSV)

How to Start a Relationship with God

The Bible teaches that all people apart from Christ are self-centered sinners. Before we can have a relationship with God, we must acknowledge the existence of God and must believe that Jesus, Who is God, died on a cross for our sin. We must ask Him to forgive us for our sins:

> If you confess with your mouth the Lord Jesus and **believe in your heart that God has raised Him from the dead**, you will be saved.   (Ro.10:9 NIV)

Next, we need to repent, which means a change of mind. For example, if I went into a store to buy a shirt but changed my mind, did I come out of the store with the shirt? No! We must turn from seeking self-gratification and sin to living to please Him:

> I preached that they **should repent and turn to God** and prove their repentance by their deeds.   (Ac.26:20 NIV)

Every journey starts with a first step. With Christianity, the first step is to be baptized. Christ died to be our Savior, but He rose from the dead to be our Lord. In baptism, we go under the water, dying to sin, self, and Satan; and we come out of the water, with Christ living in us by His Spirit:

> **Repent and be baptized** every one of you in the name of Jesus Christ **for the forgiveness** of your sins, and **you will receive the gift of the Holy Spirit**.   (Ac.2:38 ESV)

God saved us from our sin to have a relationship with Him. We must study the Bible every day. Daily, we must ask Him in prayer for His love for others, His wisdom for decisions, His holiness to transform our lives, and His power to do His will. When God's Spirit convicts us of a sin, we must promptly confess it:

> If we confess our sins to him, **He** is faithful and just **to forgive** us our sins and **to cleanse us from all wickedness**.   (1Jn.1:9 NIV)

Confessing is agreeing with God that we have sinned. We must ask Him for His mercy that forgives us and for His grace that empowers us to overcome our sin. If we fall in sin, we must respond as a toddler responds when learning to walk. When he falls, he gets up and starts walking again! So get up, confess your sins, and start walking in your relationship with Christ. Believe all that the Bible states you are!

About the Author

Ron joined the military at the age of seventeen with the hope of adventure. On the flight to boot camp, he heard God's voice: "Ron, are you going to live the rest of your life for yourself, or are you going to live for Me?" By the time the plane landed, Ron had made Christ both his Savior and Lord. During his time in the military, he was nicknamed "Reverend" because of the radical change in his attitude, behavior, and character. After an honorable discharge, Ron endeavored to serve his Lord Jesus Christ in instant, absolute obedience. Christians first recognized Ron's prophetic gift while he was working in the inner city. His heart was broken by the church's apathy to the poor and by their conformity to the world. The Bible defines the gift of prophecy:

> And if I have **the gift of prophecy**, and know **all mysteries and all knowledge**; ...but do not have love, I am nothing.   (1Co.13:2 NIV)

The gift of a prophet is used to reveal God's truth and will to man. Love does not deviate from the truth; love always tempers the truth. The Bible teaches that the truth shall set us free when it is applied to our lives. Ron's life has been committed to sharing the transforming truths of God's Word. His heart is for Christians to become fathers of the faith who can display Christ's love, share His wisdom, reveal His power, and walk in His Holiness. It is Ron's hope that after reading *The Tabernacle, The Temple, And You,* you may have a better understanding of who you are in Christ.

Milton Keynes UK
Ingram Content Group UK Ltd.
UKHW050831250324
439991UK00001B/320